YOU LOST ME

# YOU LOST ME

Why Young Christians Are Leaving Church . . . and Rethinking Faith

## David Kinnaman

### with Aly Hawkins

BakerBooks

*a division of Baker Publishing Group*
Grand Rapids, Michigan

© 2011 by David Kinnaman

Published by Baker Books
a division of Baker Publishing Group
P.O. Box 6287, Grand Rapids, MI 49516-6287
www.bakerbooks.com

Paperback edition published 2016
ISBN 978-0-8010-1589-2

Printed in the United States of America

All rights reserved. No part of this publication may be reproduced, stored in a retrieval system, or transmitted in any form or by any means—for example, electronic, photocopy, recording—without the prior written permission of the publisher. The only exception is brief quotations in printed reviews.

The Library of Congress has cataloged the hardcover edition as follows:
Kinnaman, David, 1973–
    You lost me : why young Christians are leaving church, and rethinking faith / David Kinnaman with Aly Hawkins.
        p.  cm.
    Includes bibliographical references.
    ISBN 978-0-8010-1314-0 (cloth) — ISBN 978-0-8010-1408-6 (international trade paper)
    1. Christian youth—United States—Attitudes. 2. Ex-church members—United States—Attitudes. 3. Religious institutions—United States—Public opinion. 4. Christianity—United States—Public opinion. 5. Public opinion—United States. I. Hawkins, Aly. II. Title.
    BV4531.3.K57 2011
    277.3'0830842—dc23                                          2011022322

Unless otherwise indicated, Scripture quotations are from the Holy Bible, New International Version®. NIV®. Copyright © 1973, 1978, 1984, 2011 by Biblica, Inc.™ Used by permission of Zondervan. All rights reserved worldwide. www.zondervan.com

Scripture quotations labeled NLT are from the Holy Bible, New Living Translation, copyright © 1996, 2004, 2007 by Tyndale House Foundation. Used by permission of Tyndale House Publishers, Inc., Carol Stream, Illinois 60188. All rights reserved.

Scripture quotations labeled Message are from The Message by Eugene H. Peterson, copyright © 1993, 1994, 1995, 2000, 2001, 2002. Used by permission of NavPress Publishing Group. All rights reserved.

To protect the privacy and confidentiality of those who have shared their stories with the author, some details and names have been changed.

18   19   20   21   22        7   6   5   4   3   2

In keeping with biblical principles of creation stewardship, Baker Publishing Group advocates the responsible use of our natural resources. As a member of the Green Press Initiative, our company uses recycled paper when possible. The text paper of this book is composed in part of post-consumer waste.

green press
INITIATIVE

**To the previous generation**

Donald Kinnaman (1921–1997) Esther Kinnaman (1925–2008)
Walter Rope (1917–1999) Irene Rope (1921–1991)

**and to the next**

Emily Kinnaman (1999) Annika Kinnaman (2001)
Zachary Kinnaman (2004)
Grant Culver (2003) Lauren Culver (2005)
Kaitlyn Culver (2007) Luke Culver (2009)
Oliver Kinnaman (2011)
Grace Kinnaman (2009) Isaac Kinnaman (2011)
Ellie Kinnaman (2010)
Sydnee Michael (2010)
Josh Rope (1995) Abi Rope (1997) Sarah Rope (1999)

**Psalm 100:5**

For the LORD is good and his love endures forever;
his faithfulness continues through all generations.

# CONTENTS

# YOU LOST ME, EXPLAINED

t feels as if they are reading from a script.

Young adults describe their individual faith journeys in startlingly similar language. Most of their stories include significant disengagement from church—and sometimes from Christianity altogether. But it's not just dropping out that they have in common. Many young people who grew up in church and have since dropped out do not hesitate to place blame. They point the finger, fairly or not, at the establishment: *you lost me.*

Anna and Chris are two such young people. I met them on a recent trip to Minneapolis. Anna is a former Lutheran, now an agnostic. After years of feeling disconnected, she was pushed away, finally, by the "fire and brimstone" sermon the pastor preached at her wedding ceremony. Chris is a former Catholic who became an atheist for several years, in part because of how the church handled his parents' divorce.

I met Graham on another business trip. A natural-born leader, he was attending a program for Christian students. Yet he confessed, "I'm not sure I really believe all this stuff anymore. When I pray I feel like I'm just talking to thin air."

As I was finishing the final edits on this book, I ran into Liz, a twentysomething from my home church in Ventura, California. When she was in high school, I had been an adult volunteer in the youth group.

She said that, despite her upbringing in church and attendance at a Christian college, she had been struggling with feelings of isolation and judgment from her Christian peers. She had met a family from another religious faith and was impressed by them. "A few weeks ago I decided to convert and join them."

Each story is unique, yet they have much in common with the unique stories of thousands of other young adults. The details differ, but the theme of disengagement pops up again and again, often accompanied by a sense that the decision to disconnect was out of their hands. A colleague of mine forwarded an article about Catholicism's loss of so many young people. Among the online comments, these two stood out:

> I wonder what percentage of . . . "Lost" Catholics feel like I do, that we did not leave the Church, but rather, the Church left us.

> I hung in for a long while, thinking that fighting from within was the way to go, but I ultimately realized that it was damaging my relationship with God and my relationship with myself and I felt no choice but to leave.[1]

The familiar themes that emerge from such stories do not make them any easier for parents and church leaders, who have poured much effort and prayer into young lives, to hear. In fact parents' descriptions of the you-lost-me phenomenon are also eerily similar. An earnest mom, Pam, stopped me after a conference. Her question: what should she do about her engineering-student son, who after being a committed Christ-follower for many years was now having significant doubts about the relevance and rationale of Christianity?

I had lunch with another Christian parent who was at the point of tears because his nineteen-year-old son had announced that he did not want anything to do with his parents' faith. "David, I can't explain the loss we feel about him. I am hopeful that he will return to faith because I see how good and generous he is. But it's so difficult for his mother and me. And I can barely stand the way his negative choices are affecting our younger kids. It's all I can do not to ask him to leave our home."

# THE STRUGGLES OF YOUNG CHRISTIANS

If you read my previous book, *unChristian*, written with Gabe Lyons, you may wonder where this new project fits with that research. *unChristian* looks at the reasons young non-Christians reject the Christian faith and explores the changing reputation of Christians, especially evangelicals, in our society. That book focuses on the perceptions and priorities of young non-Christians, or *outsiders*, as we called them.

*You Lost Me*, on the other hand, is about young *insiders*. At its heart are the irreverent, blunt, and often painful personal stories of young Christians—or young adults who once thought of themselves as Christians—who have left the church and sometimes the faith. The book's title is inspired by their voice and mindset, and reflects their disdain for one-sided communication, disconnect from formulaic faith, and discomfort with apologetics that seem disconnected from the real world. *You Lost Me* is about their perceptions of churches, Christianity, and culture. It gives voice to their concerns, hopes, delusions, frustrations, and disappointments.

A generation of young Christians believes that the churches in which they were raised are not safe and hospitable places to express doubts. Many feel that they have been offered slick or half-baked answers to their thorny, honest questions, and they are rejecting the "talking heads" and "talking points" they see among the older generations. *You Lost Me* signals their judgment that the institutional church has failed them.

Whether or not that conclusion is fair, it *is* true that the Christian community does not well understand the new and not-so-new concerns, struggles, and mindsets of young dropouts, and I hope that *You Lost Me* will help to bridge this gap. Because of my age (thirty-seven) and my position as a researcher, I am often asked to explain young people to older generations and advocate for their concerns. I welcome the task because, whatever their shortcomings, I believe in the next generation. I think they are important, and not just because of the cliché "young people are the leaders of tomorrow."

The story—the great struggle—of this emerging generation is learning how to live faithfully in a new context, to be in the world but not of the world. This phrase, "in but not of the world," comes from Jesus's prayer for his followers, recorded in John 17. For the next generation, the lines between right and wrong, between truth and error, between Christian influence and cultural accommodation are increasingly blurred. While these are certainly challenges for every generation, this cultural moment is at once a singular opportunity and a unique threat to the spiritual formation of tomorrow's church. Many young adults are living out the tension of *in-but-not-of* in ways that ought to be corrected or applauded, yet instead are often criticized or rejected.

In the vibrant and volatile story of the next generation, a new spiritual narrative is bubbling up. Through the lens of this project, I have come to understand and agree with some, though not all, of their grievances. Yes, we should be concerned about some of the attitudes and behaviors we encounter in the next generation of Christians, yet I also find reasons to hope in the best of what they have to offer. Apparently they are a generation prepared to be not merely hearers of doctrine but doers of faith; they want to put their faith into action, not just to talk. Yes, many young dropouts are stalled in their spiritual pursuits, yet a significant number of them are reinvigorating their faith with new ideas and new energy.

From this generation, so intent on reimagining faith and practice, I believe the established church can learn new patterns of faithfulness. *You Lost Me* seeks to explain the next generation's cultural context and examine the question *How can we follow Jesus—and help young people faithfully follow Jesus—in a dramatically changing culture?*

## A NEW MINDSET

This is a question every modern generation of believers must answer. I believe that, within the stories of young people wrestling with faith, the church as a whole can find fresh and revitalizing answers. Let's call it "reverse mentoring," because we, the established Christian generation, have a lot to learn from the emerging generation.[2]

We are at a critical point in the life of the North American church; the Christian community must rethink our efforts to make disciples. Many of the assumptions on which we have built our work with young people are rooted in modern, mechanistic, and mass production paradigms. Some (though not all) ministries have taken cues from the assembly line, doing everything possible to streamline the manufacture of shiny new Jesus-followers, fresh from the factory floor. But disciples cannot be mass-produced.[3] Disciples are handmade, one relationship at a time.

We need new architects to design interconnected approaches to faith transference. We need new ecosystems of spiritual and vocational apprenticeship that can support deeper relationships and more vibrant faith formation. We need to recognize the generational shifts from left-brain skills like logic, analysis, and structure to the right-brain aptitudes of creativity, synthesis, and empathy. We need to renew our catechisms and confirmations—not because we need new theology, but because their current forms too rarely produce young people of deep, abiding faith. We need to rethink our assumptions and we need the creativity, honesty, and vitality of the next generation to help us.

As we begin, recognize that we have both individual responsibility and institutional opportunity. Our interpersonal relationships matter. We need to allow the Holy Spirit to guide our parenting, our mentoring, and our friendships. Yet the next generation's faith cannot be addressed simply through better relationships. Institutions such as media, education, church, government, and others significantly influence the faith journeys of the next generation. Implication: we have to reexamine the substance of our relationships and the shape of our institutions.

Do you sense, as I do, that we are at a critical point for the substance and shape of the Christian community in the West? In Eric Metaxas's biography of Dietrich Bonhoeffer, he vividly describes the leadership and clarity the German pastor demonstrated in understanding the evils of the spirit of his age (the Nazis) and the tragic capitulation of the church to culture. Metaxas writes this about the toxic cultural atmosphere of Germany at that time: "The First War and the subsequent depression and turmoil had brought about a crisis in which the younger generation, especially, had lost all confidence in traditional authority and the church. The German notion of the Führer arose out of this generation and its search for meaning and guidance out of its troubles."[4]

Our research at Barna Group leads me to believe that the next generation of Christians has a similar crisis of confidence in institutions, including government, the workplace, education, and marriage, as well as the church. I am not saying that our times are ripe for the rise of a new führer—God forbid—but I do want to suggest that our cultural moment demands *of us* Bonhoeffer-like clarity and leadership. Where institutions failed the next generation, he stepped in as a mentor, confidant, and friend. Where culture demanded mindless conformity in exchange for a sense of belonging, he created deep, kingdom-centered, alternative community. Where the church accommodated Nazism's ungodly beliefs and practices, he spoke sternly and prophetically to its leaders and adherents, challenging them to repent and reform.

In coming chapters, we will explore the seismic shifts in our culture. We'll hear directly from young dropouts and situate their personal stories against the backdrop of profound cultural change, so that we can better understand their shifting worldview. If we begin to grasp their assumptions, values, and allegiances, I believe we will catch a fresh vision, as Bonhoeffer did, for how the Christian community can obey Jesus's command to make disciples in this and future generations.

Let me offer my thanks to the thousands of young Mosaics who shared their experiences for this project. (See p. 246 for generational definitions such as "Mosaic," "Buster," "Boomer," and so on.) If you are a young adult, perhaps you will see something like your story reflected in these pages. I hope this book provides you with a sense that you are not alone, that there are many Christians who are eager to listen to and reengage with you in the grand, yet often challenging, Way of following Jesus. I would like to think God could use this book to help you find your path back to Christ and his church.

If you are a parent, grandparent, educator, pastor, or young Christian leader, my goal for this book is that it serve as a resource, helping you consider how to transfer faith from one generation to the next. In addition to young people's views, *You Lost Me* includes contributions from experts and influencers of older generations. Given this multitude of viewpoints, I can almost guarantee that some of what we will discover together will make you feel threatened, overwhelmed, and perhaps even a little guilty. My aim is to provoke new thinking and new action in the critical process of the spiritual development of the next generation. As a faith community, we need a whole new mind to see that the way we develop young people's faith—the way we have been teaching them to engage the world as disciples of Christ—is inadequate for the issues, concerns, and sensibilities of the world we ask them to change for God. Whether we come from a Catholic, evangelical, mainline, or Orthodox tradition, we need to help the next generation of Christ-followers deal well with cultural accommodation; we need to help them live *in-but-not-of* lives. And in the process, we will all be better prepared to serve Christ in a shifting cultural landscape.

But first, we need to understand the dropout problem.

For a summary of the Barna data presented in this book and discussion questions for each chapter, visit www.youlostmebook.com.

Part 1

# DROPOUTS

# 1

# FAITH, INTERRUPTED

Millions of young adults leave active involvement in church as they exit their teen years. Some never return, while others live indefinitely at the margins of the faith community, attempting to define their own spirituality. Some return to robust engagement with an established church, while some remain faithful through the transition from adolescence to adulthood and beyond.

In this chapter I want to accomplish two things: define the dropout problem and interpret its urgency. A clear understanding of the dropout phenomenon will set the stage for our exploration of young adults' faith journeys. *Does a dropout problem exist? If so, for what reasons do so many spiritually active teenagers put their faith—or at least their connection to a church—on the shelf as they reach adulthood? Why do young people raised in "good Christian homes" wander as young adults?*

In chapter 2 we'll address the second set of big questions: *Is this generation's dropout problem the same as that of previous generations? What is so different about Mosaic (what some call Millennial) dropouts? Is the culture really changing all that much for the emerging generation?*

Let me start by describing my job.

## LOOKING FOR CLUES

Being a researcher means being one part listener and one part sleuth. The nearly thirty thousand interviews we conduct each year at Barna Group give our team ample opportunity to hear what is happening in people's lives. Our listening done, we then put on our sleuthing hats and piece together the trends that shape our collective lives and faith communities.

A big piece of the dropout puzzle fell into place for me back in 2003. One blustery autumn day while visiting Grand Rapids, Michigan, I wrote an article based on our findings that twentysomethings were struggling to find their place in Christian churches. When we released the piece online, it generated significant readership within just a few days. The article even sparked an *ABC News* segment featuring our research as well as an interview with Tim Keller, pastor of Redeemer Presbyterian Church, highlighting his efforts to communicate Christianity to young people in Manhattan.

A few years later, in 2007, Gabe Lyons and I released a book called *unChristian*, which explores how young *non-Christians* perceive Christianity. In addition to realizing the extraordinarily negative views of the Christian faith that young outsiders held, I was shocked that the data also revealed the frustrations of young Christians. Millions of young *Christians* were also describing Christianity as hypocritical, judgmental, too political, and out of touch with reality.

Those testimonies demanded further attention, so we focused our team on getting to know the next generation of Christians. We wanted to understand why they leave church. We wanted to hear about their difficulty with letting Christianity take long-term root. We wanted to discover how and why they are rethinking faith and whether this process is similar to or different from that of previous generations. We also wanted to identify areas of hope, growth, and spiritual vitality in the church's work with young adults.

Over the last four years, we have done all of the above. Our team at Barna Group has pored over hundreds of generational studies and related books, consulted experts and academics, and probed the perspectives of parents and pastors. We have compiled and analyzed the Barna

Group database of hundreds of thousands of interviews, conducted over a twenty-seven-year span, to understand the generational dynamics of faith formation. We have completed eight new scientific national studies, including nearly five thousand new interviews for this project alone. Our research has been tailored to understand eighteen- to twenty-nine-year-olds, asking them to describe their experience of church and faith, what has pushed them away, and what connective tissue remains between them and Christianity.

Based on all this, I invite you to meet the next generation. As we get to know them together, there are three realities we need to keep in mind:

1. Teen church engagement remains robust, but many of the enthusiastic teens so common in North American churches are not growing up to be faithful young adult disciples of Christ.
2. There are different kinds of dropouts, as well as faithful young adults who never drop out at all. We need to take care not to lump an entire generation together, because every story of disconnection requires a personal, tailor-made response.
3. The dropout problem is, at its core, a faith-development problem; to use religious language, it's a *disciple-making problem*. The church is not adequately preparing the next generation to follow Christ faithfully in a rapidly changing culture.

Let's explore these realities more deeply.

### From Passionate Teens to MIA Twentysomethings

At a recent student conference in Florida, I was speaking to a large group of eighteen- to twenty-five-year-old Christians. I began my talk with a simple question: "How many of you personally know someone who has dropped out of the Christian community?" Every single person in the room raised a hand.

The dropout problem touches countless students, parents, and faith leaders, but many of these have only a vague grasp of what, exactly, the dropout phenomenon *is*. The first step in the discovery process is to understand two simple facts:

1. Teenagers are some of the most religiously active Americans.
2. American twentysomethings are the least religiously active.

The ages eighteen to twenty-nine are the black hole of church attendance; this age segment is "missing in action" from most congregations. As shown in the chart, the percentage of church attenders bottoms out during the beginning of adulthood. Overall, there is a 43 percent drop-off between the teen and early adult years in terms of church engagement. These numbers represent about eight million twentysomethings who were active churchgoers as teenagers but who will no longer be particularly engaged in a church by their thirtieth birthday.

### The Dropout Problem

*percent of Americans of each age who report monthly churchgoing and church participation*

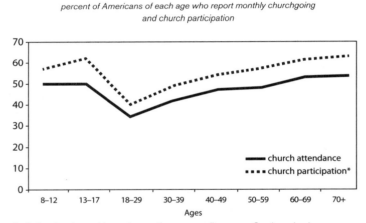

*Includes church worship service, youth group, small group, or Sunday school
Source: Barna Group, nationwide studies, conducted from 1997–2010, N = 52,496

The problem is not that this generation has been less churched than children and teens before them; the problem is that much spiritual energy fades away during a crucial decade of life—the twenties. Think of it: more than four out of five Americans under the age of eighteen will spend at least a part of their childhood, tween, or teenage years attending a Christian congregation or parish. More than eight out of every ten adults remember attending Sunday school or some other religious training consistently before the age of twelve, though their participation during the teen years was less frequent. About seven out of ten Americans recall going to Sunday school or other religious programs for teens at least once a month.[1]

In survey after survey, the majority of Americans describe themselves as Christians. Where—and *when*—do you think this allegiance begins? Early in life, before adulthood. Adults identify as Christians typically because they had formative experiences as a child or as a teenager that connected them to Christianity.

But that connection is often shallow and on the surface, having more to do with cultural identification than it does with deep faith. And our research shows that Mosaics do not share the cultural identification of previous generations.

In one of Barna Group's most recent studies, conducted in early 2011, we asked a nationwide random sample of young adults with a Christian background to describe their journey of faith. The interview population was made up of individuals who attended a Protestant or Catholic church or who identified at any time as a Christian before the age of eighteen. This included young people who were *currently* churched and those who were unchurched, as well as those who called themselves Christians and some who once did but no longer did so.

The research confirmed what we had already been piecing together from other data: 59 percent of young people with a Christian background report that they had or have "dropped out of attending church, after going regularly." A majority (57 percent) say they are less active in church today compared to when they were age fifteen. Nearly two-fifths (38 percent) say they have gone through a period when they significantly doubted their faith. Another one-third (32 percent) describe a period when they felt like rejecting their parents' faith.

Many of the perceptions of young Catholics are similar to those of young Protestants, yet we also learned that Catholics struggle with particular aspects of their faith: One-fifth (21 percent) say, "the clergy abuse scandals have made me question my faith." One-eighth (13 percent) of young Catholics say they "had a mostly negative experience in a Catholic school." Two out of every five (40 percent) say, "the Catholic church's teachings on sexuality and birth control are out of date," while one-quarter of young Catholics (28 percent) say, "it bothers me that the church does not ordain women as priests." When it comes to perceptions of their parish and the Mass, one-third (34 percent) indicate that "Mass is supposed to be meaningful but it feels like a boring obligation," and one-fifth (22 percent) say that "older people seem more important than younger people in my parish."

When it comes to young Catholics' and Protestants' perspectives about Jesus Christ, twentysomethings are the age group least likely to say they are personally committed to Christ. While they have generally favorable views of Jesus, they also harbor significant doubts about the central figure of Christianity. Young adults are more likely than any other age group to believe that Jesus sinned, to doubt the miracles Jesus performed, and to express skepticism about his resurrection. Despite their previous religious experiences, twentysomethings are the least likely to say they are confident that Jesus Christ speaks to them in a way that is personal and relevant to their circumstances.

### In Their Own Words

*How Young People Describe Their Spiritual Journeys—*
*Away from Church and Faith*
Americans with a Christian background,* ages 18–29

| | All Christians | Protestants | Catholics |
|---|---|---|---|
| **Perceptions of Church and Faith** | | | |
| Ever dropped out of attending church, after going regularly | 59% | 61% | 56% |
| Ever personally been significantly frustrated about your faith | 50% | 51% | 49% |
| Compared to age 15, less spiritual today | 29% | 31% | 29% |
| Compared to age 15, less active in church today | 57% | 58% | 65% |
| Went through period when you significantly doubted your faith | 38% | 41% | 33% |
| Went through period when you felt like rejecting your parents' faith | 32% | 35% | 25% |

* Describe themselves as having attended a Christian or Catholic church or identifying as a Christian at one point in their life.

Barna Group | 2011 | N=1,296

The conclusion: after significant exposure to Christianity as teenagers and children, many young adults, whether raised Catholic or Protestant, are MIA from the pews and from active commitment to Christ during their twenties. Even where individual churches and parishes are effectively reaching young people, the number of twentysomething attenders is a mere drop in the bucket, considering the number of young people who reside in their local community. And for every congregation that is attracting a healthy proportion of Mosaic attenders, many more churches are struggling with how to connect to and remain relevant in the lives of young adults.

## Every Story Matters

One of the things we learned from this research is that there is more than one way to drop out and more than one way to stay faithful. Every person goes on a unique journey related to his or her faith and spirituality, and *every story matters*. The reasons young people drop out, as similar to each other as they may seem, are very real and very personal to those who experience them. We in the Christian community need to bear this in mind.

At the same time, as much as every story is different and worthy of serious attention and care, there are patterns in the data that can help us make sense of the dropout problem. We discovered in our research that there are three broad ways of being lost:

- *Nomads* walk away from church engagement but still consider themselves Christians.
- *Prodigals* lose their faith, describing themselves as "no longer Christian."
- *Exiles* are still invested in their Christian faith but feel stuck (or lost) between culture and the church.

Kelly is an example of a nomad. She grew up in an evangelical Protestant church. Her father, Jack, has worked for Christian organizations during Kelly's entire life and regularly teaches Sunday school. Both her parents are committed churchgoers. Kelly describes struggling with an anxiety disorder and never feeling that she fit in at church. "The first strike against the church was the youth group, where I didn't fit in and no effort was made to help me. The second strike was in college when the campus ministry I attended started talking about their quotas for getting people saved. The third strike was the judgment my parents received from their church friends about me. They told my parents that they did a bad job raising me." Despite these negative experiences, Kelly fits the profile of a nomad because she prays and reads her Bible often. She told me, "I never lost faith in Christ but I have lost faith in the church."

Mike typifies a prodigal, an ex-Christian. He grew up in the Catholic church, but his love for science and his razor-sharp wit—which was sometimes perceived as disrespect—regularly put him at odds with the parish leaders. After a period of searching and wrestling with his faith, he says, "I just stopped believing in those Christian stories." Time will tell if Mike will return to faith later in life. But usually the attitudes of prodigals seem closed to such outcomes.

Nathan, the lead singer of a successful band, exemplifies an exile. Nathan's parents were, like Kelly's, fixtures in an evangelical church during his childhood years. Then his parents split up. "I was really volatile toward church and faith for a long time, but way more so toward church than faith." In an interview with *Relevant* magazine, this young musician described his "enormous cynicism toward all things institutional Christianity." He and his bandmates were "all really embarrassed by and ashamed of a lot of the [Christian] subculture we came from, but not necessarily ashamed or embarrassed by the beliefs we had." Nathan's faith is still intact and was largely saved by his association with other young artists who were honest about their struggles and willing to help each other heal. The magazine describes Nathan and his band as "asking questions and resisting some aspects of their own conservative upbringings—yet still searching for something more from their faith."[2]

Nathan, Mike, and Kelly represent three types of *you-lost-me* journeys. In chapters 3 (Nomads and Prodigals) and 4 (Exiles), we will delve into the research about these three groups, but there are three observations I want to make here at the beginning. First, a review. The faith journeys of the next generation are not monochromatic or one-size-fits-all. *Every story matters.* And every *type* of story matters. Perhaps you see someone you know, or even yourself, in these three broad patterns.

Second, the majority of young dropouts are not walking away from faith, they are putting involvement in church on hold. In fact, as heart-rending as loss-of-faith stories are, prodigals are the rarest of the drop-outs; most are either nomads or exiles—those who are dropping out of conventional forms of Christian community, not rejecting Christianity entirely. In other words, though I believe these issues are interconnected, *most young Christians are struggling less with their faith in Christ than with their experience of church.*

Third, there is a countertrend in the you-lost-me data—young Christ-followers who are passionate, committed, and bursting to engage the world for the sake of the gospel. (Some of these young believers have stayed deeply connected to a local parish or congregation, while others are better described as exiles.) We found, for instance, that two out of five (42 percent) eighteen- to twenty-nine-year-old Christians say they are "very concerned about my generation leaving the church." A similar proportion (41 percent) describe their desire for "a more traditional faith, rather than a hip version of Christianity." And three out of every ten (30 percent) young Christians say they are "more excited about church than at any time in my life."

I am encouraged by new expressions of worship and community, such as the Passion worship movement and Hillsong United, and the emphasis among some leaders to raise the theological and practical expectations of young people. Brett and Alex Harris, teenage twin brothers who wrote the book *Do Hard Things*, are an example of this countertrend, as is pastor Kevin DeYoung, author of *Just Do Something*. These and other young leaders are responding to the "failure to launch" that often defines this generation.[3] They realize that the pressure of increased expectations has paralyzed many of their peers and are doing all they can to help.

Yet there are also important questions raised by our research about the quality and vigor of faith among twentysomethings who do not drop out. Overall, knowledge of Scripture, doctrine, and church his-tory is poor among most Christians, not just young adult believers. But the cultural pressures faced uniquely by Mosaics make holding on to Christian faith a difficult undertaking—if their faith is shallow, how can it survive? Are their theological views and commitment to Christ deep enough? Will this be a generation to be reckoned with or one that pushes their convictions to the sidelines? How much will cultural accommodation and acclimation define their faith? Will they capitulate to faith-killing cultural norms?

The next generation is caught between two possible destinies—one moored by the power and depth of the Jesus-centered gospel and one anchored to a cheap, Americanized version of the historic faith that will snap at the slightest puff of wind. Without a clear path to pursue the true gospel, millions of young Christians will look back on their twentysomething years as a series of lost opportunities for Christ.

## Disciple Making in a New Context

On the surface, this book is about dropouts—prodigals, nomads, and exiles—but on a deeper level, it is about new pressures facing the entire Christian community as we seek to pass on the faith. I want to examine, clarify, and help us consider our response to the intense pressures that are shaping our culture and the church. Whatever our age or spiritual state, we must all respond to our new and uncertain cultural context— but Mosaics most of all.

Like a Geiger counter under a mushroom cloud, the next generation is reacting to the radioactive intensity of social, technological, and religious changes. And for the most part, we are sending them into the world unprepared to withstand the fallout. Too many are incapable of reasoning clearly about their faith and unwilling to take real risks for Christ's sake. These shortcomings are indicators of gaps in disciple making. There are three central arenas where these gaps are in evidence—and where the church has God-given opportunities to rethink our approach to disciple making.

### 1. Relationships

The first arena where there is a disciple-making gap is relationships. As we'll see in later chapters, Mosaics are highly relational in many respects (especially when it comes to peers) and many have positive relationships with their families. At the same time, twentysomethings frequently feel isolated from their parents and other older adults in the realm of faith and spirituality. Many young people feel that older adults don't understand their doubts and concerns, a prerequisite to rich mentoring friendships; in fact a majority of the young adults we interviewed reported never having an adult friend other than their parents. *Can the church rediscover the intergenerational power of the assembly of saints?*

The Mosaic generation epitomizes a me-and-we contradiction. To generalize, they are extraordinarily relational and, at the same time, remarkably self-centered. *We want to change the world! Look at me! Let's make a difference together! I want to be famous!* They want to be mentored and they want to make it on their own. They want to do everything with friends and they want to accomplish great things under their own steam. These selfish and others-oriented contradictions will certainly affect the shape of Christianity in the coming decade, but in what ways? *How can the Christian community speak prophetically to the relational-individual dissonance and help young people serve others for the sake of the gospel?*

The next generation are consummate collage artists, able to blend a diverse set of relationships, ideas, and aspirations. This includes awareness of global issues as well as maintaining relationships with people across generations, religions, sexual orientations, and ethnic backgrounds. They expect and relish diversity. (The eclectic nature of this generation's relationships and values inspired George Barna to name them "Mosaics.") *How can the Christian community understand and learn from the empathy and energy of the next generation, while also cultivating their quest for truth?*

## 2. Vocation

The second arena is vocation, that powerful, often ignored intersection of faith and calling. Millions of Christ-following teens and young adults are interested in serving in mainstream professions, such as science, law, media, technology, education, law enforcement, military, the arts, business, marketing and advertising, health care, accounting, psychology, and dozens of others. Yet most receive little guidance from their church communities for how to connect these vocational dreams deeply with their faith in Christ. This is especially true for the majority of students who are drawn to careers in the fields of science, including health care, engineering, education, research, computer programming, and so on. These young Christians learn very little in their faith communities about how to live honestly and faithfully in a world dominated by science—much less how to excel in their chosen scientific vocation. *Can the Christian community summon the courage to prepare a new generation of professionals to be excellent in their calling and craft, yet humble and faithful where God has asked them to serve?*

A related gap is the church's loss of "creatives," musicians, visual and performance artists, filmmakers, poets, skaters and surfers, storytellers, writers, and so on. In the pages of *You Lost Me,* you will meet singers, comedians, writers, and filmmakers who have found it difficult to connect their creative gifts and impulses to church culture. Frequently the modern church struggles to know what to do with right-brained talent. What has traditionally been a fertile ground for the arts—the church—is now generally perceived as uncreative, overprotective, and stifling. *Can the Christian community relearn to esteem and make space for art, music, play, design, and (dare I say it) joy?*

### 3. Wisdom

The third arena where the church must rethink its approach to disciple making is helping the next generation learn to value wisdom over information. Mosaics have access to more knowledge content than any other generation in human history, but many lack discernment for how to wisely apply that knowledge to their lives and world. Young adults are digital natives immersed in a glossy pop culture that prefers speed over depth, sex over wholeness, and opinion over truth. But it is not enough for the faith community to run around with our hair on fire, warning about the hazards of cultural entrapment. God's children in the next generation need more and deserve better.

Making sense of and living faithfully in a rapidly changing cultural context require massive doses of wisdom. But what, exactly, is wisdom? In the ancient Hebrew understanding, it is the idea of skillful living. As such, wisdom entails the spiritual, mental, and emotional ability to relate rightly to God, to others, and to our culture. Proverb 9:10 says, "The fear of the LORD is the beginning of wisdom." Wisdom is rooted in knowing and revering the God who has revealed himself in Christ through the Scriptures. We find wisdom in the Bible, in creation and the ongoing work of the Holy Spirit, in the practices and traditions of the church, and in our service to others.

But many in the next generation find it difficult to move beyond being consumers of information to become people of wisdom. For example, many young Christians admire the words and works of Jesus (information) but do not *know* him as Lord and God (wisdom). They read and respect the Bible (information) but they do not perceive that its words lay claim to their obedience (wisdom). Young Christians are the least likely generation to believe in and experience the presence of the Holy Spirit. In addition, the spiritual practices and historic traditions of the church, which serve to deepen believers' understanding and experience of God, often seem hopelessly old-fashioned to many of today's young adults.

Becoming wise does not happen by simply "saying the prayer," or by memorizing a list of dos and don'ts, or by signing a pledge, or by completing a six-week program. Instead, it is a lifetime process of deep transformation through faith in Christ, knowledge of God's Word, living by the power of the Holy Spirit, and engaging in rich community with other believers. *How can the Christian community help young Christians live wisely in a culture of mental, emotional, and spiritual distraction?*

## WHY THE DROPOUT PROBLEM IS A *PROBLEM*

Why should we concern ourselves with the faith journeys of young adults? Why does all this matter?

First, it's a matter of heart. The spiritual lives of millions of young people are at stake. That fact, in and of itself, should be reason enough to care. A person sets his or her moral and spiritual foundations early in life, usually before age thirteen, yet the teen and young adult years are a significant period of experimentation, of testing the limits and reality of those foundations. In other words, even though the childhood and early adolescent years are the time during which spiritual and moral compasses are calibrated, the experimental and experiential decade from high school to the late twenties is the time when a young person's spiritual trajectory is confirmed and clarified.

Faith switching is most likely to occur between the ages of eighteen and twenty-nine. In one study we conducted, we asked a representative sample of Americans as old as those in their nineties to identify if and when they had changed faiths. The most common response was that they had done so during their twenties, and 71 percent of those who had significantly changed faith views did so before the age of thirty.[4] This accords with a recent Pew Forum survey, which found that "most people who change their religion leave their childhood faith before age twenty-four."[5] The choices made in the first adult decade set the direction of life, as young adults make decisions about education, debt and finances, career, marriage, family, meaning, and many other critical matters. What influences will young adults choose to help them shape the lives they want to live? Will their faith—and faith communities—provide direction at these critical crossroads? It doesn't have to be faith ending for a person to disengage for a time from church or to question his or her faith; this process can actually make a person (and his or her faith) stronger. But is it the ideal?

Some faith leaders simply say they will wait until young people get old enough to get married and have their own kids. Then they will be ready to return to church. But is that really a reasonable approach, especially when the ages of marriage and childbearing are getting pushed further back? Is that what we want for young people—to have years of religious education, experiences, and relationships, only to turn away once they can decide for themselves?

Of course not.

Second, awareness of young adults' faith journeys is a matter of accuracy. Without accurate information, Christians have a choice to ignore or minimize the dropout problem or to sensationalize it. Neither approach is right or helpful. As we began our investigation on this project, one of the first things we noticed was the dispute over what is happening and what it means. There are many conflicting stories. In fact there are some who claim there is no story at all—the dropout problem is a myth, an alarmist's way of selling books and programs that promise to resolve a manufactured crisis. What we're actually seeing, according to the "dropout deniers," is the natural ebb of faith related to young adulthood in every generation. The deniers either minimize the dropout problem or explain that most twentysomethings who have lost interest in church or faith will return to the fold in later adulthood. *Move along,* they say. *Nothing to see here.*

Others clamor that not enough alarm has been raised over the dropout problem, that the crisis is deeper and more pervasive than any of us suspect. Just recently, someone called our offices to register an objection to our data, asserting that Barna Group's appraisal of the dropout numbers is off by a mile. The caller hoped we would revise our findings to reflect a *higher* number of dropouts, just to confirm his fears. *Red alert! Christianity will be gone in a generation,* proclaim the doomsayers.

I believe the dropout problem is real and even urgent but I also believe that signing the church's death warrant in the next generation is premature. I want to provide here a nuanced, data-driven assessment of young adults' faith journeys. In our evidence gathering, interviews, and data analysis, the Barna team's goal is to construct the most accurate picture we can of cultural reality, because the church is called to be the church in the real world. In this research, we have done our best to uncover the facts and the truth of the dropout problem, and this book is the compilation of our best thinking on the subject thus far—but it is hardly the final answer. There are no easy, one-size-fits-all ways to disciple the next generation or to transition faith from parents to children. If you are looking for elementary formulas or simple explanations, this is likely not the book for you. I will do my best to be clear and concise, but when it comes to questions of faith and culture, nothing is simple.

Third, it's an issue of responsibility. I am not writing this book to blame anyone for the state of the next generation or of the church. We all have a part to play, young and old, churched or prodigal. If you're a young nomad or exile or faithful Christ-follower, I would like you to remember that, as people redeemed by Jesus, we are citizens of a kingdom that unifies us with the generations of believers who have gone before. That's a lot to live up to, but I believe God's grace is sufficient for you and for me, and that he is calling us to follow Christ wholeheartedly, with courage and boldness.

If you are a prodigal, I urge you to reconsider your choice to disavow Christianity. Whatever your journey, whatever your age, whatever your gripes against Christians and the church, you at your worst are, like me, no better. Yet you and I at our best can be counted among the humble saints who have trusted that God's grace is greater than the shortcomings of his people. Together we could lovingly challenge the church from within to repent and become truly Christian again.

If you're an older believer, a parent, or a Christian leader, I am not pointing the finger of blame at you. Instead, I want us to recognize together our collective calling to love, accept, and partner with this next generation. That's not easy. Philosopher James K. A. Smith encourages parents with this poignant observation: "[Your children are] going to break your heart. Somehow. Somewhere. Maybe more than once. To become a parent is to promise you'll love prodigals."[6]

Part of that promise we make as parents and Christian mentors is to be honest with ourselves. We have to admit that we have messed up too often, attempted the impossible by our own effort, and missed divine moments of opportunity. But we don't have to miss the next ones. If we are to live in obedience to the Great Commandment and the Great Commission, we must love our young adult neighbors (rather than condemning them) and find new ways to make disciples among their number (rather than writing them off). As we look at the rate at which they are dropping out, the Christian community's challenge is to assess our culpability. In what ways are we complicit in the next generation's loss?

If you are a leader in a local church or Christian institution, you are in a position to help the faith community make course corrections on its way to fulfilling its God-given mission. I hope that the information and analysis you find in these pages will help you and your colleagues in ministry wisely discern our times and, with the Spirit's guidance, reform and renew our institutions to meet the deep spiritual needs among the next generation. How can your parish, church, or ministry expand or refine its vision to cultivate lasting faith in every generation?

Caring about the faith journeys of young adults is, finally, a matter of leadership. Every year we have the great privilege to work with many of the nation's top faith-based groups and forward-thinking leaders, including student ministries, Christian schools, denominations, faith-based colleges and universities, publishing houses, and student-focused parachurch organizations. Interacting regularly with these individuals, we see that many sense a shift happening. Many are searching for new ways to be effective in their work with this new generation, and many are waiting for the next generation of leaders to emerge. Among these groups, there is a growing sense that we need new ways of discipleship, a new way of teaching, instructing, engaging, and developing the lives of young people. We need a new mind to focus on apprenticeship in the way of Jesus.

As such, understanding the next generation is certainly relevant to stakeholders (parents, pastors, educators, employers), as well as to organizations (publishers, schools, businesses, churches, ministry organizations). To respond effectively to the spiritual needs of the next generation, established institutions and communities must understand them, and change in appropriate, biblical ways.

The evidence presented here can also make a difference for young leaders, who need to understand their peers. Young Baby Boomers in the 1960s and '70s had to know what was happening within their generation to be a part of shaping their collective influence on American religion. The same is true for leaders in the emerging generation.

Today the influences of technology, pop culture, media, entertainment, science, and an increasingly secular society are intensifying the differences between the generations. And many churches, leaders, and parents—the established generation—have a difficult time understanding these differences, much less relating to the values, beliefs, and assumptions that have spawned them. So we need younger leaders. One of the most rewarding aspects of this project has been meeting the many young Christians who are motivated by godly concern for their own generation. Their enthusiasm and hope is refreshing, and I respect their extraordinary efforts to see their peers awakened to the love and purposes of God.

Young leaders who speak the language of their peers are sorely needed because today's twentysomethings are not just slightly or incrementally different from previous generations. Mosaics are living through *discontinuously different* social, technological, and spiritual change.

In the next chapter, we'll take a long look at just how deep these differences go and what they may mean for the future of the faith.

# 2

# ACCESS, ALIENATION, AUTHORITY

Last year I met with Bob Buford, the cable television entrepreneur who made a significant midlife reorientation of his work priorities and then told his story in a popular book called *Half Time*. A few of my peers were discussing generational change, and Bob jumped in with this: "I think this next generation is not just slightly different from the past. I believe they are *discontinuously different* than anything we have seen before."

As proof, Bob turned to his files and pulled out a copy of a recent research report on Mosaics, or Millennials. He flipped to a page that showed the prevailing self-identities of each of the four primary generations in American culture and began to read the top five words or phrases each generation had used to describe itself: "Elders used words like these: 'World War II and Depression,' 'smarter,' 'honest,' 'work ethic,' and 'values and morals,'" Bob half-read, half-recited from memory. "Boomers describe their generation with terms like 'work ethic,' 'respectful,' 'values and morals,' and 'smarter.' Busters use these terms: 'technology use,' 'work ethic,' 'conservative/traditional,' 'smarter,' and 'respectful.'" He chuckled. "Everybody thinks they're smarter."

"But now, look at this," Bob continued. "The Millennials use these five phrases to describe their generation: 'technology use,' 'music and pop culture,' 'liberal/tolerant,' 'smarter,' and 'clothes.'[1] Where has *respectful* gone? Where is *work ethic*? To me, this shows that the next generation is not just sort of different; they are *discontinuously* different. I am trying to get a handle on this group because I believe God wants me to invest in this generation. But I don't know where to start."

In this chapter I argue that the next generation is so different because *our culture is discontinuously different*. That is, the cultural setting in which young people have come of age is significantly changed from what was experienced during the formative years of previous generations. In fact I believe a reasonable argument can be made that no generation of Christians has lived through a set of cultural changes so profound and lightning fast. Other generations of Christ-followers have endured much greater persecution. Others have had to sacrifice more to flourish or even survive. But I doubt many previous generations have lived through as compounded and complicated a set of cultural changes as have today's Christians in the West. The last fifty years have been a real-time experiment on the next generation, using free markets, media, advertising, technology, politics, sexuality, and so on as our lab tools. The experiment continues, but we can already observe some of the results:

Fluidity

Diversity

Complexity

Uncertainty

Today's Mosaics are being formed under the direct influence of these fast-paced changes. Their expectations, values, behaviors, attitudes, and aspirations are being shaped in and by this context. The truth is, of course, that we *all* are under the influence of this major set of shifts, regardless of our age or generation—or our willingness (or unwilling-ness) to embrace them. Today's sixtysomethings are living in the same discontinuously different culture as are today's twentysomethings. Much of the social, technological, and spiritual changes we are experiencing today began to take shape during the 1960s (more on that later). The difference is that Seniors, Boomers, and even Busters, to some extent, came of age before these momentous changes had reached maximum velocity and critical mass.

Let's return to the way teens and young adults express their disconnection from the Christian community: *you lost me*. When someone uses this idiom, they are suggesting that something hasn't translated, that the message has not been received. *Wait, I don't understand. You lost me.* This is what many Mosaics are saying to the church. As we'll see in this chapter, it's not that they're not listening; it's that they can't understand what we are saying.

The transmission of faith from one generation to the next relies on the messy and sometimes flawed process of young people finding meaning for themselves in the traditions of their parents. Prodigals, nomads, and exiles all have to make sense of the faith conveyed to them through relationships and wisdom. But what happens when the process of relationships and the sources of wisdom change? What happens to the transference of faith when the world we know slips out from under our collective feet? We have to find new processes—a new mind—that make sense of faith in our new reality.

We may take comfort in the fact that God is at work in the spiritual journeys of teens and young adults even as we are trying to figure out what to say and how to say it. Faith, ultimately, comes from God. And we can be confident that he cares more than even we do for today's young people. Nevertheless, regardless of our age, we also must commit ourselves to understanding our culture today to be effective translators of faith to the next generation. We must come to grips with the challenges and with the opportunities for the gospel to advance.

The next generation is living in a new technological, social, and spiritual reality; this reality can be summed up in three words: *access, alienation*, and *authority*.

## ACCESS

Let's take a quick trip back in time to the year of my birth, 1973. Before the end of that illustrious decade, the sci-fi adventure that defined a generation of young geeks, *Star Wars*, had hit theaters. My dad, doing his duty to shape the imagination of his young son, took me to the Cine Capri, the largest screen in Phoenix, Arizona, to see the film.

I can still remember sitting there in the darkened, air-conditioned room, mesmerized by the opening cinematic sequence: a blockade runner attempting to evade the imperial cruiser; droids shuffling about the pearl-white interior of the spacecraft; menacing Darth Vader, suffocating an officer with the power of The Force. "What have you done with the plans?" he demanded, striking fear in the heart of a small kid in a galaxy far, far away.

Recently a friend of mine, Gary Stratton, reminded me of something else that defined the success of *Star Wars*. It became a blockbuster in part because millions of people went to the theater over and over and over to see it. In what may have been a cultural first, sci-fi geeks began showing up to theaters within just a few weeks of the movie's release fully decked out in handmade versions of the character costumes.

"Okay, cool," I said. "Aside from geek-cred, why is that significant?"

"Because during the 1970s there was no guarantee we would ever be able to see the film again," Gary pointed out. "There was no such thing as a home video market or DVDs or downloadable films or Netflix. I guess we might have hoped the film would show up on network TV someday. But even stuff like HBO and cable was all pretty new at the time, and hardly something that an average guy like me expected would change our lives."

"Wow, I get it. People saw *Star Wars* multiple times at the theater because they didn't know they would eventually be able to watch pretty much any movie ever produced anywhere."

He laughed, "No, we did not. It literally felt like a once-in-a-lifetime experience."

"So how many times did you see it during the year it came out?"

"Um, probably ten. Maybe more."

"Did you dress up like Chewbacca?"

## The Challenge of Access

The first and perhaps most obvious change relates to emerging digital tools and technologies—the methods and means by which young adults connect with each other and obtain information about the world.

Hardware such as personal computers, tablets, mobile devices, and smart phones, as well as soft technologies like Web pages, apps, and software, are providing the next generation (and the rest of us) with nearly unlimited access to other people and their ideas and worldviews—at the instantaneous click of a mouse or swipe of a finger. The heightened level of *access* provided by these tools is changing the way young adults think about and relate to the world. For better and worse, they are sensing, perceiving, and interpreting the world—and their faith and spirituality—through screens. Among other things, access means the current generation can expect to enjoy nearly unlimited access to any movie at any time long after its theatrical release—and they can access so much more than movies.

One of the interviews we conducted was with a young man who described how access to the Internet as a fifteen-year-old gave him unfettered sexual opportunities, eventually leading him beyond pornography and into real-life hookups. The Internet became his portal to sexual liberty. This began a period of spiritual nomadism for him and brought him close to giving up his faith entirely as he wrestled with the notion, *Maybe I am just one of the people destined to live in this kind of sin my whole life.*

In my presentations to and work with various faith communities, the next generation's prodigious use of technology, entertainment, and media—their access—comes up again and again. Not long ago I presented on this topic at a church in southeastern Missouri. After my talks, many parents and pastors wanted to know how they should respond to the nearly symbiotic relationship they see between young adults and digital media.

Consider this episode. My son, Zack, is a talkative seven-year-old. During a discussion about some arcane subject the other day, he asked me a question. I didn't know the answer.

"Dad, give me your iPhone," he said. "Tell me how to spell it and I'll just Google it." Zack can barely spell but he knows that Google has answers. Similarly, the expectation of constant and unlimited access among those ten to fifteen years older than he is influencing who they are becoming and what they want out of life.

Simply put, technology is fueling the rapid pace of change and the disconnection between the past and the future. The Internet and digital tools are at the root of a massive disruption between how previous generations relate, work, think, and worship and how Mosaics (and, to some extent, Busters) do these activities. Mosaics and Busters, as Bob Buford described, understand technology as part of their generational self-identity.

Young people are some of the earliest adopters of technology, of course. Some have described the emerging generation as "digital natives," especially compared to their predecessors—who, for the most part, are latecomers to the technological revolution. Older adults use digital tools, but they are much less comfortable, much less conversant—as if they are learning and then speaking a second language. Mosaics, on the other hand, are native to the digital world, even compared to their tech-savvy Buster predecessors.

Busters learned to use technology as an ally against the Boomers' influence and control; if they could master technology, they had a strategic advantage. Mosaics, however, have been raised with these technologies in full supply, and that reality is facilitating new patterns of learning, relating, and influencing the world, as well as changing the way they think about church and Christianity. Technological access allows them to experience and examine content originating from nonbiblical worldviews, giving them ample reasons to question the nature of truth. It generates extraordinary distractions and invites them to be less linear and logical in their thought processes. It empowers them to think as participants, not just as consumers, of media. And it makes them both more connected and more isolated than generations before them.

## The Opportunity of Access

Access is not all negative. Thousands of young Christians are creating new venues for the gospel via new media, the Internet, podcasting, blogging, and tweeting, among many others. There is something embedded in their digital DNA that seeks a platform for influence and advocacy. Recently I met a twentysomething Christian who was keeping his blog followers informed about the protests in the Middle East and asking them to pray that this social upheaval would cultivate opportunities for the gospel in predominantly Muslim countries.

No one can begin to fully understand or accurately predict how our culture's digitization will shape our collective lives, much less how it will affect the next generation. Some have compared the proliferation of these new technologies to the invention of the printing press, which democratized access to ideas and, in many ways, enabled the rise of

## ACCESS | *Changing Technologies and Tools*

New technologies and digital tools provide unprecedented access to information, analysis, opinions, relationships, and worldviews.

### Facts | *Recognizing Access*

- The typical American consumes 34 gigabytes of data per day, an increase of 350 percent over 30 years ago.[2]
- Information is mostly visual (television, movies, and games); written words account for less than one-tenth of one percent of the total info we consume.[3]
- Young Christians, like other teens and young adults, perceive and interpret reality through screens.
- The largest university in North America, University of Phoenix, is largely powered by online learning.

### Examples | *Access in Action*

- Teachers and pastors can be fact-checked in real time.
- People *endure* jobs, school, or church and *enjoy* their "real lives" in online games.
- Software brings customized content to users so they don't have to go looking.
- Smartphones have apps for locating Thai food, checking the weather, watching movies, sending and receiving money, listening to music, shopping, blogging, tweeting, and even finding sexual hookups within a five-mile radius of your location (no, really).
- Personal news isn't "real" until it has been shared on Facebook or Twitter.

### New Reality | *Access and Spirituality*

- Young people expect to participate as well as consume.
- "Learning piracy"—young people do not see the church as the sole arbiter of spiritual content.
- Constant access—everyone is an expert—creates a "my-sized" epistemology.
- Expectation of flattened structures of hierarchy.
- Increased global awareness and connection to others in remote places, in real time.
- Desire to stay connected at all times.
- Important to broadcast yourself to the world, to express yourself, to cultivate followers.

science, capitalism, modern political theory, and so much more. One of the catalysts of the Reformation, Martin Luther, even described the printing press as "God's highest and extremist act of grace, whereby the business of the gospel is driven forward."

Hundreds of years from now, when believers look back on the early twenty-first century, will today's unprecedented technologies of access—the digitization of virtually all human knowledge, media, and relationships—be seen as an act of God's grace, driving the gospel forward? What kind of evangelists will these young digital natives be?

It is safe to say that Mosaics' affinity for technology contributes to the sense of disconnection between generations. Literally, they live in a different world than the one in which I was born a scant thirty-seven years ago, not long before my friend Gary imagined he might never see *Star Wars* again.

In sum, the changing means and methods of communicating and finding information—the digital tools of access—are one of the reasons the next generation's context is discontinuously different from the past.

## ALIENATION

The second seismic cultural shift is how alienated today's teens and young adults feel from the structures that undergird our society. We might think of *alienation* as very high levels of isolation from family, community, and institutions.

I had the chance to interview Ashley, a Christian twentysomething and young mother. She told me about finding herself on a cross-country plane trip seated next to a twelve-year-old girl whose mom had put her on the plane, in the custody of the airline, to visit her father. The young lady told Ashley that her parents were divorced and her dad had a job in Georgia. "So I visit him a few times a year. This is my second trip alone on the plane."

The two struck up a conversation that day, which turned into a "digitally aided" relationship, including cell phone calls, email, and texting. About a year later, the young girl committed her life to Christ.

That's a great ending to the story, but Ashley told me something else I still can't shake: "After we got off the plane that first day, the girl said something to me that just broke my heart. She said, 'Ashley, I think you know me better than anyone else in the world.' "

Perhaps this seems like an extreme example, but relational alienation is one of the defining features of this emerging context.

## *The Challenge of Alienation*

Alienation is rooted in the massive social changes that began in the 1960s; the drama of dislocation unfolding in the Mosaic generation is taking place on a stage set by the Baby Boomers.

If ever there was a decade when the earth seemed to tilt on its axis, the 1960s certainly qualifies, with all that happened during those years: the civil rights movement, student riots and unrest, Vietnam war, hippie culture, rock 'n' roll, women's liberation, birth control and the sexual revolution, new mainframe computer technologies, the moon landing, Watergate, FM radio, Woodstock, the Cold War, the burgeoning charismatic and Pentecostal movement, the Catholic transition to the English Mass. In many ways, what we now know as "youth culture" was born during that era, as young people embraced new forms of music and art, unprecedented lifestyles, and anti-establishment thinking; the phrase "generation gap" was first used during this period. When it comes to the church and Christianity, the Boomer generation must have seemed the most ominous of threats. John Lennon, one of the central icons of cultural change during that era, famously remarked, "Christianity will end. It will disappear."

The generation gap is bigger today than ever but it is also a *continuation*, a deepening of the rifts introduced by the youth culture of the 1960s. Essentially the Boomers popularized the church dropout phenomenon. Research from the Gallup organization that stretches back to the 1930s and '40s shows that young adults first began to look much different religiously from their parents during the 1960s. The data suggest that, prior to then, reported church attendance levels were very similar across age groups. In other words, during pre-1960s years, twenty-five-year-olds were just as likely to report weekly church attendance as were sixty-five-year-olds. In the 1960s, however, the trends diverged and young adults began to show significant disengagement compared to older adults—a trend that has continued to this day. The implication is that the dynamic of church disengagement during young adulthood was crafted by the Baby Boomers. Now their kids and their children's kids are taking a similarly circuitous route through faith and young adulthood.

What's different now compared to the 1960s? Let's explore three ways that young adults are alienated in a distinct manner.

### Family

Father absence is an example of profound social change *introduced* during the 1960s but much more common today. In the 1960s, 5 percent of live births were to unmarried women; currently, the percentage is 42 percent. In other words, today's kids are *eight times* more likely to have come into this world without married parents than were Boomers.

We will address the implications of these social changes throughout this book, but one of the most obvious is that this generation of Mosaics has grown up in a culture that affirms a multiplicity of family types—traditional, blended, nontraditional, and same-sex partnerships. This has influenced their understanding of what it means to be a family, how healthy families should function, what it means to have a good heavenly Father in their lives, and how they can find meaning, trust, and intimacy in peers, family, and romantic relationships.

A related set of changes includes alienation from the institution of marriage. Young adults are pushing marriage and childbearing to later in life (if ever). In 1970 more than four out of every five adults ages twenty-five to twenty-nine were married; in 2010 less than half this age group were married. The average age of marriage has steadily increased, moving from the early twenties to the mid-twenties over the last three decades.[4]

### Adulthood

Each generation since the Boomers has taken a longer, more circuitous path to adulthood. For many reasons, some of their choosing and others not, many young adults are postponing the complete transition to adulthood. This transition, according to research reported by one prominent sociologist, is characterized by five key developmental tasks:

leaving home, finishing school, becoming financially independent, getting married, and having a child. In 1960, 77 percent of women and 65 percent of men had completed all of these tasks—had become adults—by age thirty. In the most recent estimate, just 46 percent of women and 31 percent of men had completed the transition by the time they reached thirty years of age.[5] Think about that. "Settled by thirty" used to be the normative, typical pattern for young adults in the 1960s. Now that path represents a *minority* of today's young adults.

As much as anything, this cultural change bares the gap between church and the lives of today's next generation. Most churches and parishes are simply not prepared to minister or disciple those taking a nontraditional path to adulthood. They are most capable of guiding and helping the traditional marriage-and-career–stabilized young adult.

My friend JR Kerr, who teaches in a young congregation in Chicago, told me: "Most of the young adults who don't fit the normal Christian married mold are lovingly called 'pagans' by others and sent my way. But I love 'em and work hard to disciple them in new ways. I think they are the 'new normal' Christians."

## Institutions

A third mark of alienating cultural change launched by the Boomers and amplified in the Mosaics is skepticism about institutions. Many young adults feel "lost" from our systems of education, economics, government, and culture.

College graduates face a dismal employment outlook that is only gradually improving. *USA Today* reported in 2010 that there were "more than five job seekers for every opening,"[6] highlighting the fact that recent grads are competing for jobs against more experienced workers, many of whom have been unemployed during the recession. *Business Week* published a recent cover story on "The Lost Generation," and the subtitle says it all: "The continuing job crisis is hitting young people especially hard—damaging both their future and the economy."[7] According to the story, U.S. employers are having a difficult time finding jobs for young workers, a problem that obviously hurts the young adults themselves but which also threatens to strip their energy and creativity from the nation's economic equation.

## ALIENATION | *Changing Social Context*

Unprecedented levels of disconnection from relationships and institutions.

### Facts | *Recognizing Alienation*

- In 1960, 5 percent of live births were to unmarried women compared to 41 percent in 2010.
- In 1970 a majority had completed the transition to adulthood by age 30; this is no longer typical.
- Young people are among the least likely to vote, volunteer, and join community groups.
- Traditional media, like newspapers and nightly news, have little traction with the younger generation.
- The average young adult has worked for his or her current employer for 3 years, compared to 10 years among older adults.[8]

### Examples | *Alienation in Action*

- A fast food chain ran a promotion giving away a free burger to those who would "unfriend" 10 people on Facebook.
- Freelancing and self-employment are on the rise among young adults.
- Instead of turning to parents or older adults for advice, Mosaics consult peers.
- Recent college grads compete for jobs with millions of unemployed older workers who have more experience.
- Rising cost of living and stagnant wage prospects keep marriage and kids out of reach.

### New Reality | *Alienation and Spirituality*

- Many young adults do not have a network of older adults to help them succeed.
- Mosaics approach marriage and family pragmatically (i.e., "what works for me").
- Skepticism about "talking heads" (i.e., one-way lectures), denominations, and church structures.
- Many superficial acquaintances instead of a few intimate friendships.
- Tension between hopefulness and cynicism when it comes to politics and activism.
- Entrepreneurialism is admired over company loyalty.

Imagine how it must feel to have invested four or five years of your life in earning an education from an established institution, only to find that the piece of paper you received on graduation day is not a ticket to future success. You might be disillusioned about both the education system and the workplace. Making a living and making a difference with your life—not to mention getting married and raising a family—tend to require a paycheck.

Generational shifts are reinventing many sectors of our society, arenas that have until recently been dominated by institutions. Take media, for example. Newspapers and other forms of traditional media—"the fourth estate" of a democratic society—are hemorrhaging readers and advertising dollars. Replacing these institutions is a hyperconnected, eyes-on-the-scene social network that skips the middleman and reports "news" to each other. A decade ago, who could have predicted Facebook, let alone its social influence, continent-sized user base, and enormous market capitalization?

The music industry has been forever changed by the digitization of audio and video, which can be easily shared online. Remember Tower Records or the Virgin Megastore? Young adults don't.

Even when it's not purely due to generational changes, new technologies are changing the game for content providers like the church. Who would have guessed that one of the largest, most influential and well-funded technology companies (Microsoft) would mothball Encarta, losing the race with Wikipedia to create a comprehensive online encyclopedia to thousands of unpaid volunteer contributors, many of whom are Mosaics? It's not a one-to-one comparison, but think about which model the church most resembles—the established monolith or the grassroots network—and what that might mean for its relevance in the lives of a collaborative, can-do generation that feels alienated from hierarchical institutions.

The Mosaic generation is skeptical, even cynical, about the institutions that have shaped our society, and while they retain an undiminished optimism about the future, they see themselves creating that future mostly disengaged from (or at least reinventing) the institutions that have defined our culture thus far. Few institutions in our culture are immune to the impact of the next generation—from music to media, from the workplace to education, from politics to the church. The generational churn at play within the religious establishment is, in many ways, part and parcel of the alienation affecting every segment of our society.

### The Opportunity of Alienation

Today's young adults did not grow up in a vacuum. Like all generations, they were raised in a culture deeply influenced by its predecessors; in this case, the most significant shaping generation was the Boomers. The choices Baby Boomers made with regard to family, church, politics, business, and other institutions have had a domino effect into the emerging generation. Whatever the intent of Boomers' changing relationship with institutions, the Mosaic generation is putting their own stamp on their connections with family, adulthood, and institutions.

There is both good news and bad news for the church with regard to young adults' alienation from what used to be normative in our society. The bad news is that, where congregations and parishes are structured to meet the needs of the "old normal," it will be difficult for young people to find a meaningful place. The good news, however, is that the church is uniquely called to be the community of God—and true, authentic community banishes isolation, loneliness, and alienation and replaces them with love. What will have to change about how we "do ministry" to meet the needs of the "new normal"?

# AUTHORITY

The changing spiritual narrative in North America is the third factor in our culture's discontinuity from previous eras. Let's call this *skepticism of authority*—new questions about who to believe and why. Some have described the United States as a post-Christian nation, though that label misses the enormous size and scope of Christianity, active or not, in America. About two out of every five adults in the United States is a practicing Christian (by which we mean they attend church at least monthly and say their faith is very important to them). Moreover, nearly eight out of ten adults identify as Christian.

However, there is a new spiritual narrative on the rise that says Christianity is no longer the "default setting" of American society. The Christian faith exerted significant influence on our culture in previous generations, but much of that public role has dissipated during the past 130-plus years[9]—the acceleration of those secularizing effects has been felt strongly in the last fifty.

In the book *Will Our Children Have Faith?* John Westerhoff describes how six different arenas of culture once contributed to the socialization of faith: community, church, religious programming (such as Sunday school), public schools (which had prayer and Bible reading), popular entertainment (which was based, at least somewhat, on a biblical worldview), and stable family structures. In other words, while far from perfect, Christianity was the culture's autopilot.

Many of those socializing forces have eroded or at least significantly changed. The cultural structures that carved deep channels for the faith formation of young people are no longer available to the church. Even though they may bear the Christian label, many families don't embody faith. The culture doesn't model or esteem it. Pop entertainment rails against faith in general and Christianity in particular. The education system does its best to be neutral religiously and to instill "values" but not biblical morality.

The next generation is growing up in a culture in which the authority of the Christian community and obedience to Scripture are much less present in their developmental experiences. Mosaic Christians face an environment in which Christianity's authority has been greatly diminished in both obvious and subtle ways.

## The Challenge of Authority

Take the following example. In the early months of the music downloading explosion—the illegal "pirating" of songs digitally—the Christian music industry asked Barna Group to explore the attitudes of young Christians. Did they think that music downloading and "ripping" CDs for their friends was wrong? If not, what might be said to convince them otherwise?

I am not often floored by our data, but the study we completed qualified as a shocker. By large margins, most Christian teenagers did not see illegal music downloading as a moral issue—or if it was, they considered it a matter of fairness and loyalty to their friends rather than of right and wrong. Many of the young Christians we interviewed felt it was more important to be fair and loyal to their peers than to be loyal to the industry. Sound like *alienation* to you?

It was also a matter of—here's the other word—*access*. One young man in our research echoed a common sentiment: "If it is wrong, why would they make it so easy to do on our computers?"

The story of music piracy was also an issue of *skepticism of authority*—whom to trust and why. The students we interviewed had nothing negative to say about their parents or the Bible but they also saw little connection between these sources of authority and their attitudes or behaviors. This finding suggested that many young people maintain split selves—they are capable of holding contradictory beliefs and behaviors in multiple, even conflicting, categories. One part of them genuinely loves their parents and respects the Bible; the other truly sees no moral qualms with experiencing and sharing music as part of their natural network of relationships.

There are several observations we could make about the emerging generation's relationship to authority. Let's take a look at three arenas impacted by their skepticism.

### Scripture

The Bible's influence on this next generation is up in the air. There are certainly pockets of good news about the Good News. Millions of young people believe the Bible is the inspired Word of God, and those families who hold the highest view of Scripture seem to have the best rates of faith transference to their children. We also find that many young adults express an authentic hunger to learn from the Bible and to understand more clearly its meaning and import for their lives.

But when we examine the generation as a whole, we see challenges. Young people are skeptical about the reliability of the original biblical manuscripts; they tend to read the Bible through a lens of pluralism; their changing media behaviors and vanishing attention spans make a physical medium of Scripture less viable; and they seem less likely than previous generations to believe the Scriptures have a claim on human obedience.

As we described in chapter 1, the theological foundations of even the most faithful young believers seem, in some crucial ways, shaky or unreliable.

## Christianity and Culture

A second area of skepticism involves the role Christianity should play in public life and the broader culture. Young Christians seem to sense (accurately, I might add) that secular society makes little room for religious commitments. Questions about the proper role of faith in politics, sexuality, science, media, technology, and so on are simply being reframed to avoid debate—making people of faith irrelevant to the conversation (and, to the next generation, the only thing worse than being wrong is being irrelevant). There is a sense, across the board, of benign apathy toward Christianity. How will the next generation of believers respond to the growing hostility of our culture toward people of faith? Will they find new and meaningful ways to speak with prophetic authority, or will they grow cold to religious and spiritual conviction, like many of their peers in Western Europe?

## Christian Influencers

There are significant changes in the reach and influence of Christian infrastructure in North America, particularly in evangelicalism where Barna Group has focused many of our resources. Our studies show major drops in awareness and positive perceptions of foremost evangelical influencers, from Billy Graham to James Dobson. The nation's most prominent pastors, like Rick Warren and Bill Hybels, are virtually unknown to younger Americans. Contrast that with the relatively consistent levels of positive regard that mainstream personalities, like Denzel Washington, Oprah Winfrey, George Clooney, or Faith Hill, enjoy. Compare Mosaics' positive perceptions of Billy Graham with their positive perceptions of Paris Hilton. *The elder Christian is less favorably viewed than Paris Hilton among today's Mosaics.*

In other words, the guardians of evangelical Christianity in the public sphere are facing significantly diminished influence within the next generation. Where will the next generation of leaders come from? Will there be any? Who will young Christians, especially evangelicals, look to as their voices of Christian persuasion?

## The Gap

### Cultural Heroes versus Christian Influencers

*Percent Holding Favorable Views*

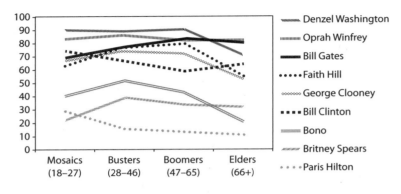

*Percent Holding Favorable Views*

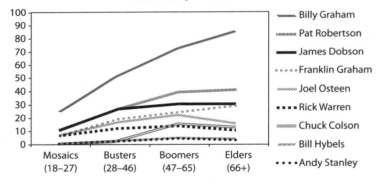

## *The Opportunity of Authority*

Here is the silver lining. A culture of skepticism is a culture of questions, and questions can lead to conversations, relationships, and truth. For instance, the next generation's questions about the Bible are an opportunity to talk about the Bible—and that's great! Tensions between faith and culture can give rise to new forms of cultural and social engagement,

## AUTHORITY | *Changing Spiritual Narrative*

New questions about who and what to believe and why.

### Facts | *Recognizing Authority Shifts*

- Young adults are friends with a more religiously diverse network of peers than previous generations of Americans.
- Young adults are among the least likely to name the Bible as sacred Scripture.

### Examples | *Authority in Action*

- Christian leaders of the previous generation are virtually unknown to today's young Christians.
- Young adults are more likely to consult the Internet than their pastor about a religious question.
- Mosaics are tech savvy, but not necessarily *truth* savvy—"I found it on the Internet" is a common claim for informational reliability.
- Everybody has an opinion, and it's hard to know who is trustworthy.

### New Reality | *Authority and Spirituality*

- Relativism—"What's true for me may not be true for you."
- Peers play an increasing role as the moral and spiritual compass for decision making.
- Young Christians are exposed to a variety of religious content, often without a grid for evaluating it.
- Young people are interested in spirituality, but on their own terms.

and the decline of the celebrity-driven Christian subculture creates space for local, real-life relationships with genuine Christ-followers.

Some Christian communities continue to monitor tightly and shape the six factors that have traditionally socialized young people into the faith: community, church, religious programming, schools, entertainment, and stable family structures. The Amish, for instance, continue a way of life very similar to that of the broader culture one hundred years ago. Some Orthodox communities maintain a similar all-encompassing approach to Christian living. They are still able to socialize their teens and young adults into their way of faith and life through traditional means.

For most faith communities, however, there is no going back. The changing spiritual narrative, and the questions of authority it raises, are akin to the difficulties immigrant cultures have between generations. The first generation speaks only the language of the country of origin. The second generation is fluent in both languages. The third generation speaks only the new language and has little esteem for the cultural traditions that have been lost in translation.

Many Mosaics are no longer interested in the authority structures that have animated Christianity. We in the Christian community need to consider our allegiance to these authorities; we must be honest enough with ourselves to determine where our allegiance is merely cultural (like first-generation immigrants) rather than biblical. We need a new mind in our approach to faith formation in a changing spiritual narrative.

## LIVING IN THE TENSION

The digital revolution, endemic social change, and a shifting narrative of faith in our culture have deeply affected the cognitive and emotional process of "encoding" faith. Because of *access*, *alienation*, and *authority*, the ability of one generation to convey the message and meaning of faith to the next generation—in thought forms, ideas, and practices they can readily understand and incorporate into their lives—has been disrupted.

This generation is, in some unprecedented ways, having to answer in-but-not-of questions. Where is the line between cultural accommodation and cultural influence? What is appropriate for Christians to participate in and what is not? Yes, these are age-old pressures; there is nothing new under the sun. But we cannot imagine that the loss of faith experienced during the 1960s occurred against the same cultural backdrop. Today an information revolution akin to the printing press—the easily accessible digitization of everything—is afoot. Fatherlessness is nearly eight times more common today than it was fifty years ago, and young adults are far less likely to attain full "adulthood" by their thirtieth birthday. And our hyperindividualized, consumer-driven, pluralistic culture invites young people to become their own king or queen, the absolute authority in their kingdom of one. How could these changes *not* affect the faith journeys of young adults?

Let's summarize the challenges and opportunities created by each of these new cultural factors:

> *Access.* Few would debate that we live in a knowledge economy, in a creative age, powered by science-fiction–like technologies. *Will the Christian community connect meaningfully with the generation growing up in this context?*

> *Alienation.* We are conducting a real-time experiment with relationships, family bonds, and institutional reinventions. *Will the Christian community cultivate a presence-centered approach to developing young people, bringing us out of our isolation and alienating pragmatism?*

> *Authority.* The spiritual narrative of our culture has shifted—slowly in places, quickly in others—toward secularism and away from the Bible and Christianity. *Will the Christian community see skepticism of authority as an opportunity or as a threat?*

Teens and twentysomethings and the church are living in the tension of deep cultural change. What a privilege we have to experience these times! Ultimately, because I trust the work of God in every generation, I believe the church can and will respond to the accelerated pace of change. Yet while I am hopeful and encouraged by some of what I see, the outcome is not a foregone conclusion. The transmission of vibrant faith from one generation to the next is still to be determined.

Now that we recognize the cultural backdrop of the next generation's faith journeys, let's meet two groups of dropouts: nomads and prodigals.

Learn how media and technology affect young adults' spiritual journeys at www.youlostmebook.com.

# 3

# NOMADS AND PRODIGALS

I n a recent article, *Rolling Stone* magazine asked one prominent entertainer from the Buster generation about his spiritual journey: "Did you ever go through a period where you lost your faith?" The comedian answered:

> Yeah. It was a college angst thing. But once I graduated from college, some Gideon literally gave me a box of *The New Testament, Psalms and Proverbs* on a street in Chicago. I took one and opened it right away to Matthew, chapter 5, which is the opening of the Sermon on the Mount. That whole chapter is essentially about not worrying. I didn't read it—it spoke to me, and it was an effortless absorption of the idea. Nothing came to me in a thunderbolt, but I thought to myself, "I'd be dumb not to reexamine this."[1]

Who is this popular celebrity who encountered Jesus (again) through the gift of a street evangelist? Stephen Colbert, satirical conservative host of the popular faux news show *The Colbert Report*.

Colbert describes a dark period of his young life triggered by family tragedy—the death of his father and two of his brothers in an airplane accident when he was just ten years old. That event, coupled with an abrupt move to a new city, impacted the young man so that, by the time he went to college, Colbert was deeply skeptical about his faith—until his encounter with that Gideon handing out boxes of Bibles on the street. A couple of decades after his return to the Catholicism of his youth, Colbert describes his nomadic spirituality like this:

> From a doctrinal point of view or a dogmatic point of view or a strictly Catholic adherent point of view, I'm first to say that I talk a good game, but I don't know how good I am about it in practice. I saw how my mother's faith was very valuable to her and valuable to my brothers and sisters, and I'm moved by the words of Christ, and I'll leave it at that.[2]

In the next two chapters of *You Lost Me*, you'll find a few celebrities' stories. I've used them because they are out-front, very visible examples of the dropout journeys we are trying to get a handle on. The last thing I want to do is objectify real people who are made in God's image, and so I point to Stephen Colbert, Katy Perry, David Bazan, and others with respect and admiration, not ridicule or voyeurism. I also do so knowing that a closer, more personal examination of these individuals' spiritual journeys would reveal an even more complex picture of their faith and motivations.

Colbert's story sets up one of the questions this book seeks to answer: *Isn't the next generation's wandering just a symptom of the same life-stage issues that all generations go through as they grow into adulthood? Isn't it just "a college angst thing"?* And closely related: *Don't young people return to church when they get older?*

We might put a more academic sheen on these questions: *Is Christianity's dropout problem a unique sociological phenomenon of the early part of the twenty-first century or just a natural part of the human life cycle in which young people experience faith maturation?* There is a good deal of debate on this matter among experts, as I have mentioned. This is also one of the most common questions I get when I speak or consult on this subject.

I want to argue that the problem is both old *and* new. That is, dropping out is both a natural part of the maturation process—of people of any generation becoming comfortable, in fits and starts, in their own spiritual and religious skin—as well as a unique, pressing reality for the church. Wrestling with faith is an enduring feature of the transition to young adulthood, as Baby Buster Colbert's story demonstrates. *And* it is a particularly urgent dilemma for the Christian community because of the profound changes to the emerging generation's social and spiritual context, described at length in the previous chapter. Many of the struggles experienced by Mosaic dropouts are not new—they have, in fact, been repeated through centuries of spiritual life within Christianity—yet they are exacerbated by the new realities of *access, alienation,* and *authority,* which combine to make today's twentysomethings discontinuously different from previous generations.

In this chapter and the next, I want to introduce you to the dropouts of the next generation, who fall into three broad categories: *nomads, prodigals,* and *exiles.* As you might expect, no two young people share the same pathway away from or toward faith; we can identify trends, yet disengagement is a rich and varied tapestry of individual experiences. Each of the thousands of young people we interviewed described personal aspects of leaving faith or leaving a church, sharing unique and specific stories, conversations, and experiences. Remember: *every story matters.*

Even given the individuality of experience expressed by those we interviewed, we can observe some significant patterns. Young dropouts are being "lost" in three distinctive ways. Two groups (exiles, whom we'll get to know in the next chapter, and nomads) are disengaging from church, while the third is rejecting Christian faith entirely (prodigals). I have intentionally rooted these labels in types of people found in Scripture, because our research uncovered significant alignment with these ancient archetypes of faith.

If you are an adult over the age of thirty, some of these templates have likely been true of your own experience or perhaps those of your peers; these forms of dropping out are not exclusive to ages eighteen to twenty-nine. Still, dropping out is concentrated among young adults, and we need to understand these patterns better to capture their particular relevance for today's context.

Let's get to know the first two types of dropouts: nomads and prodigals.

## NOMADS

Every generation since the middle of the last century has had its pop princesses and celebrity trendsetters. The 1950s and '60s made an enduring icon out of blonde bombshell Marilyn Monroe. Cher and Diana Ross, in their sequined jumpsuits and surreal headdresses, reigned supreme over the disco era of the 1970s. No one could come close to the super-stardom of Madonna in the '80s and '90s—not until, that is, a cute little Mouseketeer named Britney Spears donned a suggestive schoolgirl getup and begged America to "Hit Me Baby, One More Time."

When I set out to find a cultural icon to represent the nomads among the you-lost-me generation, I didn't have to look any further than Katy Perry, pop music's newest It Girl. Through the early months of 2011, it was nearly impossible to escape her infectious hit "Teenage Dream," just as you couldn't go anywhere in 2008 without hearing "I Kissed a Girl." (You may find the lyrics objectionable, but the tune's catchiness is undeniable.) A Southern California native, twenty-seven-year-old Perry is known almost as much for her colorful vintage style and '50s-inspired pinup girl glamour as for her frothy, radio-friendly odes to teenage crushes and heartbreaks. Perry is married to potty-mouthed English comedian Russell Brand, a recovering heroin and sex addict, who once claimed to have slept with more than eighty women in a single month.

Katy Perry is also the daughter of Pentecostal evangelical ministers.

Perry grew up singing in church, speaking in tongues, and eating "angeled" (never "deviled") eggs. By her own account, once she embarked on a career in pop music, she wanted to try everything that her strict religious upbringing had kept off-limits: "I was like, 'Wow, there are a lot of choices.' I began to become a sponge for all I had missed. . . . I was as curious as the cat."[3] For the most part, Perry sees her experimentation and exploration in very positive terms: "To grow up and come from something different than what you are now and to spread your wings . . . I think that's a beautiful thing."[4] At the same time, her Christian heritage is still very much a part of her personal belief system, hodgepodge though it may be. In an August 2010 *Rolling Stone* cover story titled "Sex, God & Katy," Perry describes her beliefs this way:

> I still believe Jesus is the son of God. But I also believe in extraterrestri-
> als, and that there are people who are sent from God to be messengers,
> and all kinds of crazy stuff. I look up into the sky . . . all those stars and

planets, the never-endingness of the universe. . . . Every time I look up, I know that I'm nothing and there's something way beyond me. I don't think it's as simple as heaven and hell.[5]

She also values spiritual ideas and pursuits but isn't sure how they fit with her adult identity: "[Spirituality] is just important to me. The details of the importance are still to be determined, I guess. . . . It's one of those things that as the older you get and the farther you try to run away from your parents, you just turn right around and they are embedded into your DNA."[6]

Perry embodies the first, and most common, category of dropout—the spiritual nomad, the wanderer. For these young adults, faith is nomadic, seasonal, or may appear to be an optional or peripheral part of life. At some point during their teen or young adult years, nomads disengage from attending church or significantly distance themselves from the Christian community. They demonstrate an up-and-down, hit-or-miss faith, like Katy Perry and Stephen Colbert, who put their faith on the shelf for a time. Most, however, do not discard it entirely.

We estimate that about two-fifths of young adults who have a Christian background will go through a period of spiritual nomadism. This spiritual drifting, either a little or a lot, through the twentysomething years is the most common dropout experience of young Christians coming of age. Many of these young people will discontinue church participation, although not all will do so. This period of wandering is corroborated by other research we have done at Barna Group that shows that half of all born-again adult Christians say they have gone through a prolonged period in their lives when they felt very distant or spiritually removed from God. Much of this occurred during their young adult years.

Frequently nomads among the Mosaic generation say that leaving church was less an intentional choice and more of a "slow fade," a period of increasing detachment that took many months or years. For some, faith was never very deep; they were "in the building" but never really committed to following Christ. Yet for others, the opposite is true. Many nomads describe a personal history of intense commitment.

One of the defining characteristics of this group of dropouts is that they have a mix of positive and negative feelings about their "native" faith.

Most nomads are disenchanted with religion on some level but they have not cut all ties that bind them to Christianity. Most nomads consider themselves to be Christian, even when they are disengaged from church. Whether they are actively following Christ is another matter entirely; many have pushed their faith so far to the sidelines that they look little like a faithful Christian to those observing their behaviors and priorities.

Nomads can be particularly frustrating to parents and church leaders because they are neither inside nor outside the church. The parents of nomads may have an acute sense of anxiety over their children's wandering, but what can they do? Many feel helpless to affect their dropout's choices. Nomads can also frustrate researchers because, depending on what question we ask in our surveys, they can appear to be quite spiritual. But ask any pastor or church leader and he or she will tell you that, while nomads may show up every once in a while, they are missing from the faith community in the ways that matter most and are not actively pursuing a deeper relationship with Christ.

Sometimes disengagement happens in the late high school years or right after high school; in other instances it may kick in during the decade of the twenties. How long does the nomadic journey last? It can be a few months or a few decades—and sometimes a lifetime, morphing into a more entrenched posture toward the church or Christianity. Our research suggests that the average nomad is "out of commission" for about three years, though it is sometimes much longer. Some of these young people may hover on the edges indefinitely and never invest in a truly vibrant and growing spirituality. Others may encounter another group of dropouts—the exiles, whom we'll get to know in the next chapter—and make a serious, deep-level commitment to Christ (though they may never return to the institutional church).

Here are some characteristics of the nomadic mindset:

- *They still describe themselves as Christian.* They have not disavowed Christianity but are no longer particularly committed to their faith or especially to churchgoing.
- *They believe that personal involvement in a Christian community is optional.* They see going to church or being with Christian friends for spiritual purposes as options, not requirements.

- *The importance of faith has faded.* They admit that Christianity was more important to them at some point in their past. If they describe it as important, it is on their own terms. About one-quarter (24 percent) of the young Christians we interviewed say they may be willing to return to church later in life, but it's not particularly urgent to them.

- *Most are not angry or hostile toward Christianity.* They tend to find their personal history with the faith amusing, or perhaps distressing, but they are not generally angry about their past. Frustrated and disillusioned, yes—especially with Christians. Hostile, no.

- *Many are spiritual experimentalists.* Nomads find meaning and spiritual stimulation from a variety of activities in their lives, which sometimes include trying on other religious experiences for size.

## Nomads Describe Their Faith Journeys

*Percentage of 18- to 29-year-olds who have a Christian background*

|  | completely true of me | completely or mostly true of me |
|---|---|---|
| I think going to church or being with Christian friends is optional. | 21% | 43% |
| Faith and religion are just not that important to me right now. | 15% | 25% |
| I may return to church when I'm older but I have no interest now. | 9% | 24% |
| I used to be very involved in my church but I don't fit there anymore. | 8% | 23% |
| Church meant a lot to me when I was younger but it doesn't make sense in my life now. | 8% | 20% |
| I grew up as a Christian but since then I have tried other faiths or spiritual practices. | 6% | 14% |
| I made an emotional decision to be a Christian early in life that didn't last. | 5% | 14% |

Barna Group | 2011 | N=1,296

## PRODIGALS

The second category of dropout consists of young people who leave their childhood or teen faith entirely. This includes those who deconvert (including atheists, agnostics, and "nones," those who say they have no religious affiliation) and those who switch to another faith. For the sake of simplicity, I refer to both as *prodigals*.

Prodigals' views of Christians and churches are all over the map, largely dependent on how positive or negative their experiences were. Many prodigals are quite nuanced and logical in their reasons for disengagement. Most are more defined by and committed to their distance from Christianity than they are to their current spiritual perspectives. In other words, one of the identity-shaping characteristics of prodigals is that they say they are *no longer Christian*. While nomads may bounce from church to church or from active to inactive, the typical prodigal is either holding firmly to "no faith" or espousing a different faith entirely.

Our research finds that many prodigals' negative experiences with Christianity run deep. One such prodigal, singer-songwriter David Bazan, formerly of the band Pedro the Lion, is a deconverted Christian. His first solo album, *Curse Your Branches* (2009), was reviewed as a "harrowing breakup record—except he's dumping God, Jesus, and the evangelical life."[7] In an interview about his journey away from Christianity, Bazan describes the devastation of leaving the faith: "It's like I have to go through life with a scalpel. What do you cut out? My whole identity since I was twenty-five years old was completely intertwined with the Christian faith."[8] And later in the article: "My parents were the biggest [spiritual] influences. Their expressions of Christianity, love, service, and compassion really impacted me. They are deeply ethical and compassionate people. If it weren't for their authentic example, I would have bailed on Christianity much earlier than I did."[9]

Of the criticism he has received from his Christian fans, Bazan says, "What I've done is unforgivable to some: You don't break ranks. But in the longer arc of the faith, I think what I've done falls in the tradition of people shaking their fists at God."[10]

The term "prodigal" harkens back to the famous story Jesus told of a father and his two sons (see Luke 15:11–32). The younger son, as the parable goes, becomes a *prodigal* when he leaves his father's household and throws away his inheritance on wild living and partying. Yes, the prodigal in Jesus's narrative returns home, and that is the hope we can have for present-day prodigals. For now, however, they are lost, disconnected from their parents' faith. I recently heard a mom describe one of her daughters in this way: "Janey is our prodigal. And it breaks our heart."

The fact that many modern-day prodigals don't "flame out" like the son in Jesus's parable does not lessen the feelings of anxiety and even grief experienced by the parents, church leaders, and religious educators they leave behind. It's my desire that, as we get to know two distinct groups of prodigals and their reasons for leaving "home," we can respond with the patience and compassion that the father in Jesus's parable displayed. (After all, as Tim Keller points out in his book *The Prodigal God*, the story of the apostate son is also the story of a father's prodigal—that is, extravagant, even reckless—grace.)

Bazan typifies the first breed of prodigal, those who come to a point where Christianity is intellectually untenable. We might call them "head-driven prodigals," because their reasons for abandoning the faith are rational and, many times, well-reasoned—even if many of them also feel hurt by their church experiences.

The "heart-driven prodigal," on the other hand, embodies most fully the concept of prodigal, with all the emotional punch that term implies. These are young people whose faith burns out in an extreme fashion, usually as a result of deep wounds, frustration, or anger, or of their own desire to live life outside the bounds of the Christian faith. They express their rejection of childhood Christianity in emotionally strong terms and may feel bitterness or resentment for many years after leaving the fold.

Frequently head-driven prodigals define themselves by their new faith choices, while heart-driven prodigals focus on their denunciation of Christianity. There also seems to be something open-ended and unresolved about heart-driven prodigals, as though their spiritual flame could reignite at any moment; head-driven prodigals, by contrast, seem to be more settled in, perhaps even resigned to, their distance from the faith.

As you might expect, many prodigals maintain a mix of head- and heart-driven factors that led them away from faith. Both kinds of prodigals (and nomads too) often struggle with sex, alcohol use, or drug abuse. Our research does not allow us to determine whether these factors are cause for religious wandering or symptomatic of a deeper search for meaning.

### Prodigals Describe Their Faith Journeys

*Percentage of 18- to 29-year-olds who have a Christian background*

|  | completely true of me | completely or mostly true of me |
|---|---|---|
| Christian beliefs just don't make sense to me. | 10% | 21% |
| I had a negative experience in church or with Christians. | 9% | 20% |
| My spiritual needs cannot be met by Christianity. | 10% | 19% |
| I don't plan on ever returning to the church. | 12% | 18% |
| When I was a Christian, I wasn't encouraged to think for myself. | 7% | 18% |
| I used to be a Christian but now I'm not. | 9% | 15% |
| My parents probably feel as though I rejected their faith. | 5% | 14% |

Barna Group | 2011 | N=1,296

Here are some characteristics of the prodigal mindset:

- *They feel varying levels of resentment toward Christians and Christianity.* Many still have positive things to say about specific people (such as their parents), but the overall tenor of their perceptions is negative.

- *They have disavowed returning to church.* They feel deeply wounded by their church experience and do not plan to ever go back.

- *They have moved on from Christianity.* Prodigals describe themselves as "over" Christianity, saying it just does not make sense to them. Their spiritual needs, such as they sense them, are being met elsewhere.

- *Their regrets, if they have them, usually center on their parents.* In other words, they recognize that their faith choices have made a significant impact on their parents yet they feel as though they were compelled to deconvert.

- *They feel as if they have broken out of constraints.* Many prodigals feel that the Christianity they experienced kept them stuck in a box or demanded that they become someone other than their true self. They experience leaving as freedom.

## *WHAT* ARE YOUNG PEOPLE LEAVING?

Here is a snapshot view of nomads and prodigals side by side:

| Nomads | Prodigals |
| --- | --- |
| Wandering from church, wrestling with faith | Rejecting or switching faith |
| Disengaging from church, Christian community, or other conventional forms of faith | Switching from one faith to another or to no faith/deconversion |
| Going through a period of distraction, disobedience, or disconnection from God, or becoming disillusioned or frustrated with their church experience or with their parents' faith | Significantly changing faith views, rebelling or overtly distancing themselves from the faith of upbringing |
| | May be head-driven (intellectual questions) or heart-driven (emotional experience) |
| Terms that might describe these individuals:<br>• nomads<br>• backsliders<br>• spiritual wanderers<br>• church dropouts | Terms that might describe these individuals:<br>• prodigals<br>• skeptics<br>• faith dropouts<br>• ex-Christians |

Those who drop out of church (nomads) are far more common than prodigals—roughly four times more common. Yet it is easy to imagine why three-quarters of pastors and youth workers believe that most young people are putting their *faith* on the shelf during their twenties, rather than recognizing that most dropouts are pressing pause on *church*. In one sense, church leaders are accurately reading the situation. By their measures of involvement, the church has lost these young adults. Many stakeholders, such as parents, pastors, priests, and youth workers interpret this loss as a massive exodus from the faith, but the sociological reality is that most of those absent young adults are going through a period of nomadism. Only 11 percent of young adults say that they grew up as a Christian but have deconverted entirely or converted to another faith; this number is offset somewhat by the 4 percent who convert to Christianity after a childhood in a different faith. All things considered, a young Christian has about 1:9 odds of losing his or her faith entirely. While this is a rare outcome, it is a very high number when you think about the estimated five million eighteen- to twenty-nine-year-old ex-Christians encompassed by this statistic.[11]

From the perspective of many Christians, prodigals are the more acute problem—and in one sense, that's true. To put it crassly, prodigals no longer count in the "Christian column." Yet this line in the sand ignores an important point: a nomad who self-describes as a Christian is not necessarily in a better state of faith than a non-believer. In fact the Bible serves up special criticism for those who are "lukewarm," neither in nor out (see Rev. 3:16). *Lukewarm* would certainly describe many of the young nomads we interviewed. They think of themselves as spiritual but have little orthodoxy, meaningful accountability, or faith vitality in their lives. Furthermore, we should be careful not to define someone's spiritual life as better or worse than another, because it is not always obvious who is moving in which direction.

All this reaffirms what we described in chapter 1, an important insight based on the research for this project. The dropout phenomenon is most accurately described as a generation of Christians who are disengaging from institutional forms of church. Young people are leaving established congregations. Many young Christians—even as they express generally positive associations with Jesus Christ—are alienated from the institutional forms of faith in which they were raised.

## A NEW REALITY

At the beginning of this chapter, we asked if the dropout phenomenon at work in the Mosaic generation is any different from the pattern of young adult disengagement in earlier generations. I believe it is. Beginning with the Boomers, a period of nomadism in young adulthood became a normative experience for twentysomethings; yet the new social and spiritual reality in which Mosaics live makes it less likely that they will follow their predecessors back to church in the same numbers or in the same ways.

Given their *access* to all kinds of information and a wide variety of worldviews, many young adults no longer believe that the local church and Christianity provide the only or even best avenues to spiritual growth and maturation. Nomads and prodigals are able to get spiritual input from a variety of sources, unmediated by the delivery systems common in the established church.

Mosaics' *alienation* from our society's institutions—including the traditional family, educational and economic structures, and the church—means that they are deeply skeptical about the relevance of these structures to their lives. When the Christian community functions according to the priorities and protocols of previous generations, there is little resonance in the minds and hearts of today's twentysomethings.

Finally, young adults' location in a post-Christian culture encourages them to reject the *authority* of the Bible and of spiritual leaders and even to question the existence of truth. Many prodigals and nomads seek and find sources of authority outside of conventional Christian forms.

Dropouts reject Christianity or church involvement for a variety of specific and personal reasons. Some of their rationales may seem myopic, self-absorbed, and petty, the ultimate expressions of the narcissistic "Me Generation." Others—such as stories from young people wounded by church life and repelled by poor embodiments of the faith—are gut-wrenching. In part 2, we will take a look at the six most pressing reasons Mosaics give for dropping out and at how these connect to issues of access, alienation, and authority that shape the world inhabited by the next generation.

But first, let's meet one more segment of the you-lost-me generation—the exiles.

# 4

# EXILES

Ryan was, in his words, "born on the pew." That's only a slight exaggeration. He grew up in a charismatic megachurch in Southern California, attending four worship services and Bible studies per week, plus two or three church-centered social events. His family's life revolved around church, and Ryan, like his parents, was very serious about faith. At the age of twelve, he asked his youth leader, "Why do we do so many pointless activities like car rallies and lock-ins when people are on their way to hell because they don't know Jesus?"

Hell figured prominently in Ryan's childhood theology. He says, "I learned that I was a sinner in constant danger of the fires of hell but I could avoid eternal torment and instead go to heaven if I acknowledged Jesus as my personal Savior. This 'salvation' depended on me repenting of every specific sin I committed before I died. So, starting around age seven, I would lie in bed at night and tearfully confess every sin I could think of, begging God to help me remember them all, in case I died in my sleep."

Ryan was gifted in music and decided to study at a Christian university to prepare for worship ministry. Even though he had misgivings about the gospel he'd grown up with, he "wanted to live as significant a life as possible and I still believed serving in ministry was the primary way to do it."

He got married and was hired by a large church to launch a "modern" worship service, an idea not everyone in the congregation supported. (Ryan once laid a hand of support on an older lady's shoulder because she was obviously in the throes of intense intercession, only to realize, when she began to pray aloud, that the "apostate, heretical kid who introduced Satan's music into our church" was the subject of her petitions.) Despite that, his ministry went well for several years. During the same time, Ryan and his wife, Dawn, got to know many non-Christians in their neighborhood. Their nonbelieving friends seemed always to want to talk about God, Jesus, spirituality, and how to do good in the world, and Ryan and Dawn began to wonder why their church friends, in contrast, seemed obsessed with church programming and conservative politics. There was increasing tension between the part Ryan felt he had to play to keep his church job and the calling he sensed to rethink what it means to "act justly and to love mercy and to walk humbly with your God" (Micah 6:8).

Then Dawn began to have major problems with depression and anxiety, making home a very stressful place to be. About the same time, things at work took a turn for the worse, due in large part to negative leadership. Ryan tried to juggle both crises for about a year, but the pressure spun him into a dark depression. Eventually he resigned from the church, which had become increasingly dysfunctional, and focused his remaining energy on Dawn and their marriage.

That was three years ago.

After everything he has experienced in church, Ryan has not given up on Jesus—but he doesn't plan to work in a church long term. He leads worship part-time in a small faith community while he works toward a degree for a nonchurch career. Ryan says, "I want to build loving friendships with those in the church, but my main focus will be anyone who cares about the things I believe Jesus calls us to care about, whether they label themselves Christian or not. I've had too many negative experiences in church and I don't see myself working inside the institution over the long haul. But I still want my life to be about the way of Jesus."

Ryan is an example of a person on a third type of spiritual journey, those who feel stuck between two worlds, pushed out and pushed away from something familiar—the exiles.

## MODERN-DAY EXILES

In the previous chapter, we got to know nomads and prodigals, two types of dropouts who may be found in any generation but who have certain cultural particularities when they come from the Mosaic generation. In this chapter I want to consider a third way of being "lost" from the church—the path of exiles. For our purposes, let's define exiles as those who grew up in the church and are now physically or emotionally disconnected in some way, but who also remain energized to pursue God-honoring lives. They feel the loss, in many ways, of the familiar church environment in which they once found meaning, identity, and purpose.[1] They feel lost, yet hopeful.

One hallmark of the exiles is their feeling that their vocation (or professional calling) is disconnected from their church experience. Their Christian background has not prepared them to live and work effectively in society. Their faith is "lost" from Monday through Friday. The Christianity they have learned does not meaningfully speak to the fields of fashion, finance, medicine, science, or media to which they are drawn. Ryan originally thought his calling to music was best expressed through working in a local church. Yet his growing desire to make a difference outside the walls of the church, along with the negative aspects of working inside the church, left him feeling lost and listless.

Before we get to the latest Barna Group research on next-gen exiles, I would like to explore some boundaries for this discussion. This may be a difficult category for you to grasp—it has been for me. So I would like to help you understand what I mean—and don't mean—when talking about exiles.

First, my use of the term "exile" comes from the Old Testament biblical narrative, most notably the lives of Daniel, Ezekiel, and their less famous friends. These young Hebrews were, as you may know, taken captive or forced into political exile when the nation of Judah was overrun by the kingdom of Babylon, an event that occurred hundreds of years before the time of Christ.

Second, I think the metaphor of exiles works especially well, given the modern-day North American parallels with Babylon. Our cultural backdrop of access, alienation, and authority isn't far removed from the spirit of Babylon nearly three millennia ago. At its worst, today's western culture is indulgent, distracted, idol-following, and hedonistic. The time and place may be different, but the tension of living in-but-not-of lives describes the challenge for the faithful both then and now.

The late Richard John Neuhaus, a prominent Catholic thinker in the late twentieth and early twenty-first centuries, and theologian Walter Brueggemann, among others, have shown the common challenges faced by modern Christians and ancient exiled Jews. Neuhaus's last book before his death was *American Babylon*, in which he suggests that Christians live in exile in a foreign land, for our citizenship is in the kingdom of God. Similarly Brueggemann draws parallels between the "dislocation, uncertainty, and irrelevance of the Old Testament Jewish exiles in Bablyon"[2] and the tensions felt by North American Christians today. Expounding on Brueggeman's work, Australian leader Michael Frost writes, "The experience that faced the Jewish exiles mirrors the church's experience today. In fact, the biblical metaphor that best suits our current times and faith situation is that of exile. Just like the Jewish exiles, the church today is grieving its loss and is struggling with humiliation."[3]

I believe the Christian community must come to grips with its current cultural setting, understand the ways in which our collective experience is like (and unlike) Babylon, and respond faithfully to the new opportunities afforded by exile. Eugene Peterson, translator of the popular biblical paraphrase *The Message*, writes this: "Every generation faces a changed culture, different social problems and challenges, new patterns of work, evolving economic and political conditions. Much of what a Christian community in each generation does is learn together how this is done in its particular circumstances."[4]

The desire to tackle this task is strong in exiles, who sense the church's calling to counter the culture by living Christ-shaped lives. They want to inform and transform the "foreign" culture that surrounds them, rather than withdrawing from it. But many don't know how. They are trying on new ways of Christ-following that make sense to their communities and careers. Their rejection of some mindsets and methods common to the North American church stem from this desire. They sense that the established church has internalized many of "Babylon's" values of consumerism, hyperindividualism, and moral compromise instead of living in-but-not-of as kingdom exiles. As a consequence many of today's exiles, while they are not *political* exiles in the Old Testament sense, feel isolated and alienated from the Christian community—caught between the church as it is and what they believe it is called to be.

## A PROFILE OF EXILES

In our research among young Christians, we encountered a number of views that can help us identify the reality of being stuck between two worlds. As we have for nomads and prodigals, let's look at some of the characteristics of young exiles and their perspectives about the faith. Then we'll meet a few exiles who are following Jesus on the frontiers of cultural change.

- *Exiles are not inclined toward being separate from "the world."* Exiles want their faith to matter. One-third of young Christians (32 percent) identified with the statement, "I want to find a way to follow Jesus that connects with the world I live in." They long for their spiritual lives to be connected, to be whole, and to make sense.
- *They are skeptical of institutions but are not wholly disengaged from them.* Even while they sense God at work outside of church, not all are post-institutional in their faith. Just one-fifth of young Christians (21 percent) say that the institutional church is a difficult place for them to live out their faith. Many young exiles are infrequent participants in conventional faith expression, such as regularly attending a church worship service, but most of them remain connected in some way to a faith community.
- *Young exiles sense God moving "outside the walls of the church."* This was among the most common views of any we assessed in our

research—God is moving outside the church and exiles wanted to be a part of it. As Ryan's story at the beginning of this chapter illustrates, many young people want to participate in ministry outside of conventional forms of Christian community. We explore their perceptions more fully in later chapters, but in a nutshell, exiles are dissatisfied with a church that is a weekend event, not a movement of God's people on mission for Christ.

- *They are not disillusioned with tradition; they are frustrated with slick or shallow expressions of religion.* In some of our research, we discovered a common theme to be "I want to be part of a Christian community that is more than a performance one day a week." Similarly a frequently expressed sentiment was they "want a more traditional faith, rather than a hip version of Christianity."

- *Exiles express a mix of concern and optimism for their peers.* This generation is certainly self-centered but they are also very communal and peer-oriented. A related concern is the feeling of loss many young Christians reported *about their peers.* Many described being very concerned about seeing so many of their generation leaving the church.

- *They have not found faith to be instructive to their calling or gifts.* One of the recurring themes in our research with young exiles is the idea that Christianity does not have much, if anything, to say about their chosen profession or field. The ways career and calling connect to faith and church community seem to be missing pieces in the puzzle for many young exiles.

- *They struggle when other Christians question their motives.* A final characteristic of these young exiles is that their fellow Christians—particularly older believers—frequently have a hard time relating to their choices and concerns. This can be the young person's parents, but often is the *friends* of parents or other well-meaning Christians who can't get their head around their unique calling. In fact, many times these young exiles end up staying under the radar, as both fellow Christians and nonbelievers often misunderstand their faith and their calling.

Estimating the proportion of young exiles is a more complicated task than trying to gauge the proportion of prodigals and nomads. The latter groups are much easier to categorize because they have a discrete profile in terms of leaving church (nomads) or leaving faith (prodigals). I think it's best to define exiles based on their attitudes and perspectives. As such, our research suggests that about one in ten of eighteen- to twenty-nine-year-olds with a Christian background qualifies as having a strong exile-like perspective on their faith. At the same time, nearly half of today's young Christians demonstrate at least some inclinations toward an exilic posture.

This brings up another point. We discovered back and forth movement among nomads and exiles (and occasionally prodigals). Young people move between categories based on their level of engagement with church *and* their sense of personal commitment to and intensity of faith.

### Exiles Describe Their Faith Journeys

*Percentage of 18- to 29-year-olds who have a Christian background*

|  | completely true of me | completely or mostly true of me |
| --- | --- | --- |
| I want to find a way to follow Jesus that connects with the world I live in. | 15% | 38% |
| God is more at work outside the church than inside, and I want to be a part of that. | 12% | 33% |
| I want to be a Christian without separating myself from the world around me. | 14% | 32% |
| I want to help the church change its priorities to be what Jesus intended it to be. | 12% | 29% |
| I am a Christian, but the institutional church is a difficult place for me to live out my faith. | 8% | 21% |
| Christian community is important, but I want to do more than get together once a week for worship. | 10% | 23% |
| I feel stuck between the comfortable faith of my parents and the life I believe God wants from me. | 4% | 11% |

Barna Group | 2011 | N=1,296

# EXILES IN THE FLESH

This profile of exiles is research based, but who are these young people in the flesh? Early in the process of writing this book, I presented the findings on prodigals, nomads, and exiles to an intergenerational church group. One twentysomething young woman came up afterward and said that the exile category reassured her about her brother. "Really? What does he do?" I asked.

"He's an artist, a writer. And he's really been trying to push our church to do things differently. I think he's getting under some people's skin. What you said about the church not understanding his calling in the world and people questioning his motives—that sounds like my brother. He really loves the church, but no one seems to bother to figure out what makes him tick."

This story illustrates one of our findings from this study. We have learned that most exiles feel tremendous tension between their work, usually in mainstream arenas of society (the arts, media, science, fashion, law, and so on), and their faith. In large measure, they don't feel supported or equipped by the Christian community to follow Christ in these endeavors. With this in mind, read the following descriptions of a few young exiles I have encountered during the past several years.

## Exiles in Hollywood

Justin attended the Peter Stark Producing Program at the University of Southern California's film school. He is one of the few evangelicals who completed that prestigious graduate level program. His father is a senior leader at one of the nation's largest megachurches. Since Justin's graduation, his parents—though enthusiastically supportive of his calling—have struggled with some of their friends to "justify" his films, which have language and other content that seem foreign to his Christian upbringing. His mother says, "I feel like he's taking on the culture in order to influence it. I wish the church-at-large would understand that our children are called to mission fields that aren't located on a globe but may be more culturally impacting than mission fields we currently recognize. I wish families like ours would be better understood, supported, and encouraged by the church community." Justin's take is that in order to influence the world of entertainment, he has to be willing to learn how to make great films. "A film isn't Christian just because it has inserted the gospel message in there somehow. A film can point to Christ when it honestly portrays our human condition and invites us to experience something about redemption that each of us needs."

## Exiles in Science

Kathryn has a PhD in computational cell biology (don't feel bad; I don't know what that is either). She is actively involved in both the scientific community and in her church. She laments, "Many people I talk to think it's impossible to embrace both mainstream science (especially evolutionary biology) and traditional Christian faith. Scientists tend to scoff at faith as being anti-intellectual, while Christians tend to reject scientific conclusions out of hand if they don't fit with their view of the world. This should not be! Christians, of all people, should pursue truth with a spirit of confidence, and the church should take a more active role in encouraging that pursuit." Kathryn is passionate about challenging the church to deal well with science, but not everyone in the Christian community is convinced she's headed in the right direction.

## Exiles in Music

A few years ago, I spoke to a roomful of young Christian musicians and artists. The meeting was convened by my friend Charlie Peacock at the Art House, a beautiful, old renovated church in Nashville where Charlie and his wife, Andi, offer hospitality and mentoring to young artists. After my talk, I had a chance to get to know some of the up-and-coming musicians. One of them told me that she had been pressured by people in her church not to license her music to a secular television show because "the message would get lost." She said, "That just seems backwards. I mean, isn't the message more likely to get 'found' if people actually have a chance to hear it?" One of the common denominators among the young musicians I have met is that they want their art to speak for itself, without having to call themselves a "Christian band" or a "Christian musician."

## Exiles in the Newsroom

Eugene is a journalist based in Phoenix. He's no slouch; some of his work has appeared in national newsmagazines such as *Newsweek* and *USA Today*. I met him at a conference, and he said my description of exiles portrays his challenge. "In the newsroom, I am constantly trying to help my editors tell accurate stories about religion and faith communities. So that's a tough place to be heard. But I am also hit on the other side—Christians who can't understand why I would work here or why I would work in media at all. Because it's what I am good at! It was really hard finding a church where I could learn about how to be a good Christian in the middle of this tension."

## Exiles in the Military

I met a U.S. military chaplain a few years back at an Air Force base in Washington, D.C. Gary described the incredible privilege of being a spiritual guide to men and women in the armed forces. "It requires cooperation without compromise, which is different than most ministry settings." As he described it, chaplains are required to lead worship for various religious traditions. They must understand and appreciate Catholic, Protestant, Jewish, Buddhist, and Muslim traditions and cooperate with adherents to these faiths while not compromising their own faith convictions. "The chaplaincy is a place where we regularly have to navigate cultural and hierarchical tension in ways that are off the map for most religious workers."

## Exiles in University

Michelle and Paul are savvy leaders and strong believers. They live in Canada, an environment that is struggling at least as much as the United States with the cultural changes of access, alienation, and authority. Michelle mentioned to me the last time we were together that their eldest daughter is going to a public university in Vancouver. "I know we raised her right, but Vancouver and university are tough places to remain Christian. We pray for her and talk with her regularly, and she's doing well. But we often wonder how her faith will hold up. And because we have a lot of confidence in her, we wonder how her development will stretch our faith when she's done."

## Exiles in Ministry

Jay Bakker is the son of televangelists Jim and Tammy Faye Bakker, former hosts of *Praise the Lord Club* or *PTL*, a religious television talk show. Jay's dad was caught up in a sex scandal and went to prison after revelations of accounting fraud in the ministry. In the aftermath of his family's downfall, Jay turned away from church to substance abuse yet eventually he found his way back to Christ. He founded a church called Revolution, "for those who feel rejected by traditional approaches to Christianity . . . to show all people the unconditional love and grace of Jesus without any reservations due to their lifestyles or background, past or future."[5] His very public stand in favor of gay marriage has won him few friends in the Christian establishment.

**Exiles**

Rejecting "cultural Christianity" to seek deeper faith in Christ

Feeling stuck between the security of the Christian subculture and the realities of life in today's society

Struggling to see how their faith connects to their calling or professional interests

Seeing the best in culture and desiring to redeem and renew it—sometimes experiencing the worst in the church

Terms that might describe these individuals:
- exiles
- creatives
- culturally engaged
- reformers

## EXILES IN CONTEXT

These stories may make you feel angry or at least uncomfortable—some exiles are pretty far off the reservation, if by "reservation" we mean "acceptable to the Christian establishment." It is not my intention to defend their views or activities, a handful of which I can't, in good conscience, endorse. Instead, through their stories, I hope to focus our attention on the larger exile phenomenon these young adults represent.

From exiles in the next generation we often hear such words as "uncertainty," "improvisation," and "adaptability." To the ears of the established Christian generations, these words may sound a lot like "relativism." Sociologist Robert Wuthnow calls Mosaics a generation of "spiritual tinkerers." But when we connect the dots between our modern-day "Babylon" and that experienced by the exiles of old, I believe we will see a picture emerge of faithful young adults doing their level best to follow Christ in an upended cultural context—and even showing the church how to be the community of God in a new world.

Let's take a brief look at the social and spiritual context that faced Daniel, one of history's most famous exiles, in Babylon. He faced the challenge of living in tension in a discontinuous culture, just as we do now. In his story, we find the familiar themes of access, alienation, and authority.

### Access

When Daniel was forcibly moved to Babylon, his world got bigger. Judah, his home country, was a small-town backwater compared to the cosmopolitan Babylonian kingdom—and Daniel was dropped almost directly into the corridors of political, cultural, and academic power. Scripture tells us that he was fed a steady diet of the language and literature of the Babylonians. He experienced instant access (relatively speaking) to ideas and worldviews from across the empire, which stretched from the border of Egypt in the west to Persia in the east. Dealing with that massive influx of new information must have been overwhelming.

### Alienation

The minute he arrived in Babylon, Daniel's upbringing in a particular way of life and faith had to be reevaluated in light of his new reality. He had to make decisions about his faith and purpose, about what to hold on to and what to negotiate—and he had to make those choices very quickly. What had been his default positions were, in this new context, alien.

Exile causes disassociation, which is just another way of saying that, in a new cultural reality, significant relationships, social connections, and other forms of identity are cut off. Daniel had to find new ways to be faithful because the forms and traditions of faithfulness with which he'd grown up were, in Babylon, foreign and often irrelevant.

## Authority

Daniel faced the balancing act of submitting to an earthly authority that was set against God while, at the same time, trusting God to sustain him. Reading Daniel's story centuries later at a safe distance, walking that line looks almost easy; when Daniel chose to pray, knowing that he risked the lions' den, his trust in God's sustaining grace was never in question (see Daniel 6). But we should remember that his courage through that episode came after decades in Babylon, during which he had learned, day by day, how to serve the earthly king while trusting the authority of the eternal King.

Here's the point: the early years of Daniel's exile in Babylon were not so cut-and-dried. In Daniel 1 we see a young believer not quite so willing to draw a firm line in the sand between what he would and wouldn't do under Babylon's authority. It is clear from early on that his intention was to remain a faithful servant of Yahweh, but figuring out how to do so, in exile and under Nebuchadnezzar's authority, didn't happen overnight. As young Jewish nobles, Daniel and his friends were carried off from Judah to serve in King Nebuchadnezzar's court. The young men were forced to adopt Babylonian customs, even taking on new names as part of the indoctrination process—Daniel was called Belteshazzar, while his friends Hananiah, Mishael, and Azariah are even today better known as Shadrach, Meshach, and Abednego. This was no small sacrifice, because the new names were derived from pagan deities such as Bel, one of the Babylonian gods; imagine being devoted to the one true God, Yahweh, and having your name forcibly changed to "Bel Worshiper." On top of that, at least a few biblical historians have suggested that the young Israelite exiles may have been forced to become eunuchs![6]

Daniel's wisdom and insight garnered him esteem in the Babylonian king's court, which led eventually to his increasing power and opportunity. With every new promotion, the temptation to capitulate his faith, values, and allegiances to his new cultural reality must have been enormous. Yet Daniel was willing, in order to serve God, to be fully *in* this foreign culture—even as he had to figure out how not to be *of* it.

## SAME SONG, DIFFERENT MILLENNIUM

Based on our research and a close study of exiles in the Bible, I believe that the number and impact of exiles rises during times of tumultuous social and spiritual transition. Although all dropouts, including nomads and prodigals, are affected to some extent by the environments that surround them, periods of social, technological, and spiritual change give rise to an increased number of exiles from the religious establishment.

That's a good thing, because the generational patterns of alienation, access, and authority in our day are making these strategically disengaged young people increasingly important to the church's future. As Christianity moves from the mainstream to play a more marginal role in our culture, and as North America becomes more religiously pluralistic, I believe that exiles are the people most able to help us navigate these changes. When the Christian faith is no longer autopilot for the broader culture, Christians who are comfortable in two worlds can orient the Christian community toward faithfulness in a new setting.

Again for insight, let's consider the ancient exile's life. Once in Babylon, Daniel was put on a dietary and training program that was to last three years and include the replacement of his religious upbringing with "the language and literature of the Babylonians" (Dan. 1:4 NLT). This was, obviously, a significant threat to the young Israelite's beliefs, traditions, and faith. Rather than totally resisting their reeducation, however, Daniel and friends chose, in those early days of their exile, to refuse only the diet proposed by the court officials. And even in this small resistance, we are told that Daniel deferred the final decision to the Babylonian official: "Test us for ten days on a diet of vegetables and water. . . . *Then you can decide* whether or not to let us continue eating our diet" (Dan. 1:12–13, emphasis added). That certainly doesn't sound like the Daniel of the lions' den fame!

The young Israelites seem to have cooperated with many elements of their indoctrination program, and I want to suggest that they did so because they had to find a way to navigate a new cultural reality. The spiritual choices that had been automatic back at home in the nation of Judah were now uncertain, fluid, and almost certainly dangerous. They were pushed into a period of spiritual improvisation. The world they inhabited—much like the one in which we find ourselves—was characterized by greater complexity and more religious pluralism, as well as competing spiritual and political narratives of truth.

To God-fearing people in different circumstances, the adjustments that Daniel and other biblical exiles made may have appeared to be inexcusable or even unforgivable compromises. Yet in Daniel's case, and in the cases of Esther, Ezekiel, and others, God blessed the exiles during times of cultural and spiritual upheaval—not because they did exactly as their parents would have done, but because they *found new ways to be genuinely faithful.* And not only that. The work of the exiles led eventually to spiritual renewal within their faith community. God used exiles like Daniel and Esther to restore his people.

Patrick Whitworth, a Christian leader in the UK, writes on the role of exiles during transitional periods:

> For much of the last two millennia the church, in conjunction with [political] rulers, created paradigms of power which it later had to change or abandon, if it was to reflect in any way the Lord it claimed to serve. Often these essential changes were only brought about through exiles—individuals, groups, or movements willing to go into different kinds of exile to bring about renewal of mission, or reformation of the ministry of the church.[7]

The challenge for the Christian community is how to respond to the growing number of exiles. Will we do what we can to equip them to make the choices that faced Daniel in Babylon—choices about balancing cultural accommodation and faithful, Christ-centered living? Will we listen to and take to heart their prophetic critiques of the church's posture toward our increasingly pluralistic society? Will we change our structures, guided by the unchanging truths of Scripture, to nurture their gifts and unique calling into a world deeply loved by, yet in many ways hostile to, God?

If so, I believe we will see the next generation flourish in a new cultural context as they find new ways to be faithful, new ways to be *in*, not *of*. And I believe their efforts will bear fruit for all of God's people, just as the Babylonian exiles blessed and renewed the people of God in ancient days.

You'll find videos of prodigals, nomads, and exiles at www.youlostmebook .com to use for small groups, public talks, or personal viewing.

Part 2

# DISCONNECTIONS

# DISCONNECTION, EXPLAINED

We were looking for a single "smoking gun." Instead, we found many. I suspected that our investigation would uncover one big reason that young adults disconnect from the church or walk away from their faith—maybe two or three. I expected we would find, for instance, that going away to college is a faith killer—but it turns out that's just not the case for most young people.

Instead of one or two "biggies," we discovered a wide range of perspectives, frustrations, and disillusionments that compel twentysomethings to disconnect. No single reason pushes a majority of young adults to drop out. Each person has his or her own set of unique and mundane reasons—that is, both deeply personal and rather pedestrian. Yet the everydayness of these reasons does not make them unimportant or uninteresting. Every nomad, prodigal, and exile has a story. And as we have observed before, *every story matters*.

While we explore the reasons many young adults disconnect, keep in mind that our research examines primarily their *perceptions* of what's gone wrong. Research is not infallible and it requires interpretation. Most people are not fully cognizant of what, exactly, causes them to leave church or faith, and part of our job as researchers is to analyze all the responses and look for themes to emerge. In doing so, we use not only our professional expertise but also our spiritual discernment. Part 2 is the result of our best efforts to identify the reasons young people disconnect and our humble recommendations for some ways the body of Christ can respond in love and on mission.

# IDENTIFYING DISCONNECTION

In sifting through our research findings and individual stories, we were able to identify six themes that capture the overall phenomenon of disconnection between the next generation and the church. I want to reiterate that people in every generation may experience similar feelings. However, the combination of our cultural moment and the discontinuity of the next generation, explored in Part 1, make these attitudes among young adults particularly combustible. Many twentysomethings are not hesitating, as have previous generations, to burn the bridges that once connected them to their spiritual heritage.

Here are the broad reasons they offer for dropping out. They find the church to be:

1. *Overprotective.* The impulses toward creativity and cultural engagement are some of the defining characteristics of the Mosaic generation that are most obvious. They want to reimagine, re-create, rethink, and they want to be entrepreneurs, innovators, starters. To Mosaics, creative expression is of inestimable value. The church is seen as a creativity killer where risk taking and being involved in culture are anathema. *How can the church peel back the tamper-resistant safety seal, making space for imaginative risk taking and creative self-expression, traits that are so valued within the next generation?*

2. *Shallow.* Among Mosaics, the most common perception of churches is that they are boring. Easy platitudes, proof texting, and formulaic slogans have anesthetized many young adults, leaving them with no idea of the gravity and power of following Christ. Few young Christians can coherently connect their faith with their gifts, abilities, and passions. In other words, the Christianity they received does not give them a sense of calling. *How can the church nurture a deep, holistic faith in Christ that encompasses every area of life?*

3. *Anti-science.* Many young Christians have come to the conclusion that faith and science are incompatible. Yet they see the mostly helpful role science plays in the world they inhabit—in

medicine, personal technology, travel, care of the natural world, and other areas. What's more, science seems accessible in a way that the church does not; science appears to welcome questions and skepticism, while matters of faith seem impenetrable. *How can the Christian community help the next generation interact with science positively and prophetically?*

4. *Repressive.* Religious rules—particularly sexual mores—feel stifling to the individualist mindset of young adults. Consequently they perceive the church as repressive. Sexuality creates deep challenges for the faith development of young people. *How can the church contextualize its approach to sexuality and culture within a broader vision of restored relationships?*

5. *Exclusive.* Although there are limits to what this generation will accept and whom they will embrace, they have been shaped by a culture that esteems open-mindedness, tolerance, and acceptance. Thus Christianity's claims to exclusivity are a hard sell. They want to find areas of common ground, even if that means glossing over real differences. *How can the Christian community link the singular nature of Christ with the radical ways in which he pursued and included outsiders?*

6. *Doubtless.* Young Christians (and former Christians too) say the church is not a place that allows them to express doubts. They do not feel safe admitting that faith doesn't always make sense. In addition, many feel that the church's response to doubt is trivial and fact focused, as if people can be talked out of doubting. *How can the Christian community help this generation face their doubts squarely and integrate their questions into a robust life of faith?*

## THE TURN TOWARD CONNECTION

Once we begin to understand the problems the next generation experiences with the church and Christianity, our second task is to determine how these areas of disconnect are challenging the Christian community to change. Are there ways in which the struggles of the next generation ought to shift our thinking and practice? If we ignore or discount the spiritual journeys of the young, could we be at risk of missing a fresh move of God in our time?

The Spirit-inspired interplay between generations is a common theme in Scripture. As one example, consider the story of Eli (the older generation) and Samuel (the younger generation) described in 1 Samuel 3. You may recall the episode. In the middle of the night, God calls to Samuel, but the young prophet-in-training repeatedly mistakes God's call for the voice of his mentor, Eli. Finally it occurs to Eli, after Samuel has interrupted his sleep several times, to instruct his protégé to say, "Speak, Lord, your servant is listening."

Once I heard present-day leader Jack Hayford observe that the younger generation needs the older generation to help them identify the voice of God, just as Samuel needed Eli to help him know God was calling him. Hayford also observed that helping in this way requires that we recognize, as Eli did, *that God is speaking to the younger generation.*

If you are a younger Christian, this means it's *your* turn to listen.

If you are a "well-established" believer, maybe it's time to trust in a deeper way that God is working in the next generation.

My hope is that *You Lost Me* can, in some way, catalyze this vital dynamic between generations. Each chapter in Part 2 explores one of the six broad reasons Mosaics give for disconnecting from church or the faith. Toward the end of each chapter, I offer "the turn"—some suggestions to help young dropouts *turn* their reason for leaving into a hunger for deeper faith, and to help us in the church's older generations *turn* our frustrations and occasional feelings of failure into renewal.

Let's examine the six areas of disconnection, starting with the perception that the church is overprotective, more concerned with safety than its mission to transform the world.

For a summary of the Barna data presented in this book and discussion questions for each chapter, visit www.youlostmebook.com.

# OVERPROTECTIVE

*Disconnection*: "A lot of [our upbringing] was very fear-based to get you to do something as opposed to giving you logical reasons why you should or should not do something."

—Nathan

*Reconnection*: "Our son is teaching us, his ministry parents, how film can reveal the truth about our human condition and our need for redemption in ways that are as powerful and provocative as any sermon."

—Valerie

As I listened to the young worship musician, I thought, *He's better than most of the people I see on* American Idol. *I wonder if he's ever auditioned.*

After the worship service, as Sam and I waited in line at a restaurant in Missouri, I asked if he had ever considered going on the megapopular TV talent show.

"Nope, you can't qualify if you've already had a recording contract," he said without any hint of haughtiness.

As he talked about his previous work, I discovered that one of Sam's songs—not a worship tune, a love song—hit it big a few years ago. He had composed the song for his bride and performed it for her on their wedding day. It had a catchy refrain, and the studio recording was chosen as the soundtrack for an episode of a popular teen television drama.

For some of the churchgoers Sam knows, the song's success was a disappointment. They made it clear to him that he should never have agreed to have his song on secular TV—especially not in a scene depicting teen sexuality.

Sam told me, "I don't get it. Most of my time *is* spent on worship music, but not every song I write is about faith. I thought the idea of being a musician—of being a Christian musician—is to write songs that matter to people, songs that matter to our culture because they tell the truth. But when I write a song that's not used in a way every Christian agrees on, I get hammered for it. What am I supposed to be using my talents for exactly?"

## HELICOPTER CULTURE

You have probably heard about "helicopter parents" who hover over their children to keep them safe from every conceivable danger. They keep a vigilant eye on the little (and not-so-little) ones, protecting them, insulating them from the hots, colds, and sharp edges of life. Helicopter parents try to protect their child not only from physical danger but also from failure and negative consequences of every kind.

The rise of the helicopter parent corresponds to a rising culture of protectiveness across the board. When I was growing up during the 1970s, car seatbelts were an upgrade. Over-the-counter medications came in bottles that anyone—including toddlers with poor motor skills—could open. "No smoking" signs were the exception not the rule. Jungle gyms and playground slides were made of rusty metal, and merry-go-rounds and teeter-totters still existed. Helmets were worn by racecar drivers and BMX pros, not by kids taking an after-school spin around the neighborhood on their Huffys. Only the winning Little League team got trophies, not every kid who put on a uniform.

I'll move on before I get too nostalgic.

Toy, food, and packaging safety are now front-page news. Nearly every product on store shelves is labeled with fine print absolving the manufacturer of liability. Businesses spend billions each year on quality checks and regulatory fulfillment to avoid litigation or prosecution. Even churches go to great lengths to protect their congregants' safety, whether by performing in-depth background checks on all prospective children's ministry workers or carrying liability insurance in case anyone is injured on church property.

Protectiveness has become a way of life in our culture—and an argument can be made that much of it is, on balance, a good thing. No one wants his or her child playing with a toy coated in harmful substances or mistreated by an unqualified childcare worker. But it should not surprise us that our culture's obsession with safety has shaped two generations of Boomer and Buster parents who are deeply risk-averse when it comes to their kids.

Is it possible that our cultural fixation on safety and protectiveness has also had a profound effect on the church's ability to disciple the next generation of Christians? Are we preparing them for a life of risk, adventure, and service to God—a God who asks that they lay down their lives for his kingdom? Or are we churning out safe, compliant Christian kids who are either chomping at the bit to get free or huddling in the basement playing *World of Warcraft* for hours on end, terrified to step out of doors?

Here are some of the criticisms that young Christians and former Christians level at the church:

- *Christians demonize everything outside of the church.* The next generation feels as though many Christians characterize every non-Christian thing as bad. For example, they perceive that the church's underlying message about non-Christians—adherents to other religions, atheists, and agnostics—is that these people are categorically evil.

- *Christians are afraid of pop culture, especially its movies and music.* Many young Christians complain that they have been conditioned to fear "the world." The problem is that, as they explore "the world," they come to believe (rightly or wrongly) that the world is not nearly as hopeless or awful as they've been told. They discover movies, music, and other art and media that sometimes describe the reality of human experience much better than the church does.

- *Christians maintain a false separation of sacred and secular.* Many of the interviews we conducted among young Christians focused on the false dichotomy they feel between the church world and the outside world. Our research shows that this generation does not see a divide between the sacred and secular, at least not in the same way their parents do.

- *Christians do not want to deal with the complexity or reality of the world.* To young Christians, the church can feel rigid and unreal. Christians' black-and-white views seem not to reflect the world as it really is. "It's complicated" is a phrase I hear a lot from young people. Often I am impressed with their ability to make finely tuned arguments, to highlight shades of meaning and nuance—at least when it's something important to them. For these young people, matters concerning "the world," relationships, and faith are rich and textured.

### Overprotective | In Their Own Words

*Percentage of 18- to 29-year-olds who have a Christian background*

| | completely true of me | completely or mostly true of me |
|---|---|---|
| Christians demonize everything outside of the church. | 11% | 23% |
| Church ignores the problems of the real world. | 9% | 22% |
| My church is too concerned that movies, music, and video games are harmful. | 9% | 18% |
| Church does not offer opportunities to artists and creative people. | 5% | 13% |
| I am involved in social causes that the church doesn't seem to care about. | 6% | 12% |

Barna Group | 2011 | N=1,296

## THE RISKS OF OVERPROTECTIVENESS

In short, many young Christians feel overprotected. Millions of young believers perceive that the church has kept them fearful of and detached from the world—a world, mind you, that they are called by their faith in Christ to redeem. Let's look at how this sadly ironic risk aversion is causing major disconnections.

## Alternate Thrills

One of the most significant consequences of being overprotected is that millions of young people look for excitement outside traditional boundaries. This may be pornography or sexual experimentation, drugs and other addictive substances, extreme thrill seeking (YouTube is fueled by high-octane, stupid human tricks), total immersion in video game universes, under- and overachievement, hyperexercise and eating disorders, and so on. I believe that self-harm among teens and young adults is also connected to their longing to take risks. Some young people cut themselves *just to feel something.*

Risk-free Christianity also inspires the pursuit of other forms of spirituality. One out of every four young adults (27 percent) told us that they "grew up a Christian, but since then have tried other faiths or spiritual practices." We encountered one young woman, a nomadic Catholic, who is curious about Baha'i. "It just seems really different than what I got in catechism," she said. "Jesus was taught as this miracle worker, but that wasn't my experience. This guy told me about the Baha'i faith. And while I kinda felt like he was trying to convert me, he described a spiritual adventure that was pretty appealing."

Yes, some young people are driven to thrills because pop culture is constantly seeking to outdo the spectacle of itself: "You've *Never* Seen Anything Like *This*!!!" every ad seems to promise. But the church must own up to the part it has played in passing on a faith that is yawn-worthy instead of Christ-worthy.

## Failure to Launch

The culture of heightened expectations—as well as more significant economic and professional hurdles for young people to clear—is making it harder than ever to "launch," to get going in life. As we discussed in chapter 2, most twentysomethings have not completed the major transitions that have come to define adulthood: leaving home, completing higher education, achieving financial independence, getting married and starting a family, and so on.

Although there are many social and economic reasons for this delay (for instance, the increasingly common view that marriage should be postponed), I believe that the Christian community is complicit in young adults' failure to launch. We have not provided a clear, compelling, prophetic voice to answer the issues that cause young people to stay "stuck." A few years ago, Barna Group conducted research for a mainline denomination. We interviewed young people who were *de*-churched (former churchgoers) and discovered that one of the major reasons they had left the church was that their faith community had not been able to help them deal with the life issues they faced. Too often, we have not provided practical coaching on marriage, parenting, vocation and calling, and all the smaller choices emerging adults must make along the road to maturity.

One bright young man we interviewed described how one of his high school teachers was shocked to discover that he was planning to attend a Christian college. "She told me I would forfeit tens of thousands of dollars in annual earning power by not choosing a 'higher profile' university. As I processed her advice, it never occurred to me that I should talk to anyone at my church about it."

## Paralyzing Self-Doubt

A friend of mine recently told me about a young woman she is mentoring. Chris, who is twenty-six, is terrified to make a decision—*any* decision. Her insecurity and fear of regret are intense and constant, whether she is choosing between brands of pasta at the grocery store or deciding to accept her boyfriend's proposal of marriage. Sometimes Chris thinks she senses a call to missions or full-time ministry, but other times she's not so sure. Recently she told my friend she would rather work her minimum-wage job and live with her college roommate for years than make the "wrong" decision about the next phase of her life.

Chris is an extreme example, but many twentysomethings experience self-doubt severe enough to keep them in personal, professional, relational, and spiritual paralysis. Think about it. For their entire lives, young adults with helicopter parents have been shielded from failure and regret. To their mind, negative consequences are truly unthink-able—maybe not even survivable! Why else would their parents protect them so completely?

Some church-raised young adults experience similar self-doubt when it comes to making spiritual judgments. Instead of equipping them to make thoughtful, prayerful decisions and then to trust God for the out-come, the church has instilled a debilitating fear of sin or "stepping out of God's will." How can we expect the next generation to move forward with confidence into God's future when they are scared of making a misstep?

## Loss of Creatives

A fourth consequence of overprotectiveness is the loss of many of the most talented, creative individuals from the church community. This perception—that the church is overprotective—is most common among young exiles, those who feel stuck between the safe, comfortable world of their church experience and the dangerous, all-encompassing faith they believe God requires. Exiles want to follow Jesus in a way that connects with the world they inhabit, to partner with God outside the walls of the church, and to pursue Christianity without separating themselves from the world. Many of these exiles are also creative types—artists, musicians, entertainers, and filmmakers—who feel their calling is out of tune with their Christian upbringing. They think the church doesn't know what to do with creatives like them.

Many of the church's brightest talents, like Sam, have been asked to confine their gifts to the service of the Christian community. As a con-sequence, many young creatives have headed for the hills; it's no small coincidence that many of today's hottest entertainers and artists left behind a churchgoing heritage. The church has a hard time preparing these young people for service to the world, while also keeping them grounded in and deeply connected to the body of Christ.

Recall Katy Perry (we met her in chapter 3), whose Christian family ate "angeled" eggs when she was a child—and who is now a twentysome-thing "curious as the cat," ready to try everything she was denied by her overprotected upbringing. Or consider the Grammy-winning rock band Kings of Leon, made up of the three Followill brothers and their cousin.

Nathan, Caleb, and Jared did much of their growing up on the road with their dad, a Pentecostal preacher, "barnstorming churches and tent revivals in Tennessee, Arkansas, Louisiana, Mississippi, and Oklahoma."[1] According to *Rolling Stone* magazine, "The boys' religious mandate was strict: no movies, no music but church music, no 'mixed bathing,' no competitive sports, no short pants (even while waterskiing)."[2] In an interview with *Relevant* magazine, Nathan Followill said, "We didn't even own three CDs. . . . I think my mom had this guy named Leon Patillo and I can remember Russ Taff. Oh, then there's Shirley Caesar." While the brothers wouldn't change how they were raised—"There would be no Kings of Leon without our upbringing," Nathan says—they point to the overprotectiveness of their upbringing as a factor in their dropping out. "A lot of that was very fear-based to get you to do something as opposed to giving you logical reasons why you should or should not do something."[3]

Not long ago I had the privilege of visiting my friend Charlie Peacock's Art House in Nashville. (Charlie doesn't talk much about it but he has enjoyed an accomplished recording and performing career, and has mentored a number of highly successful young artists, such as Switchfoot and The Civil Wars.) I spoke to a group of seventy or so young musicians and artists, and then they shared their formidable talents with me and each other.

I was struck to find out that very few of these young creatives are pursuing careers in the Christian music industry; most of them are attempting to "go mainstream" with their gifts. I was also impressed by their eagerness to learn how to live faithfully outside the Christian subculture. Charlie and the other convener of the event, Mark Rodgers of The Wedgwood Circle, coached them on how to follow Christ while navigating the cannibalistic, ego-infested waters of the secular entertainment industry. During breaks between sessions, some of the musicians expressed to me their frustration with the lack of support from their home churches, which are ambivalent at best and condemning at worst about their dreams for a mainstream career.

And it's not just young musicians. Our study has found a desire among many young Christian creatives to engage in the broader world. I have interviewed young actors and film directors, fine and graphic artists, designers and activists, as well as young adults from other creative careers, who believe the Christian community has been unnecessarily insulating. They don't want to be consigned to the "Christian ghetto," a phrase that consistently comes up in our interviews. Most echo the sentiment that the church is not a safe place to take risks and not welcoming to the creative compulsion so ubiquitous among the next generation.

## OVERPROTECTIVENESS TURNS TO DISCERNMENT

Let's think back to one of the central arguments of this book: the next generation is living through a period of compressed social, cultural, and technological change. This environment invites them to live out their faith in new and sometimes startling ways.

I want to suggest that the widespread desire for a life in the mainstream is one of the consequences of monumental change. This is not the first time mainstream credibility has inspired faithful believers. Think back to the biblical account of Daniel. Life in Babylon gave the young Hebrew the platform and opportunity to influence the broadest circles of political and societal power. God used Daniel and his peers, exiles in a pagan culture, to bring about his purposes. Could it be that the growing desire for mainstream influence among the younger generation is the work of God—preparing them to bring restoration and renewal to our culture?

I believe so.

Yet this hopeful potential in the next generation also comes with a number of very real challenges. An aspiration to influence culture begs the question of how to embody in-but-not-of faithfulness, and how to deal with the poison pill of cultural accommodation that the pull toward mainstream influence makes available. Let me put it this way: gaining credibility for its own sake is vanity; gaining credibility to participate in God's work to redeem his world is a mission. I am concerned that too many Mosaic Christians are so interested in pursuing the good, the true, and the beautiful that they forget to acknowledge and draw near to the source of those pursuits—Jesus.

The church must help the next generation live into the difference, by *turning* our overprotectiveness into discernment. Here are some examples:

*Overprotectiveness* characterizes everything that is not Christian as evil.

*Discernment* helps young people understand that other people are not our enemies, but that there is fundamental brokenness in humans and an adversary who intends to derail us in every possible way.

*Overprotectiveness* makes strict rules about media consumption to "save the kids from smut." It avoids watching, reading, and talking about current events and pop culture in the hope that they will just go away.

*Discernment* reads "the Bible and the newspaper," in theologian Karl Barth's famous formulation (we might update this to "the Bible and the Internet"). Unless we choose to live in secluded Christian community—which is a viable option for only a few—exposure to media-driven culture is inevitable. Rather than steering clear of secular films, music, websites, books, and television shows, let's watch, listen, and read together and do "cultural exegesis" as a faithful community.

*Overprotectiveness* oversimplifies the tough stuff of life—suffering, failure, relationships—and offers formulas instead of honest, contextualized answers.

*Discernment* is transparent about the hazards of being human and teaches the full witness of Scripture, which is messy, complex, and, ultimately, wonderfully true.

*Overprotectiveness* discourages risk taking and uses fear to "protect" the next generation.

*Discernment* guides young people to trust God fearlessly and follow Christ in the power of the Spirit, even at the risk of their lives, reputations, and worldly success.

*Overprotectiveness* tries to convince young people that the only (or best) way to serve God is by working in a church, parish, Christian nonprofit, or mission field.

*Discernment* recognizes that there is no difference between sacred jobs and secular professions. Yes, we need called and prepared young people to serve as priests, pastors, evangelists, and missionaries. But we also need to affirm the powerful sentiment captured by Dutch theologian *and* politician Abraham Kuyper: "Oh, no single piece of our mental world is to be hermetically sealed off from the rest, and there is not a square inch in the whole domain of our human existence over which Christ, who is Sovereign over *all*, does not cry: 'Mine!'"

*Overprotectiveness* paints a false picture of reality that hurts young people much more in the long run than honesty would in the short run. Many teens and young adults have been told they can be, do, and have anything they want—only to find the "real world" not quite so obliging.

*Discernment* develops a robust theology of calling that recognizes each person's unique purpose and gifting as nothing less (or more) than what God has ordained. Let's recognize that the Holy Spirit has plans for the next generation that are bigger than what they can dream for themselves, and let's make it our business to tune their hearts to hear his voice, not just ours.

## *The Risks of Following Christ*

I have heard hundreds of sermons but I still remember this line from one of my father's: "When you have a child, you open up a grave." Sounds morbid, but Dad was reminding his listeners, as Scripture does in many places, that our lives are fleeting.

This way of thinking is exactly the opposite of our security-oriented, prepare-for-the-future mindset. And I believe that at the heart of our problems with overprotectiveness is our very human need to control.

But God refuses to be controlled.

An overprotected generation has been sold the lie that "Christian living" means material blessing, automatic protection, and bulletproof safety. Two millennia of Christian martyrs beg to differ, and many young adults today are interested in those martyrs' lives of jeopardy and fulfillment. They are desperate for a new way to understand and experience the worthy risks of following Christ. Life without some sense of urgency—a life that is safe, incubated, insular, overprotected, consumptive—is not worth living. The next generation is aching for influence, for significance, for lives of meaning and impact. Think of your favorite film or novel. Invariably the best stories, regardless of medium, involve significant hazards for the characters. We care about characters for whom the stakes are high—yet we have done all we can to lower the stakes for the newest real-life protagonists in God's grand, risky story.

Let's reorient our thinking about the proper role of risk in our contemporary Christian witness.

## The Risks of Parenting

Unfortunately, no Christian parent earns a reward in heaven for coaching his or her kids to live long and secure lives. Sure, we all hope to make it to a ripe old age—and there is nothing wrong with managing not to die young! But ameliorating risk is not how God measures effectiveness among parents. God looks at how we shape our children's hearts and minds to be responsive and obedient to him.

This means taking seriously Jesus's words: "If you try to hang on to your life, you will lose it. But if you give up your life for my sake, you will save it" (Matt. 16:25 NLT). Are we willing to embrace this truth on behalf of the children God has entrusted to our care?

My friends Britt and Kate Merrick have been fervent and tireless in fighting the cancer that has invaded the body of their smart, sassy, seven-year-old daughter, Daisy. God has blessed her recovery thus far, but Britt, a pastor in Southern California, has been very clear in his teaching during the last year that the hope of the church and of parents is not that every child lives. *It's that Jesus is Lord.* That kind of faith takes my breath away, and I truly believe it is the kind of faith to which all Christ-following parents are called. We never stop interceding on our children's behalf but we put our hope only in Jesus, who is Lord of all.

Of course, there are times when and places where we should shield our children from danger and unwelcome content. We have a biblical responsibility to nurture our children—especially young children—in safe and godly environments. But we must not use our fear for their safety as an excuse for not properly preparing them to be used by God. Jesus prayed to the Father for his disciples, "I'm not asking you to take them out of the world, but to keep them safe from the evil one" (John 17:15 NLT). Might we have the grace and courage to pray the same for our kids?

What if God is preparing this generation for great exploits in his name? What if a new renaissance of global mission could be realized by this generation? Is our preoccupation with safety keeping our children on the sidelines? Or are we willing partners in preparing them for what God has planned?

## *The Risks of Cultural Influence*

A growing sentiment of this generation is that they want to be, in the words of my friend Gabe Lyons, a "counterculture for the common good." For many young Christians, there is a realization that they want to follow Christ in a way that does not separate them from the culture. They want to be culture makers, not culture avoiders.

This kind of influence comes at a cost. Sometimes being a cultural influencer comes at the cost of acceptance within the Christian community, as Sam found when his love song hit it big in the mainstream. Those who seem too cozy with secular business, media, entertainment, social sciences, and politics are viewed with skepticism by many devout Christians.

By a similar token, I know some young believers who are reluctant to be linked to the "Christian tribe," which has a decidedly negative reputation in many sectors of our society. There is a talented Broadway actress who feels she must keep her Christian bona fides in the background. A well-known singer-songwriter in his twenties feels the need to be publicly cautious about his faith connections. Similar sentiments are repeated by other young Christians in science, government, business, and the academy. It's not that they hide their faith, exactly; they are just *intentional* about when and to whom they reveal it.

I can almost hear what some readers are thinking at this point: *Aren't they just ashamed of the gospel? Are these young Christians willing to stand up for Christ or not?* I understand these questions but I want us to imagine for a moment that these young adults are missionaries to a group of people who know next to nothing about Christ, God, or the Bible. Suppose that they are missionaries in an Islamic dictatorship where their livelihood and even their life are at stake. While they do not aspire to live long lives for their own sake—they want above all else to live for God's purposes—they do not want to be reckless with God's gifts of life, talent, relationship, and opportunity. In such an environment a missionary must be discerning about how and when to reveal his or her faith. I want to suggest that we should see young people who are using their gifts in our broader culture as missionaries. They are helping to re-create, to renew, to redeem the culture by adding their voices to the wider conversation about what it means to be human. No, most are not handing out religious tracts, but by living into their calling to reflect the Creator's image, they point the way to him—which is harder than it sounds. Perhaps those of us who are older need to cut them some slack and let them minister as God directs in a culture that is so different from the one in which we grew up.

Christ-followers contend with two opposing temptations. The first is *cultural withdrawal.* When we remove ourselves completely from the surrounding culture, we neglect Jesus's calling to be "the light of the world" (Matt. 5:14). We have a duty, a healthy Christian obligation, to bless the world around us. The prophet Jeremiah gave this challenge to God's people exiled in Babylon: "Build homes, and plan to stay. Plant gardens, and eat the food they produce. Marry and have children. Then find spouses for them so that you may have many grandchildren. Multiply! Do not dwindle away! And work for the peace and prosperity of the city where I sent you into exile. Pray to the LORD for it, for its welfare will determine your welfare" (Jer. 29:5–7 NLT). Read that last line again. Let's make music, movies, tools, services, and ideas that bless people around us, Christian or not. We are blessed to be a blessing.

The second temptation is *cultural accommodation.* A healthy desire to influence culture can turn too easily into an unhealthy preoccupation with acceptance by mainstream culture. When this happens, we consume what the world has to offer and end up with lives no different from anyone else's. Some Christians in every generation have succumbed to this temptation, including Mosaics—some of whom would rather be cool than Christlike.

In the critical tension between cultural withdrawal and cultural accommodation, we need new, better ways—a new mind—to equip a generation to live in-but-not-of the world. This may mean that parents and faith leaders should allow young people to take bigger risks. It may mean trusting that their calling is different from our own and requires them to live in a greater degree of tension than would make us comfortable. It certainly means we need to facilitate transparent relationships and conversations so we can all find the God-spaced ground between withdrawal and accommodation.

My friends Steve and Valerie have modeled this "new mind" as their son, a filmmaker, has grown into a man. (We briefly met their son, Justin, in chapter 4, "Exiles.") Steve and Valerie have served some of the most influential Christian organizations in the U.S., and when Justin decided to study moviemaking in a secular film program after finishing seminary, they heard lots of concerns: "Christians and Hollywood don't mix." "But he had such a bright future as a church leader!" Their family had always been culture-engagers—public school supporters, theater- and moviegoers, actively involved with their secular friends and neighbors—and willing to take risks, so they thought they were prepared.

But Steve told me, "You should see some of the major films he's worked on to build his credibility in mainstream Hollywood, David. It's mostly great stuff. But sections are also jarring. The first movie that hit national theaters with his name in the credits opens with a sex scene that is not visually explicit but left no question what was happening. I thought, *Whoa! Who do I feel comfortable inviting to see this? How many Christian folks will understand how strategically he's placed? That he may be the only Christ-follower some of these Hollywood-types ever meet, one of the only believers with inside access?"*

"When some Christians tell us they are praying for him," Valerie said, "I'm guessing they really mean they hope he doesn't go to hell in Hollywood. We wish they would pray for him to find favor and work for God's pleasure. You know what? Our son is teaching us, his ministry parents, how film can reveal the truth about our human condition and our need for redemption in ways that are as powerful and provocative as any sermon."

Steve continued, "Were we younger and braver, we like to think we would follow a similar path. But Justin is following the unique calling of God on his life, and we are more convinced than ever about the strength of his faith, even though it is expressed in his professional life differently than in ours."

## The Risks of Holiness

Cultural influencers embrace risks for the sake of the gospel, but I am concerned that many in the next generation do not fully appreciate the importance of holiness and obedience. It is right for young Christ-followers to pursue lives of mainstream influence, yet it's dangerous—and not in the good way—to do so without understanding our culture's powers of seduction.

We must steer young cultural influencers away from the temptation to measure their faithfulness, personal worth, effectiveness, or gifted-ness by the level of mainstream acceptance they achieve. When the world's standards of success become the yardstick, Christians with the best of intentions cave to the pressure to cut corners, cheat just a little, lie to protect their reputation, take a favor under the table, ignore the marginalized to please the in-crowd, or blow by their own boundaries of behavior—all to measure up to society's standards. Gaining credibility with the world must never become more important than obedience to God. The apostle John wrote, "Do not love this world nor the things it offers you, for when you love the world, you do not have the love of the Father in you. For the world offers only a craving for physical pleasure, a craving for everything we see, and pride in our achievements and possessions. . . . And this world is fading away, along with everything that people crave" (1 John 2:15–17 NLT). Living a creative, Spirit-filled life, set apart for the Lord's holy purposes, is not for the weak-willed.

Looking again at Daniel's life, we see that holiness both defined him and gave him influence in the world around him. His access to the Babylonian cultural elite afforded him an opportunity to speak truth to power. But it was his commitment to holiness that made him worth listening to—and that landed him in the lions' den (see Daniel 6). God shut the mouths of the lions and vindicated Daniel before the Babylonian politicians who had conspired to see him dead.

Risking holiness doesn't always have a happy ending, however. During World War II, German pastor Dietrich Bonhoeffer took a stand against Adolf Hitler and the Third Reich—and against the German church, which ignored and even supported the Nazi regime. Bonhoeffer was convinced that followers of Christ have an obligation not to withdraw from culture (even when it's as wicked as the Nazis) but *to be in it*, and not to accommodate the culture (like the German church did) but *not be of it*.

Three weeks before the war ended, Dietrich Bonhoeffer was hanged for plotting against the government. He had risked everything to obey in holiness, but God did not "shut the lions' mouths."

Bonhoeffer's "Daniel moment" got him killed.

His life and death stand as a stark challenge to anyone who believes that following Christ is the easy road to blessing, riches, comfort, and acceptance. And the widespread, ongoing influence of his life and writings represents a rebuke to a church that has too often failed to prepare the next generation for the grand, terrifying, exhilarating adventure of God's mission to the world.

Each of us will face a "Daniel moment" sometime in our life. Maybe more than one. Will we—and those whom God has called us to disciple—know what to do when it arrives?

**6**

# SHALLOW

*Disconnection:* "It just feels like in America everyone keeps faith separate from work and life."

—Tracy

*Reconnection:* "I am focusing on going deep with a lot fewer young people."

—Jon

Tracy was coming home from Tanzania. I sat next to the twenty-three-year-old young woman on a flight from Washington, DC, to Denver, Colorado, the last leg of her twenty-nine-hour journey back from Africa. Despite her taxing trip, she was enthusiastic about what she had seen and done, filling the last hour of our flight with interesting details about her experiences.

The journey had been part of Tracy's master's degree in international affairs from a university in the Denver area. "It's the same program that Condoleezza Rice went through," she told me with pride. Tracy was raised Catholic and attended a Catholic undergraduate college, and she fits the nomad profile described in chapter 3. She considers herself a Christian, though she attends Mass only occasionally with her boyfriend. "My boyfriend is much more into church than I am. I'd say he is more into spiritual stuff than I am, even though I am spiritual. Like, whenever I say 'Oh, God!' he quickly chimes in 'loves you.' It's cute and also annoying."

What excites Tracy most are her experiences internationally. "Working with vulnerable people is so cool. My boyfriend is a math geek. He does loans and accounting—stuff I don't understand. And he loves it. But I see my work as more than just a nine-to-five thing. I mean, I think this is so important. I don't think I will ever see development as just a job."

"It's a calling," I said. When her expression showed confusion, I added, "I mean, it seems like God has put it in your heart. You were made for it."

"Oh, huh. I never thought of my interest in helping the poor around the world as a calling from God. It just feels like in America everyone keeps faith separate from work and life. That's not how it is in Africa, certainly not in South America and Central America. I've spent a lot more time in those countries, and faith is definitely woven into the lives of the people there."

She paused for a long, thoughtful moment and then said, "I guess maybe it is a calling for me."

My conversation with Tracy illustrates one of the significant forms of disconnection that plagues this generation of students: the separation of faith from their "real lives." The faith too many of them have inherited is a lifeless shadow of historic Christianity, which insists that following Jesus is a way of life, not a laundry list of vague beliefs that have little meaning for how we spend our lives. I think the next generation's disconnection stems ultimately from the failure of the church to impart Christianity as a comprehensive way of understanding reality and living fully in today's culture. To many young people who grew up in Christian churches, Christianity seems boring, irrelevant, sidelined from the real issues people face.

It seems *shallow*.

The shallowness equation has two sides. On the one, we find young adults who have only a superficial understanding of the faith and of the Bible. The Christianity they believe is an inch deep. On the other, we find faith communities that convey a lot of information *about* God rather than discipling young believers to live wholly and deeply in the reality *of* God. Thus the Christianity some churches pass on is a mile wide. Put the two together and you get a generation of young believers whose faith is an inch deep and a mile wide—too shallow to survive and too broad to make a difference.

Let's start with the inch-deep side of the equation.

## ROOTLESS AND SUPERFICIAL

Our research shows that most young people lack a deep understanding of their faith. The trend of biblical illiteracy, which is problematic among most age-groups, has been on the increase since my mentor George Barna wrote his books on the younger generations, including *Baby Busters: The Disillusioned Generation, Generation Next,* and *Real Teens.* Other researchers have explored these challenges as well, including Kenda Creasy Dean, who shows in *Almost Christian* that most teenagers embrace beliefs that are Christian on the surface—but once you dig a little deeper, you find they are not quite orthodox. Perhaps the best description of this superficiality is found in Christian Smith and Melinda Lundquist Denton's book *Soul Searching.* They famously label the religion of today's young Americans as *moralistic therapeutic deism*, vividly described like this: "God is something like a combination Divine Butler and Cosmic Therapist: he is always on call, takes care of any problems that arise, professionally helps his people to feel better about themselves, and does not become too personally involved in the process."[1]

This inch-deep, not-quite-Christian understanding of God has been demonstrated in Barna Group studies as well. One project we conducted in 1999 examined the views of teenagers who shared their faith in Christ regularly with others—"teen evangelists." We found that the faith they were trying to spread was, in fact, more akin to moralistic therapeutic deism than to historic Christianity. Few of these youth evangelists could identify a single portion of the Bible as the basis of their faith in Christ.[2]

This type of shallow faith that most Christian young people embrace does not require the nurture of a faith community to thrive. Certainly it is not a holistic way of life that demands we die to ourselves for the sake of Christ. And while it is indeed easier than following Jesus, I believe this uniquely American take on faith among young Christians is a core reason so many of them are disengaging from church to become nomads or prodigals.

Consider some of the perceptions young Christians maintain. Nearly one-third (31 percent) described the church as boring. One-quarter indicated that faith is not relevant to their career or interests (24 percent), that the church does not prepare them for real life (23 percent), that the church does not help them find their purpose (23 percent), and that the Bible is not taught clearly or often enough (23 percent). One out of five young people (20 percent) expressed that God seems missing from their experience of church. These may not seem like large percentages but they represent millions of young prodigals, nomads, and exiles.

### Shallow | In Their Own Words

*Percentage of 18- to 29-year-olds who have a Christian background*

|  | completely true of me | completely or mostly true of me |
|---|---|---|
| Church is boring. | 16% | 31% |
| Faith is not relevant to my career or my interests. | 13% | 24% |
| My church does not prepare me for real life. | 9% | 23% |
| My church does not help me find my purpose. | 9% | 23% |
| The Bible is not taught clearly or often enough. | 7% | 23% |
| God seems missing from my experience of church. | 7% | 20% |

Barna Group | 2011 | N=1,296

Some young adults, like Tracy, are doing all they can to create meaningful lives yet cannot see how the feel-good god they believe in has anything to do with making a difference in the world. (Who can blame them?) Others have not even considered what a meaningful life might look like, much less how faith could be the unifying feature of a life filled with purpose. They have such a shallow understanding of Christianity and the Bible that their roots of faith cannot survive the weather systems of real life. It's difficult to imagine them anchored as "oaks of righteousness" (Isa. 61:3) whose spiritual, relational, and vocational roots are planted deep in Christ.

## Misplaced Confidence

As we look at the problem of shallow faith, we need to consider where to assign responsibility. This is not an exercise in finger-pointing; we need to understand the causes of shallow faith in order to find God-ordained solutions. The Christian community may share the blame for superficiality of faith among the next generation (more on that in a moment). However, young adults' ability to grow in faith withers when they persist in narcissism, entitlement, and out-of-proportion self-confidence. The results of a study conducted by Barna Group captures this phenomenon. The vast majority of churchgoing teenagers said they understand the teachings of the Bible "very well." But when we asked specific questions about the basic content of those teachings, most teens in the study performed quite poorly. In other words, their self-confidence was totally out of proportion with their actual knowledge.

One seventeen-year-old from Oregon typifies this sort of imbalance. When we asked him to describe his life goals, he said, "I don't know. I am really good at a lot of things. I am also really interested in a lot of things. I'm thinking of starting a college. I feel I have a lot to teach others about many subjects." It's admirable that this young man has big dreams, but his outsized self-confidence comes across less as ambition and more as naïve arrogance.

Some overindulgent parents are partly to blame for their kids' unrealistic self-assessments, but young people have been aided and abetted by a culture that glorifies youth as inherently beautiful, valuable, and wise. Have you ever noticed the degree to which youth and young adults are featured in advertisements? This is true even for products and services targeted to a general audience—that is, ads for soft drinks, cosmetics, alcohol, automobiles, clothing, pharmaceuticals, amusement parks, restaurants, and many other items frequently feature twentysomethings, even though many other age-groups are included in the target market.

Simply put, there is something amiss and superficial in the marketing media's obsession with youth and young adults, an obsession that has at least two negative consequences. First, it reinforces the very modern notion that the next generation—the arbiters of cool—must be catered to before all else. Second, it fuels the damaging misperception that older people don't have much of value to offer younger generations, thereby increasing generational fragmentation in our cultural imagination. In other words, there is little doubt that our culture contributes to the shallowness of the generation.

### Missing Ingredient

All this leads to a faith that lacks one essential ingredient: *humility*. If you already know all there is to know, if you've been told your entire life that you're "just right" exactly the way you are, if the main job of the god you believe in is to make you feel good about yourself (because you're entitled to great self-esteem, along with everything else), then there are not a lot of compelling reasons to sit in the dirt at the feet of Jesus and live the humble life of a disciple.

To follow Jesus, young adults in the next generation—just like the generations before them—will have to learn humility. From whom will they learn it? When they look at us, do they see humble servants and eager students of the Master?

# BROAD AND TRIVIAL

Even though there is some blame to assign to young people (unrealistic self-regard) and to our culture (media-driven superficiality), congregations and faith communities must also share some responsibility for the shallow faith of many young adults. It is a tragedy that so many of them come to such a tepid conclusion about their faith communities—places that should breathe meaning and hope into their lives as they connect with God and with others.

As we look at the experiences facilitated by faith communities in the lives of young Christians (found in the table on p. 119), we discover a mix of good news and bad in four areas: relations, mission, education, and vocation.[3]

## What Happens in Church Stays in Church?

Survey question: Thinking about your experience at church during high school, which, if any, of the following did you experience through your church or faith community?

*Percentage of 18- to 29-year-olds who have a Christian background*

|  | Catholics | Protestants |
| --- | --- | --- |
| **Relational Outcomes** | | |
| Had a close personal friend who was an adult at church or parish | 28% | 39% |
| Had an adult mentor at church, other than the pastor or church staff | 12% | 17% |
| **Missional Outcomes** | | |
| Served the poor through my church | 24% | 20% |
| Went on a trip that helped me expand my thinking | 16% | 19% |
| Found a cause or issue at church that motivates me | 11% | 15% |
| **Educational Outcomes** | | |
| Received helpful input from a pastor or church worker about my education | 11% | 11% |
| Received a scholarship for college through church | 4% | 3% |
| Learned about schools or colleges I might want to attend through my church | 4% | 3% |
| **Vocational Outcomes** | | |
| Learned about how Christians can positively contribute to society | 28% | 28% |
| Learned to view my gifts and passions as part of God's calling | 25% | 26% |
| Better understood my purpose in life through church | 23% | 25% |
| Learned how the Bible applies to my field or interest area | 10% | 16% |
| **Experienced none of these** | 44% | 46% |

Barna Group | 2011 | N=1,296

Let's look first at relational experiences. Most young Protestants and Catholics do not recall having a meaningful friendship with an adult through their church, and more than four out of five never had an adult mentor. This is true of enough young Christians that we must ask ourselves whether our churches and parishes are providing the rich environments that a relationally oriented generation needs to develop deep faith. I believe we need a new mind to measure the vibrancy and health of the intergenerational relationships in our faith communities.

Our research focused as well on missional, educational, and vocational experiences. Did young people discover a sense of mission through their church? Did their faith community help them make significant educational choices? Did their church or parish family help them navigate their calling and career trajectory? You can see for yourself that these kinds of experiences are relatively rare among young Christians. There are significant opportunities for the Christian community to improve in these important areas of discipleship.

As we look at four of the factors that contribute to the problem of shallow faith, you will begin to sense some of the ways that the church needs a new mind to engage this generation. Later in this chapter, we will explore how we can "turn" the experience of spiritual shallowness into something deeper and more akin to historic Christian discipleship. The "turn" is what motivates me as a researcher and writer. There are many churches, organizations, and families doing great work developing disciples, and my aim is to inform and equip many more for the kingdom work of passing on the faith.

To move forward, however, we need to look at the unfortunate role we in the Christian community sometimes play in passing on shallow faith to the next generation.

## Mass Production of Disciples

After more than a decade and a half of research into American faith, I believe that the Christian church in the United States has a shallow faith problem because we have a discipleship problem. Moreover, diagnosing and treating shallow faith among *young* adults is urgent because we have a shallow faith problem among *all* adults.

I suggested earlier in this book that we have a mass-production approach to faith development. Taking our cues from public education, among other sectors of society, we have created a conveyor belt of development that industrializes the soul formation of young people—who eventually become adults with inch-deep, mile-wide faith. The outcome is adult Christians who were not transformed by their faith as children, as teens, or as young adults. How can we expect more after they turn forty?

Some are tempted to believe that spiritual effectiveness is connected to the size of our institutions and the sophistication of our content, but nothing could be further from the truth. Can you imagine a human civilization with a more developed spiritual infrastructure than the United States today? We have Christian camps by the handfuls, Christian media companies by the hundreds, Christian schools by the thousands (from daycare to graduate schools), local churches by the hundreds of thousands. Today Christians in North America use the most advanced communication technology and media that have ever been known to humankind.

But does this infrastructure yield more and better discipleship automatically? Our research says no. Colleges, publishers, camps, and schools are not bad things—and I believe such institutions are absolutely vital for the future of Western faith. In fact one of the outcomes I hope emerges from this book is action for institutional decision makers. Your efforts to rethink and reimagine your church, business, nonprofit, or denomination—cultivating a "new mind" for what you do and how you measure success—will bear significant fruit for the future of the next generation.

Still, despite their size and reach, institutions can serve outcomes that are antithetical to genuine discipleship, especially to the approach found most often in the Scriptures. Yes, the Bible records instances of large events in which many made a commitment to follow Christ, and it is absolutely clear about the need for sound teaching, which can and should be delivered to groups large and small. But compare the mentality of today's Western church to Jesus's work with his disciples, which was characterized by life-on-life mentoring and apprenticeship. Can we really conclude that by embracing an industrialized, more-is-better approach, we have improved on the Lord's results?

## Missing Rituals

A second way our communities of faith contribute to shallow faith is by failing to provide meaningful rituals—or, when rituals exist, failing to provide a clear sense of their meaning and importance. Not long ago, I attended the Bat Mitzvah ceremony of my daughter Emily's friend, Kelsey. I was deeply impressed by the way the rabbi involved the entire family in the service. Kelsey read from the Torah, demonstrating to her faith community the hours of work she had invested in learning Hebrew. Then she gave a short talk about the importance of faith in her life and about the meaning of the verses she had read. Kelsey's grandparents stood at the front and passed the Torah scrolls to her parents, Dan and Debbie, who passed them to Kelsey, symbolizing in a tangible way the passing of the Scriptures from one generation to the next.

When Jewish kids become Bar or Bat Mitzvahs, they are no longer children in the eyes of their religious community. They accept full responsibility as adults under Jewish tradition, including being accountable for their moral choices and serving their local synagogue in public Scripture reading and prayer.

Most mainline and Catholic parishes have a similar ceremony for young teens called confirmation, the "sacrament of maturity"—yet many do not follow the ceremony with a meaningful expectation that the confirmed will contribute to the spiritual growth of the community. The majority of evangelical churches lack such a rite of passage completely, though they may have an occasional "youth service" when teens are invited to lead the congregation in worship. Most of the time, however, teens and young adults are consumers of the church's services, not servants of the church.

My point is not that every church should have confirmation but that Christian communities of all kinds must find ways to include teens and young adults in the spiritual life of the church, rather than relegating them to the game room. We need a new mind for facilitating meaning-filled rites of passage. How might young people be involved in Scripture reading, praying, leading worship, giving testimony, or providing a short teaching to the congregation? What would happen if teens and twenty-somethings knew they had a responsibility to visit the sick or shut-ins of their church, or to become a "big sister" or "big brother" to younger kids, mentoring and discipling their spiritual growth?

A related challenge is the lack of opportunity for young people to participate, commensurate with their abilities, in decision making for or leadership of the congregation. Many schools and civic groups have youth councils that participate in policy decisions. Of course, elder boards should not be replaced with youth boards, but isn't it unrealistic of us to expect young people to claim a stake in the church's mission without having a seat at the table? What can congregations do to appropriate the energy and passion of young adults to benefit the whole body?

## Expecting Too Little

A third problem found in many churches and families is expecting too little of the next generation. This is a point driven home in Kenda Creasy Dean's book *Almost Christian*. In a review of the book, Eve Tushnet draws the following contrast between the expectations placed on Protestant teens and those placed on Mormon teens.

> [Protestant] parents who show, by their words or their actions, that the tenets and practices of their faith are vague, unimportant, or only tenuously related to daily life, produce teenagers whose faith is vague, marginal, and unlikely to shape their actions and plans in any significant way. Parents who ask little of their children in terms of faith formation, but a great deal in terms of, say, getting into a good college, make a statement about priorities which their children trust and follow. Churches, youth ministries, and similar groups that trade "send[ing] young people out" for "rop[ing] young people in" wind up with teens who think church is fine, a good place to be—"nice." And who then leave church to act just like all of their friends.
>
> Mormons, by contrast, challenge their teenagers and require a lot of time, study, and leadership from them. Mormon parents rise at dawn to go over their church's history and doctrine with their children. More than half of the Mormon youth in the study had given a presentation in church in the past six months. Frequently they shared public testimony and felt that they were given some degree of decision-making power within their community. They shape their plans for the immediate future around strong cultural pressures toward mission trips and marriage.[4]

In our research, we find clear evidence that many parents and churches have expectations of young people that are much too low or much too driven by cultural ideas of success. Often we misread youth involvement in church as growth in faith. However, teen attraction to the newest flash-bang-wow at church may be a misleading indicator of success. Teenagers' excitement about church, their willingness to attend, and the friends and social connections they make at church are not the same thing as spiritual growth. We must not equate youth attendance at programs with discipleship.

Not only do we tend to expect too little of our young people, we expect too little of ourselves, and those low expectations spill over onto our students. If faith in Christ is not shaping every facet of our lives, transforming us into people who love God with heart, soul, mind, and body (see Luke 10:27), why would we expect more from the next generation?

## Quantity over Quality

A fourth practice that contributes to shallow faith is the fact that many of our youth ministries fixate on numbers of attendees rather than measuring spiritual growth and transformation. We emphasize quantity over quality. I was describing some of this research to my friend Jon Tyson, who is now a pastor in New York City. For many years, this Australian worked as a youth pastor in Nashville. Recently as I explained our research findings, I suggested that some large youth groups actually do damage to young souls by taking the "factory" approach to faith development. "It's not wrong to have big youth groups, of course," I said. "Good ministry can result. But it's really about the issues of apprenticeship. Are young people learning to live like Christ or just coming to see friends and hear an entertaining speaker?"

Jon stared intently at me. I thought for sure I had ticked him off, but then he said, "I've had to repent of focusing on myself and my own success. I have come to realize that I was subconsciously more concerned with how many teens were in the room rather than how many were becoming like Jesus. I have had people come to me since then and tell me that the largeness of our youth group ended up pushing them away from God. I couldn't believe it at first. But God has shown me that my own ambition for success actually hurt my ministry."

Then he added: "Now I am focusing on going deep with a lot fewer young people."

If you have a hard time believing that size matters, think about the field of education. There is considerable evidence that class size is a major factor in the effectiveness of learning environments. That is, smaller classes increase the quality of education. Why would we assume the same rules do not apply to the church's training of junior high and high school students? I realize there is some debate about this. Still, most small colleges promote small class sizes and teacher-student ratios as a benefit of these collegiate settings.

Or imagine that you are starting a new career. Would you prefer to attend a lecture series with hundreds of other new employees or to be mentored by a twenty-year veteran of your chosen industry? Yet somewhere along the line, many of us decided bigger is better. We chose big attendance numbers over young lives shaped in the "classroom" of deep-level discipleship.

The truth is that it is much easier to put on events for large groups of kids than it is to mentor each and every one of them into a mature and holistic walk with God. If our churches are too big to provide that level of life-on-life focus, can we grow the next generation of Jesus's disciples?

## SHALLOW TURNS TO APPRENTICESHIP

The Parable of the Sower in Matthew 13 is helpful when considering what it takes to develop sustainable faith. I've often thought a better title would be the Parable of the Soil, because Jesus's focus in the story is the various kinds of ground on which the seed of his message falls. There is packed-down dirt where birds gather to steal the truth. There is rocky ground where the seed can't put down deep roots and so it withers under the sun's scorching rays. There is soil with weeds and brambles that choke out the message. Finally, there is rich, loamy earth in which the seed can take root.

People of deep faith are the metaphorical equal of deeply rooted trees, an image used throughout Scripture (see Ps. 1:3 and Isa. 61:3, for instance). It is appropriate, then, to ask what it takes to cultivate young Christians who are deeply rooted in the faith. The simplest answer is that to grow big, solid, thriving "trees," we need to prepare rich, fertile, soft-hearted soil. The task of growing spiritual redwoods is God's work. Yet we can partner in that effort by tilling and tending the soil of the young lives God entrusts to us.

We must rethink what it means to "make disciples" (Matt. 28:19) in a context of massive, compounded cultural change (access, alienation, and skepticism of authority). I believe we need to change from an industrialized, mass-production, public-education approach and embrace the messy adventure of relationship. We need a new set of ideas and practices based on *apprenticeship*.

We see in the Gospels that, while Jesus had many followers at various times in his earthly ministry, he invested himself fully in just twelve disciples, who went on to change the world. We find in the book of Acts that the early church grew through both the public proclamation of the Good News and a network of relationships. In the apostle Paul's letter to the fledgling church in Corinth, we discover a shining example of deep-level faith mentoring: "Even though you have ten thousand guardians in Christ, you do not have many fathers, for in Christ Jesus I became your father through the gospel" (1 Cor. 4:15). Today in North America we have thousands of "guardians in Christ" in our church culture but we do not have many spiritual fathers and mothers. Yet it is people with that level of commitment who make disciples.

As a starting point, let's consider three areas where the potential for deepening faith is most obvious.

## Meeting God

Millions of young Christians, represented by those in our survey, admit that they have been frustrated with their faith because "God seems missing from my experience of church." In a related critique, many students point out the gaps between the miracles and faith-fueled exploits described in the Bible and the flat, lifeless experience of church in today's world. If people who want to meet God are not meeting him in church, we need to consider why this is and how we can make a different experience possible.

God can, of course, meet with anyone anywhere. Some family friends, Mike and Maureen, recently told my parents that their

twenty-three-year-old daughter served at a Christian camp last summer, where she found greater depth in her faith than ever before. Many
times God shows up without any help from us. Yet he has also called
us to be about the business of making disciples, which means showing
(not just telling) them how to trust Jesus, live for God, and participate
in the Spirit's work. People *want* to meet God, so let's make sure we're
helping not hindering.

## Restoring Knowledge of Truth

This generation wants and needs truth, not spiritual soft-serve. According to our findings, churches too often provide lightweight teaching
instead of rich knowledge that leads to wisdom. This is a generation
hungry for substantive answers to life's biggest questions, particularly
in a time when there are untold ways to access information about *what
to do*. What's missing—and where the Christian community must come
in—is addressing *how* and *why*.

Dallas Willard, in his excellent book *Knowing Christ Today*, suggests
that there are two important challenges for what and how we teach.[5] First,
we must connect spiritual wisdom with real-world knowledge. Churches,
Dr. Willard argues, have ceded the realm of knowledge to academics
and institutions of higher education. Essentially, we make little effort
to help disciples connect the dots between their vocation—whether in
medicine, journalism, city planning, music, sales, computer programming, or any other—and their faith. We in the church focus on matters
of belief and commitment, which may be divorced from any impact
these make on the whole of life. Willard illustrates the disconnect by
pointing out that no one wants a brain surgeon who has merely a belief
in or commitment to medicine. We want a surgeon with knowledge
of and experience in surgery! Likewise, Christians must connect our
commitment to God with real-world knowledge and experience—and
we need to teach young people to do the same.

Second, Willard contends that we must teach through experience,
reason, and authority—*all* are important to our apprenticeship efforts.
Churches tend to emphasize one element over the others, and this leads
to insufficient discipleship. For example, some churches rely too much

on experience (events and activities) and not enough on authority (the Bible) or reason (reflection and application). Others emphasize Bible teaching but do not connect the Word with experience or reason. We need to be holistic in our approach to discipleship so that young people can think about and respond to truth in various ways.

## God Calling

Another way we can cultivate apprenticelike training for the next generation goes to the very heart of apprenticeship—finding what young people are gifted for and called to do, and doing all we can to nurture that calling. Most youth ministers and volunteers have some sense that this is important and do the best they can. But I believe young people need a much clearer, definitive, objective, and directional approach to finding their calling in Christ's body. This is not likely to happen through a simple weekly message. It's a whole mindset that needs to pervade our faith communities.

Callings may include science, math, medicine, business, congregational ministry, art, music, or any number of other vocations. Our guidance in the area of vocation should take both learning style and spiritual giftedness into consideration. Additionally, all of these factors must be wedded to a strong sense of mission. *What has God called you to do, in partnership with the community of Christ-followers? How can you be on mission for Christ in the world, based on what you're gifted to do?*

We also should reconsider our metrics of success. A woodworking artisan does not employ hundreds of protégés. He could hire any number of laborers to mass-produce furniture, but his goal is not thousands of cookie-cutter headboards or tables. His aim is to pass on the fine art of carpentry, so he selects one or two apprentices who want to learn the craft. He goes on making beautiful, one-of-a-kind pieces of furniture. And he spends time making future craftsmen.

What if, instead of measuring our success by the numbers, we changed our metrics? What if we said that the hallmark of mature Christianity is a willingness to invest in a young person for a period of two to four years, teaching him or her the fine art of following Christ?

I think an apprenticeship would have made a difference in Tracy's life, back when she was first discovering her passion for helping developing communities in Africa and South America. Instead of feeling disconnected from her Catholic upbringing, today the blossoming international humanitarian might understand her vocation as a vital outgrowth of a thriving faith.

Jesus has commanded us to make disciples. We can obey that call by helping young people answer their callings.

# 7

# ANTI-SCIENCE

*Disconnection:* "To be honest, I think that learning about science was the straw that broke the camel's back. I knew from church that I couldn't believe in both science and God, so that was it. I didn't believe in God anymore."

—Mike

*Reconnection:* "Students need a place to ask questions about science . . . we cannot expect them to ignore the issues of science all around us."

—Richard

Millions of young Christians perceive Christianity to be in opposition to modern science. What does this mean? Two episodes will help define the contours of the problem.

The first comes from an experience I had while assisting in our church's youth ministry a few years ago. Colleen, one of the students in the group, had just graduated from high school and asked the youth pastor what he thought about her becoming an egg donor to pay for college. She could donate some of her reproductive capacity for a surprisingly large payday.

Colleen had been told her entire life that going to college was a top priority for her long-term success, but her family could not afford to pay her way—so she was evaluating her options to make up the difference. If she could avoid saddling herself with a mountain of debt, she would. She had read on the Internet that fertility clinics and childless couples were willing to pay top dollar for eggs donated by healthy women under the age of twenty-five. Yet Colleen wondered if selling her eggs would be morally or spiritually questionable. Did the Bible say anything about it? Would God be angry with her?

In another incident, during a dinner party in the early months of 2011, I heard a prominent scientist lament his interactions with the next generation of believers.

"Every week, I am contacted by young Christians who tell me that their faith cannot survive their interest in science. They feel the church has forced them into an either-or decision—they can either stay true to the Christian faith or become an intellectually honest scientist." This observation aligns closely with Barna Group's findings, as we will see in this chapter.

He went on, "That's a false choice, of course. And it's heartbreaking that we aren't helping young Christians pursue their calling in science in a way that affirms both science and faith. It's not a simple task. Yet if we don't take this job seriously, I am afraid we're going to lose a generation of scientists and a generation of Christians."

Then, whether or not it was intentional, the scientist demonstrated the remarkable coexistence of his passions. First, he captivated dinner guests with a fascinating description of his team's discoveries, which may save the lives of thousands of people who suffer from a rare medical disorder. Then he brought the dinner to a worshipful close by playing the guitar and leading us in "How Great Thou Art."

Issues of science are one of the significant points of disconnection between the next generation and Christianity. Many times churches are unprepared to help young adults navigate an increasingly complex world where scientific breakthroughs seem to happen every day. This lack of preparation is due in part to the perceived long-running culture war between science and religion that has been fought, on various battle-grounds, for centuries. Might it be that the church is so used to being science's debate opponent that we've forgotten how to be anything else? If so, we have a problem.

The two stories that open this chapter reveal two main areas in which we see the rift between science and faith undermining the church's efforts to make disciples among the next generation. The first, illustrated by Colleen's story, is the challenge facing all believers to live biblically in a culture im-mersed in science. The second area, shown in the scientist's remarks, is the challenge of nurturing and supporting young science-minded Christians.

First, let's look at the broader challenge.

## CHRISTIANS LIVING IN A SCIENCE CULTURE

Science has come to dominate and define our collective culture. Digital and mechanical technology, medical research and treatment, survey and conservation of the environment, study of the human brain and mind, genetics, physics, and discoveries about our universe—these areas of scientific inquiry, and so many more, shape our reality. Tools and methods developed by science significantly impact our daily lives—our world would be all but unrecognizable to someone transplanted here from the early twentieth century. As we observed in the chapter on access, alienation, and authority, the pace of change has dramatically increased. The amount of information available, the connectedness of human cultures, and the ways we explore and understand our world are vastly different than at any point in human history.

Today's teens and twentysomethings have been even more profoundly influenced by these developments than previous generations. From their earliest days, science and technology have had a hand in nearly every area of their lives—from food production and distribution to medical treatment, from computers at home and in the classroom to easy and affordable air travel. Think about this—American teens and young adults have always lived in a world with email, cell phones, fast food, plastic surgery, cars with airbags and antilock brakes, and digital music, video, and photography. I could go on, but you get the idea.

Not only do the sciences have incredible reach, but information about science is also more readily accessible than ever before. When I was a kid, our family subscribed to *National Geographic* magazine and our shelves held a set of rarely used encyclopedias. Now teens and young adults have this morning's world-changing discovery at their fingertips, and have science entertainment, such as *MythBusters* and the Animal Planet cable channel, available to them 24-7. All this access to (loosely) science-related content gives many young adults the feeling that they are quite well-informed about scientific matters.

## Popular Science

Another dimension of our scientific culture is the many scientists today who enjoy rock star status. Well-known scientists who promote atheism, such as Sam Harris, Richard Dawkins, and Stephen Hawking, are front and center in our culture today. They have gained popular attention not only because of the post-Christian zeitgeist, but also because the Internet amplifies provocative voices, enabling them to reach devoted niche audiences and leverage their powers of persuasion to generate mainstream attention.

The popularization of science has several implications. First, as the previous paragraph suggests, it invites scientists to seek not only legitimacy within their own community—what is commonly called "peer review"— but also publicity in the mainstream. This is not inherently a bad thing, but it's not too hard to imagine why the race for an audience could invite some scientists to rush responsible inquiry. We hear all the time about supposedly ironclad scientific knowledge overturned by a newer discovery. Gordon Pennington, a former marketing executive for Tommy Hilfiger's clothing line, once observed that "science is also a fashion industry, with theories changing regularly, although not as often as hemlines."[1] With so many contradictory "facts" flying around, it can be difficult for young adults to find out what is true. And with ubiquitous media constantly declaring "world-changing" and "revolutionary" news, it's hard to sort out truth from the fashions that masquerade as legitimate scientific discoveries.

Second, the popularization of science has, in many ways, democratized science. In the introduction to *Science Is Culture: Conversations at the New Intersection of Science and Society,* Adam Bly, editor of *Seed* magazine, writes:

> The burgeoning "citizen science" movement coupled with the rise of mobile devices and social media allows anyone to participate in the process of science. . . . Science is necessarily flat and open. Any idea can be overturned at anytime by anyone. . . . Although they must ultimately hold up to the other tenets of science—reproducibility and falsifiability among them—the best ideas can come from anywhere.[2]

Because anyone can participate in science, it's sometimes hard to figure out who is worth listening to and who isn't. A young Christian might watch a debate between a Bible professor and an evolutionary biologist on YouTube, read a series of blog posts on Intelligent Design, and then crack open her biology textbook to study for tomorrow's exam—after which she'll go to a local Bible study, where the leader may go on at length about how you can't believe in evolution and the Bible at the same time. How can she know which of these sources is trustworthy? What makes someone an "authority"?

Although it may seem counterintuitive, the very fact that science invites participation lends its authority more weight than areas of inquiry that don't. Dialogue, creative problem solving, living with questions and with ambiguity, group brainstorming, the opportunity to contribute—these are highly valued by the next generation. To the extent that we in the Christian community insist that young adults should just accept our "right" answers, we perpetuate a needless schism between science and faith.

## Faith and Scientism

One reason young Christians feel acutely the antagonism between their religion and science is that there is animosity on both sides—Western science has often seen itself as an opponent of faith. We could call this opposition "scientism," the assumption that science has cornered the market on knowledge, and something can only be true if it can be tested by scientific methods. Unfortunately, scientism's epistemology (theory of knowledge) has come to dominate our culture. "True" has come to mean "verifiable in the lab."[3] For scientism, what is reasonable *just is* what is scientific.

The number of atheists (many of whom affirm scientism) is disproportionately larger in higher education than in the culture at large, which means that many undergrads each year are unknowingly subjected to the false dichotomy of "faith versus reason." Add to this the fact that "big science," like "big business," struggles with corruption; more than a handful of research scientists have admitted to falsifying or skewing data in their favor at some point in their career. To add insult to injury, it is not uncommon for those in the academy who question the scientific party line to be ostracized, denied tenure, or even fired. On these and other grounds, the church has reason to feel antagonized by the scientific establishment.

Still, if we are serious about living biblically in a science culture and about helping the next generation do the same, putting up our dukes or sticking our fingers in our ears are not viable options. Because science has come to play such a defining role in our broader culture, it is shaping young adults' perceptions of the church. It is these perceptions that we must deal well with if we truly desire to make young disciples.

In our research among eighteen- to twenty-nine-year-olds with a Christian background, one-third (35 percent) suggested that Christians are too confident about knowing all the answers. In a related thread, one-fifth (20 percent) said they believe Christianity makes complex things too simple. Nearly three in ten (29 percent) said that churches are out of step with the scientific world we live in, while one-quarter (25 percent) described Christianity as anti-science. One-quarter of those surveyed report that they are turned off by the creation-versus-evolution debate (23 percent) and one-fifth are disillusioned with Christianity because it is anti-intellectual (18 percent). It may not surprise you to learn that many prodigals—those who no longer identify as Christian—hold these opinions. However, a significant number of nomads and exiles embrace these notions too. And while these are not majority views among young Christians, neither are they fringe perspectives that can be easily dismissed.

The ferocity with which some of the research respondents hold these views is likely influenced, at least in part, by the cultural power wielded by scientism. There is broad acceptance of the idea that science (or rather scientism) "tells it like it is." Questioning this premise—as the church often does—is culturally hazardous. These factors do not negate the problem we are called to address, however, and they do not absolve God's people from acknowledging where we have fallen short. The underlying sense of these perceptions is that many in the next generation do not see Christians as humble partners with today's science-driven culture—and I believe there is some truth for us here.

### Anti-science | In Their Own Words

Percentage of 18- to 29-year-olds who have a Christian background

| | completely true of me | completely or mostly true of me |
|---|---|---|
| Christians are too confident that they know all the answers. | 17% | 35% |
| Churches are out of step with the scientific world we live in. | 12% | 29% |
| Christianity is anti-science. | 9% | 25% |
| I have been turned off by the creation-versus-evolution debate. | 11% | 23% |
| Christianity makes complex things too simple. | 9% | 20% |
| Christianity is anti-intellectual. | 8% | 18% |

Barna Group | 2011 | N=1,296

# THE LOSS OF SCIENCE-MINDED CHRISTIANS

There is a second challenge facing the Christian community as it relates to science—the disconnect between the faith and those who are particularly science-minded. The church is losing too many young scientists.

If the Christian community desires to equip young people to follow Jesus faithfully in the real world, we need to understand the challenges facing young science-minded individuals. Those who have specific gifts, abilities, and passions in the realm of science appear to be some of the most likely to struggle with their faith. They have a difficult time connecting the claims of Christianity with scientific evidence and methods.

Mike's story is an example of a young science-minded prodigal. I met Mike in Vancouver, British Columbia, at a daylong seminar for pastors. He was raised in a Catholic home but is now an atheist. The seminar organizer, Norm, wanted to "get a real, live young person who doesn't believe in God in front of these folks." Mike, who fit the bill, was about two years out of high school and was joined by his pal Brandon. The plan was for Mike to spend the day, along with his still-Christian friend, trying to help Christian leaders understand why he does not believe in God.

That day in Vancouver, Mike ventured into a room packed with clergy. I sat in the front row, watching Mike's body language as he spoke to that group of professional communicators. In the first few minutes of his soul-baring story, Mike looked understandably uptight. His confession was mixed with the discomfort of public speaking. But finally he put everyone at ease, including himself, with the comic relief highlight of the day: "Sheesh, I'm as nervous as an atheist at a pastors' conference."

After the laughter died down, his story came in spurts—but that made it no less compelling: "It was tenth grade. I started learning about evolution. It felt like my first window into the real world. To be honest, I think that learning about science was the straw that broke the camel's back. I knew from church that I couldn't believe in both science and God, so that was it. I didn't believe in God anymore."

## Stories of Loss

I have interviewed scores of teens and young adults who are pursuing careers in science and I've also had occasion to meet many parents of students gifted in these areas. In the majority of cases, there is a deep sense of conflict within these young people—and sometimes with their parents—about staying faithful, given their interests and capabilities. In my observations, the nomad-scientist simply puts his or her faith involvement on the shelf, compartmentalizing spiritual pursuits away from career. The prodigal-scientist feels forced to choose his or her affinity for science over faith and may resent the church for "forcing" the choice. The exile-scientist attempts to reconcile competing narratives of a life of faith and the life of the mind.

A mother in Honolulu told me about her son. A formerly passionate Christian, this twentysomething is an engineering student at a prestigious Ivy League school. Recently he disavowed his faith in Christ—making a journey we could label as prodigal.

Another mother described her son, a twenty-three-year-old molecular biology student who is still interested in faith but hasn't found a Christian community in his new college town. His faith, though not abandoned entirely, has been moved to the margins. This is classic nomadism.

Scientifically inclined exiles seem to be among the most common when it comes to feeling lost between science and faith. Remember that exiles are those whose calling and faith seem disjointed and irreconcilable. Their sense of being exiled cuts both ways: they feel that their faith commitments are disrespected by popular science and their scientific interests are marginalized by the Christian community. A young computer programmer who designs video games has not quite gotten used to raised eyebrows from fellow Christians. A young research assistant is called "superstitious" by her peers, and feels that her intellectual rigor is always on trial.

These tensions are not entirely unhealthy. Every person of faith must learn how to live the in-but-not-of discipleship that Christ calls us to. Managing the tensions between science and faith is part of that journey. We need to develop young leaders who can capably serve *in* science, but not be so *habituated* to scientism that faith becomes untenable.

### Stewarding Young Scientists

Let me describe a significant gap in most faith communities. More than half of churchgoing thirteen- to seventeen-year-olds say they hope to train for a science-related career. This includes medical and health-related industries (23 percent), engineering and architecture (11 percent), research science (8 percent), technology (5 percent), and veterinary studies (5 percent).

Yet issues of science are a surprisingly rare topic in U.S. churches. Only 1 percent of youth pastors told us that they have addressed a subject related to science during the last year. I am not suggesting that churches should change their entire mission approach to address science, but if only 1 out of 100 youth workers are talking about issues of science, how can we possibly hope to prepare a generation to follow Jesus in our science-dominated culture?

### Science: Youth Aspiration versus Youth Ministry

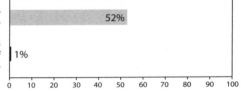

Youth group teens who aspire to science-related careers* — 52%

Youth pastors/youth workers who have addressed issues of science in the past year — 1%

\* Includes medical- and health-related careers, engineering, science, technology, veterinary medicine.

Barna Group, YouthPoll[SM], 2009, N=602 | YouthLeaderPoll[SM], 2009, N=508

As we described in chapter 6 (Shallow), the vast majority of young churchgoing Protestants and Catholics never received a sense of how the Bible applies to their calling or interests; only a small minority discovered a mentor in their faith community; and few ever had helpful coaching from religious leaders pertaining to their educational choices. In other words, young science-minded adults are not finding much guidance from the faith community in matters of vocation or calling. Neither are they likely to find meaningful support from older science-minded Christians. These are huge gaps and they significantly affect the ability of the Christian community to transfer faith to the next generation.

Let's look specifically at college experiences. Is going to college—particularly to a secular or state school—an automatic faith killer? Our research suggests not. Yes, it is a challenge for many students, but the blame is often overstated. First, most students who are likely to experience loss of faith do so *before* college; they begin to feel disconnected from their faith or from the church even before high school ends. Second, those who lose their faith or wander during college do so for a variety of reasons, not merely because of *intellectual* challenges to their faith.

Millions of young Christians get through college with a flourishing faith. One of the marks of these individuals is a meaningful connection to some form of Christian community—whether a worshiping congregation, a Christian campus group, or a Christian-oriented college—which makes them less likely to become nomadic or prodigal. The key here is a *meaningful* connection, not merely showing up at religious activities.

Young adults who do find it difficult to keep their faith growing through college do so, I believe, because of relational, educational, and vocational gaps that were left unaddressed in the years prior to and during college. In other words, when students struggle in college, many times it is because the Christian community has not provided a sufficiently strong set of relationships, sense of purpose, or whole-life coaching. This is particularly true in the lives of science-minded students. We should not assume that the tough questions of a hostile professor are at the root of lost faith. Rather in many instances, I believe the Christian community has failed to disciple its science-inclined students to become responsible, intelligent, capable, resourceful, and faithful followers of Christ. We need to do a better job stewarding the intellect of this generation.

## ANTI-SCIENCE TURNS TO STEWARDSHIP

The concept of stewardship permeates Scripture. According to God's Word, our lives and our resources are gifts from God to be given back to him in service to others. I believe we need to see this generation as a gift to the church to be given to the world for God's purposes. What are some ways we should care for these gifts so they are prepared for service in our science-obsessed culture?

To find out, we should look again at Daniel, the young Hebrew exile who is famous for being stuck in the lions' den. Much earlier than his encounter with the beasts, we are told that he and his peers were taught "the language and literature of Babylon" (Dan. 1:4 NLT). "Literature" here encompasses the written literature of Babylon as well as the knowledge that lay behind it.[4] In fact the text actually describes a scientific inclination in their pursuit of such knowledge. It says that God gave them "an unusual aptitude for understanding" these skills and subjects (v. 17 NLT).

The first chapter of the book of Daniel gives some background on why and how Daniel was later able to speak prophetically in the throne room of the Babylonian king. As a young man he was apprenticed into the Babylonian way of seeing and communicating about the world. With his intellectual gift and knowledge, and applying himself to learn all he could in these arenas, he could eventually speak with authority on these subjects with colleagues and superiors in the king's court.

Our modern economy, language, media, and society are dominated by science, whether we like it or not. If we are to be shapers of culture, rather than blind consumers of it, we must prepare our young people to be in-but-not-of science. What does this mean? Young Christians who are called into positions of scientific inquiry and pedagogy ought to be encouraged by the Christian community to follow their callings to the utmost of their abilities. We need to help them discover how their chosen field of study and work is closely connected to God's design for the world and for them.

Rather than being encouraged by the Christian community to investigate God's good creation with wonder and reverence, too many young science geeks, like Mike, have been told that their curiosity is dangerous. I recently heard a pastor declare that intellectual questions are a defense mechanism used by those who don't want to accept Christ. That may be true in a few cases, but at its root, isn't this pastor's argument a rejection of God's gift of human reason? Intellect should not be used to diminish our reverence for God, but subjugating intellect to avoid sticky questions about our world also steals from God's creative glory.

We must do a better job challenging and training all young Christians—not just the science geeks—to think clearly, honestly, and comprehensively about matters of science. This includes understanding the various philosophies that undergird science, scientism, and knowledge. Teaching philosophy to teens and young adults is not easy, but if we don't we may be asking too little of the next generation and setting our expectations of them too low.

Yet the first step is to take a hard look at our rhetoric. By no means are all Christians or Christian leaders openly antagonistic toward the scientific community, but the perceptions measured by our research indicate that *the way* the church takes its stand in our culture is as important as the stand itself.

If how the church has responded to and interacted with science is a problem, what needs to change? What should be the response of the Christian community to a science-dominated culture? I believe that people of faith have a responsibility and an opportunity to speak positively and prophetically to issues of science, rather than responding out of hostility or ignorance. We must work together to offer a viable, respectful Christian voice to our culture's collective dialogue about stem cell research, cloning, animal testing, pharmaceuticals, technology's impact on the human brain and soul, cosmetic and elective surgery and beauty enhancement, nutrition, agriculture, weapons and military technologies, and many other matters of science and ethics. This will not be easy—the learning curve will be steep for many of us—yet if we desire to steward the next generation for faithful service, we must tackle this complex challenge.

Here are some ways we might become credible, trustworthy partners in dialogue with the scientific community.

## More Science, Not Less

Many students do not know how or where within the Christian community to bring up their questions about science. With some pastors making claims like the one above—that intellectual questions are the enemy of faith—it is easy to see why. I know some leaders who believe they are providing space for evenhanded, open dialogue on scientific issues. But that is not always how it appears to students, most of whom want to work together toward an answer, rather than being told what to believe.

One church in Oregon is creatively integrating science into their broader conversations about faith. An ornithologist (that's a bird scientist) in the congregation serves as their director of apologetics. He specializes in the study of raptors and is a passionate advocate, as many in the Northwest are, for the environment—specifically for the natural habitats of birds of prey. He is also finishing his MA in theology and serves his faith community by leading online and in-person discussions about the intersection of science and faith. Richard commented in a telephone conversation, "I have come to recognize that students need a place to ask questions about science, that we cannot expect them to ignore the issues of science all around us."

Not every church has an ornithologist in the second row, ready to dialogue about scientific questions that are out of the pastor's league, but what about the high school biology teacher who goes to church down the road? Or the community college physics professor who sponsors an on-campus ministry? There are plenty of Christians in the scientific community who would love to serve the body of Christ with their gifts and knowledge, and there are many young adults who need a scientifically credible Christian mentor who will walk alongside them as they reason through competing truth claims.

## Scientific Apprentices

While high school and college can be years of awkwardness and confusion for many students, they are also a season when young adults take steps toward becoming who they are meant to be. Many young people decide what they are going to do and be during these years. Unfortunately, many of these same young people have no meaningful interaction during high school and college with Christian adults who work in their field of choice. As a result, Christian twentysomethings often do not connect their career choices with a sense of calling or vocation; their faith and work decisions are bifurcated, rather than holistically entwined.

What if churches made a concerted effort to identify scientific and mathematical inclinations in young people (as well as other skills and gifts), and then connected young believers with older Christians who are living out their faith in related careers? This could provide a dramatically different understanding of science and technology, not as adversaries of or disconnected from faith, but as domains where faith compels us to make a difference.

## Good Thinking

Our research suggests that students who see the world for themselves through a biblical lens are best prepared to face intellectual challenges. The best-prepared young Christians are encouraged to think for themselves, with Scripture as the viewfinder through which they interpret the world around them, including the world of science. And God's natural revelation, interpreted through the lens of their scientific aptitudes, helps them expand their understanding of God as well. They are taught *how* to think well, not simply *what* to think.

In contrast, too many young believers are not given good intellectual tools with which to interact with science. Scientists and others who oppose what the faith community believes may be made into straw men whose arguments, whether made in good faith or not, are ignored or rejected rather than dealt with honestly. Sometimes this happens because Christian leaders lack the expertise needed to tackle the topic. How could the typical youth worker, for instance, be prepared to deal with every question that comes up, such as the ethical implications of egg donation?

This goes right to the issues of access and authority that we discussed in chapter 2. The fact is that no single pastor, youth worker, parent, or Christian teacher can begin to master every scientific or intellectual dilemma that presents itself to today's young adults. This is the reason we must rethink our efforts to teach young people *what* to think about issues of science, ethics, politics, and even theology and consider how we can help them learn *how* to think. As stewards of their considerable gifts, we must prepare them for careful, prayerful, collaborative reasoning with Christians and non-Christians alike.

## Humble Disagreement

Earlier I mentioned that the tone of our disagreements matters. We need to be models for the next generation not only of intellectual rigor, but also of humility and generosity of spirit. True wisdom is confident in knowledge yet humble in the awareness that there are limits to our knowledge. Only God is God—a fact that should lead us to trust in him rather than in our own rightness on any given topic.

A good place to start this endeavor is with fellow believers. Many sincere, passionate Christians disagree on matters of science. Collegial and vigorous debate is a good thing for the Christian community, as we seek a prophetic voice with which to speak into our broader culture. Yet over and above our debates, we should cultivate a spirit of Christian unity, purpose, and mission. This means assuming the best of each other and loving and praying for one another, even as we speak the truth. It also means taking care not to toss around emotionally charged words and phrases that escalate tensions and divide Christ's body. For example, young-earth creationists may want to rethink accusations of apostasy when they talk with (or about) old-earth creationists or those who hold to theistic evolution. Likewise, Christians who believe evolution is God's chosen mechanism for creation must be cautious of intellectual condescension toward their sisters and brothers who believe differently. The issues and debates are not unimportant, but the relationships in Christ are of paramount importance.

My point is that all kinds of Christians are hard at work trying to discern the mysteries of the universe—and we need each other. Refusing to sever the ties that bind us, even as we disagree, can help keep us all humble before our God, trusting him to guide us into all wisdom and truth.

The same is true for our engagement with the next generation. The fact is, many of them will not come to the same conclusions we have settled on—especially if we do a really great job equipping them to think well for themselves! Some of them may never find answers that are completely satisfying, and this is another area where we can help; we can teach them to understand and manage the unresolved tensions that are an inevitable reality in our modern world. (It turns out that unresolved tension is also a tool God can use to grow our trust in him.)

### History Lessons

In 1687, when Sir Isaac Newton published *Principia*, his masterwork of classical mechanics that defined science's understanding of the physical universe for the next three centuries, he did so as a devout Christian. While some of his religious beliefs were outside the mainstream of orthodoxy—some historians believe Newton was anti-Trinitarian, for instance—the Bible was his greatest passion, over and above science. He once said, "I have a fundamental belief in the Bible as the Word of God, written by those who were inspired. I study the Bible daily."[5] His curiosity about the world was deeply entwined with his reverence for the Creator, whom he credited with the existence of the universe.

Newton's mechanical model of the universe also helped to broaden the divide between the community of faith and the scientific community. The universe is held together by force of gravity, many later scientists came to believe, not by God. Yet Newton, along with many other fathers of the scientific revolution, was able to hold his discoveries in tension with his faith, rather than replacing God with natural laws.

I want to suggest that the same posture is possible for believers today—that a sense of wonder and thoughtful inquiry can lead us to worship, rather than to deny, God. We honor the Creator when we apply our God-given intellect to the investigation of the universe, and what we discover there invites us to give him glory. How can we recapture the curiosity and devotion that drove Newton—and so many other faith-filled scientists—and pass them on to the next generation?

## MODELING A NEW MIND

In a way, my unlikely career path illustrates how the faith community can get things right. I am a scientist of sorts—a research geek—and a committed believer. I majored in psychology and thrived in my science-related classes, like statistics, measurement, social psychology, sociology, learning theory, and multivariate analysis. My father, a lifelong pastor, encouraged my pursuit of this field, even though it meant I was not going to follow his path into full-time church work. Today he remains incredibly supportive despite the times our research at the Barna Group generates findings that are not flattering to the Christian community.

My faith in Jesus is the lens through which I live out my career. I am able to participate in and contribute to my field in part because my dad was and is supportive. When I was growing up, he allowed my curiosity to flourish without questioning my faith and he gave me books to read that did not always conform to the worldview of my family and church.

When I came home from youth group with rather simplistic views, he suggested that there might be other perspectives to consider.

I do not know where I would have ended up without his influence. To be candid, the church my father led did not always encourage students who were interested in science. I don't remember learning anything about science in youth or college group. And while that faith community was generally neutral or silent on the subject, its skepticism was occasionally more overt. When I decided to major in psychology, some churchgoers wondered aloud how that fit with my faith: *Why was I forsaking the "real" influence of congregational ministry?*

It was about twenty years ago when I attended a youth group. Since then the influence of science and technology have grown exponentially, but still many faith communities operate with ambivalence or even enmity toward science. Young adults like Mike and Colleen, whom we met early in this chapter, need the community of faith to reconsider its posture toward science. If twentysomethings like them are to grow into prophetic people of faith who speak with authority and live wisely in our science-immersed culture, they need models of the Christians we pray they become.

Read more about stewarding the next generation of scientists and creatives at www.barna.org/vocational-discipleship.

# 8

# REPRESSIVE

*Disconnection:* "It just feels like the church's teaching on sexuality is behind the times. My lifestyle may not be perfect, but you know . . . *it's just sex.*"

—Dennis

*Reconnection:* "Even though many of my Christian friends told me to cut off contact with my friend after she had the abortion, I couldn't do it. I still love her. I still accept her. I still believe in her. I still believe in what God wants to do in her life."

—Amanda

Let's get right to it. Sexuality is one of the greatest expressions of God's creativity and of his intention for human flourishing. It is also confounding and confusing to teenagers and young adults on their spiritual journeys. Marriage and childbearing, if they happen, are coming later in life for most young adults—but sex is in the picture earlier than ever.

Among many of those with a Christian background, the perception is that the church is out of step with the times. Many, though not all, view the church as repressive—controlling, joyless, and stern when it comes to sex, sexuality, and sexual expectations. On the other hand, many are also dissatisfied with the wider culture's pressure on them to adopt lax sexual attitudes and behaviors. They feel torn between the false purity of traditionalism and the empty permissiveness of their peers.

The Christian community needs a "new mind" to engage the next generation in the arena of sexuality. I will do my best to describe the situation in this chapter but I want to recognize at the outset that the subject of sexuality can be contentious and divisive because it is so personal. My posture here—as in the entire book—is grounded on two desires: to clearly explain what we have discovered in our research and to humbly call the Christian community to a new place of faithfulness in a changing world. I hope you will read what follows with these intentions in mind.

Let me begin by briefly describing four encounters.

I sat on our couch across from Dennis, who is in his early twenties, and tried to help him reconnect with his Catholic upbringing. Some of his misgivings and hesitation related to his sexual habits. Dennis loves to have sex, especially with older women.

"I understand what you're saying about faith and about Jesus, David. But it just feels like the church's teaching on sexuality is behind the times. My lifestyle may not be perfect, but you know . . . *it's just sex.*"

A friend of mine, Aly, told me about a young Christian woman with whom she recently had lunch. Jenna told Aly that she went into marriage as a virgin three years ago with high hopes that sex would be perfect—because that's the picture her youth leaders and college pastor had painted.

"It didn't take too long to realize that sex is nothing like that. Sometimes it's incredible but sometimes it's hard work, just like the rest of the relationship. In fact I'm learning it's all related . . . good sex doesn't happen in a vacuum. It's entwined with every part of my life. But I feel like my church and youth group compartmentalized everything, and so I did too. Here's your faith in this pigeonhole. Here's your education. Here's your work cubicle, and there's your family. Over there is sex, all by itself behind the curtain. I feel like becoming an adult is this painful process of decategorizing my life. There are no categories. There's just life."

Not long ago I met a young Christian man, Keith, who had become addicted to online pornography as a teenager. He told me that a thought had occurred to him: *What if this stuff wasn't just on a computer screen? What if I could really have sex right now?* "So a few clicks later," he said, "I had tracked someone down who lived nearby. I was ready for action." The resulting sexual addiction ran rampant for several years and involved dozens of hookups. He is in recovery now, but Keith will deal with the addiction for the rest of his life, just as recovering alcoholics and drug addicts do.

One of the most unsettling things about Keith's story is that his sexual activities had, at first, no effect on his involvement in church and youth group. He said, "I stayed active. I still led worship and was involved in leadership. I just literally led a double life, between sex and church."

I met Max, a distinguished older gentleman, when I was invited to present research to his firm about the next generation. You would be amazed how effortlessly Max commands a room. He has built million-dollar businesses and world-changing ministries and he exudes confidence. After my presentation, Max had some thoughts he wanted to share. "David, I appreciate your coming all the way from California to speak to us, but you're wrong about the next generation. I don't have as much hope as you do. They are not following God. They are sexually promiscuous. They are living the lives Scripture warns us about."

I asked, "If you don't mind my asking, did you embody biblical values as a young man?"

"Well, no," he said. "In fact I had my fair share of 'experience' as a young man. But that was a long time ago." Max didn't seem exactly ashamed of the wild oats he had sown. "The difference is, I didn't flaunt it. I knew how to keep private things private. Kids nowadays have no shame."

## SEXUAL DISCONNECT

These conversations reflect the broad issues at stake when we begin to talk about sex, the life of faith, and the next generation. They also suggest the complicated feelings young adults (and older generations) have about both sex and the church.

Recently a Catholic friend of mine who is also a lawyer emailed me about this book project. He expressed his theories about why young people leave the church. "It's usually for one of two reasons: bad catechism or sex. The former is the fault of priests and bishops; the latter is, well, the way of the world, and when it's the latter, it's almost always disguised under a claim of other reasons (boring, rigid, etc.). They so insist on justifying their sexual choices that they invent a thousand other reasons to explain why they have left. No one leaves the church because of the Doctrine of the Immaculate Conception. They leave for pelvic reasons."

There is probably some truth to this, though our research shows it's not quite that simple. Twelve percent of young people told us that it is "completely" or "mostly" true that they are less interested in faith as a result of becoming sexually active. This doesn't mean that only 12 percent of Christian young adults are having sex. Recent studies have shown that most evangelical teens and young adults are surprisingly similar to national norms in terms of sexual behavior. According to one recent study, four out of five unmarried evangelicals ages eighteen to twenty-nine have had sex.[1]

We humans are complicated and multilayered beings, and my strong impression from face-to-face interviews is that often sexuality intersects a person's faith journey in subconscious, below-the-radar ways. The story of a generation and sex is complicated and layered too, filled with judgment, rules, old and new media, hypocritical religious leaders, values turned on their heads, a world saturated with sexual images, and double lives trapped between soul and pelvis.

While few young Christians admit that their sex life specifically caused them to drop out, many perceive the church and the faith to be repressive. One-fourth of young adults with a Christian background said they do not want to follow all the church's rules (25 percent). One-fifth described wanting more freedom in life and not finding it in church (21 percent). One-sixth indicated they have made mistakes and feel judged in church because of them (17 percent). And one-eighth said they feel as if they have to live a "double life" between their faith and their real life (12 percent). Two-fifths of young Catholics say the church is "out of date" on these matters (40 percent). Add it all up, and millions of young Christians feel torn between two ways of understanding and experiencing sex.

### Repressive | In Their Own Words

*Percentage of 18- to 29-year-olds who have a Christian background*

| | completely true of me | completely or mostly true of me |
|---|---|---|
| The church's teachings on sexuality and birth control are out of date.* | 23% | 40% |
| I do not want to follow all the church's rules. | 14% | 25% |
| I want more freedom in life and cannot find it in church. | 12% | 21% |
| I have made mistakes and feel judged in church because of them. | 8% | 17% |
| I have to live a "double life" between my faith and my real life. | 5% | 12% |
| I am sexually active and now less interested in faith as a result. | 5% | 12% |

* This question was only asked young adults with a Catholic background (N=562).

Barna Group | 2011 | N=1,296

# TRADITIONALISM VERSUS INDIVIDUALISM

Christian teens and young adults are caught between two narratives about sexuality. The first we will call *traditionalism* and the second *individualism*. I am indebted to Dale Kuehne's *Sex and the iWorld: Rethinking Relationship beyond an Age of Individualism* (Baker, 2009) for the framework I sketch here, and I commend this excellent book to anyone interested in a more thorough exploration of this multifaceted topic.

## Traditionalist Sexuality

The traditionalist view can best be summed up this way: *Sex? What sex?* I am not the first person to point out that, in the landmark 1950s television show *I Love Lucy*, Lucy and Ricky shared a master bedroom with a pair of twin beds. The fact that Little Ricky came into their lives after a few years only made this unlikely scenario all the more ridiculous. The morality police in Hollywood agreed that even a whiff of a suggestion that a married couple might have sex should be absolutely avoided.

Traditionalists are quite numerous among the Elder generation (born before 1945). My grandparents (were they alive) would undoubtedly shudder at the content of this chapter. That's because the traditionalist policy is to exclude sex and sexuality from polite conversation. Even if a person sleeps around, as Max apparently did as a young man, one should never mention it.

I want to clearly distinguish between traditional*ism* (or traditional-*ist*) and *traditions*. Christian traditions, such as chastity and fidelity, are significant features of spiritual and sexual wholeness emerging from an understanding of God's revelation in the Bible. Traditionalism, on the other hand, is an ideology that seeks to replace a thriving, grace-filled relationship with Christ with human-made rules and regulations. Unfortunately, traditionalist narratives about sexuality have mingled legalism with Christian tradition. As such, what many churches have taught about sex is steeped in traditionalism, not biblical tradition.

For traditionalists, *shame* is the watchword when it comes to sexuality. There is something dirty about all sexual pleasure—even within marriage. Sex is so shameful that it would be best for everyone if sexual activity were confined to procreation, its most basic utilitarian function.

The traditionalist focus on making babies, while affirming the Christian tradition of family and the biblical mandate to "be fruitful and multiply" (see Genesis 1:28), has a dark side, especially for women. If sex should be limited to fulfilling one's obligations—to obey the church, to marry and stay married as a social responsibility, to bear and rear children—there is little room for self-giving love, which requires the freedom of personal choice. Until the last fifty years in the West (and in many places around the world still today) the freedoms of women were limited, if not by law, then by societal expectations. The traditionalist paradigm made sex (at least for women) into a duty.

Anyone who does not comply with the rules written by traditionalists are outcasts. But when the Boomers came of age in the 1960s, they were sick and tired of traditionalism's "repressive" notions about sex.

During that decade of social upheaval, Boomers attempted to replace the traditionalist narrative with something new—the individual's personal journey toward sexual fulfillment.

## Individualist Sexuality

The new narrative, which has come to define our broader Western culture, is that of the individualist: *Sex is about me*. In the individualist narrative, sexuality is about personal satisfaction. Pornography is the most blatant case in point. "You don't even need anyone else to enjoy it! Or if you want to use porn to 'get revved up' for a real-life sexual encounter, go for it! You be the judge. Your own intuition will tell you where to draw the line."

The rules of individualist sexual encounters are self-defined. The highest goals of sex are not just pleasure, but freedom and self-expression. At best, young adults' "rules" for sex are loose, self-driven, and self-oriented guidelines. These "new rules" are described by Mark Regnerus in his book *Forbidden Fruit*: "(a) don't be pressured or pressure someone else into sex, (b) don't sleep around for the sake of your own reputation, (c) the only person who can decide whether a sexual relationship is OK is you, and (d) sex should optimally only occur within the framework of a 'long-term' relationship: at least three months."[2]

At worst, however, the "rules" are whatever everyone else in the social circle says is "normal." In the preface to *Sex and the Soul*, professor Donna Freitas recalls the day when the students in her undergraduate dating class decided to start a sexual revolution. They had just returned from spring break, where "they'd partied hard. They'd hooked up. They'd drunk until the wee hours of the morning and then dragged themselves onto the beach by noon, only to start the cycle over again."[3] The students recounted their exploits that morning in class until something unexpected happened. One young woman admitted "that the campus hookup scene made her unhappy, even depressed, though she embraced it as if it were 'the best ever,' just a normal part of the college experience. She thought she was supposed to like it, but to be honest, she actually hated it."[4]

To Dr. Freitas's surprise, other students chimed in. "Hookup culture," they agreed, promotes "reckless, unthinking attitudes and expectations about sex. . . . After a few years of living in this environment they felt exhausted, spent, emptied by the pressure to participate in encounters that left them unfulfilled."[5]

Unfortunately, the determination to swim up the cultural stream, as Freitas's students decided to do, is in short supply among many young adults. It's easier to just go with the flow. The irony, of course, is that individualism is supposed to be about personal choice. In my grandparents' generation (born in the 1910s and '20s), people who did not conform to social norms were outcasts. Today young people who do not conform to social expectations are prudes, quaint anachronisms from a bygone era. In fact noncompliance with the individualist sexual ethic is one of the reasons the church is perceived as out of touch. "Repressive" is how individualists describe traditionalists.

Our rapidly changing culture has been hard at work relieving the traditionalist narrative of its relevance. One way it does so is by identifying those who abstain from sex outside of marriage as hopeless relics from yesteryear. Sexual attitudes and practices have obviously become more cavalier—and those attitudes have become much more widespread—since the sexual revolution of the '60s and '70s. Individualism has sparked the concepts of casual sex, hooking up, friends with benefits, and one-night stands. As Dennis, the nomadic and sexually active Catholic, said, "It's just sex."

If fading traditionalist morality was about private confinement of (shameful) sex, today's mindset is about free and public expression. Oral sex and other forms of "nonintercourse" sexual practice are considered normal and healthy for teens, and much more so for twentysomethings. "Sexting"—the use of a cell phone or mobile device to send text messages with sexual content—has become a common practice among both teens and young adults. Other tech tools, as well, give access to new ways of expressing sexuality and desire. "Put it out there. Put it on Facebook. Don't make yourself look too slutty, but don't be too inhibited."

The changing narrative of sexuality, like the other areas we've explored in this book, has been shaped in the next generation by the three As, covered in depth in chapter 2. Young people have grown up with unprecedented *access* to sexual content via the Internet, television, movies, music, and video games, which have brought sexuality into their lives earlier and more easily than was true for previous generations. Their *alienation* from formative relationships (especially from absent fathers) has created a host of emotional issues, many of which are manifested in their sexual decision making. And their suspicion of *authority*, inherited from their Boomer predecessors, invites them to dismiss "old-fashioned" traditions without wondering first whether they might be healthy and life-giving.

The women's liberation movement, which ran parallel with the sexual revolution of the 1960s and '70s, sought to achieve more leverage for women in our culture. In many ways, the movement was a reaction to traditionalism's insistence that women have an obligation to marry and have children and so do not need opportunities to participate in business, politics, and other arenas of cultural power. Unfortunately, the positive goals of women's lib were soon bound up with individualism's approach to sex. One could easily make an argument that the real winners, in the aftermath, have been men, who are no longer bound by traditionalism's demands for commitment in sexual relationships. Rather than empowering women, it can be argued that the sexual revolution and women's lib combined to make them even more vulnerable to exploitation.

To an individualist, marriage is—like everything else—one option among many. It is an alternative best saved for later in life, because choosing one person means you're *not* choosing a lot of other people. After the wedding, divorce is also an option, especially if the other person is not meeting your needs, sexual or otherwise. "Sex is about me. Commitment, chastity, fidelity, family—these are options to exercise if and when I believe they are right for me."

# TORN

Young Christians are torn between two competing narratives—and neither of them is the Christian story of sex (more on that in a moment). Most young people think of their communities of faith as traditionalist, because a hyperconservative ethic is, in reality, quite common among older churchgoers. "Don't talk about it. Keep it in the bedroom."

To the typical Mosaic, the traditionalist view seems quaint and old-fashioned, or even repressive and controlling. The individualist culture around them, by contrast, is bursting with invitations for self-fulfillment and personal expression. "Get what you need. Find yourself. Express your sexuality." Young Christians—whether Catholic, evangelical, or mainline—are immersed in a culture that highly values all manner of sexual freedom.

The unsustainable tension between the traditionalist and individualist views has led to profound cognitive and behavioral dissonance in the next generation of believers. Young Christians hold more conservative *beliefs* about sexuality than the broader culture (for example, that one should wait until marriage to have sex, that homosexuality is not consistent with Christian discipleship, and so on). Yet their sexual *behavior* is just as libertine as non-Christians in most ways.[6] In other words, they *think* in traditionalist terms, but most young Christians *act* like individualists.

Here is how Mark Regnerus describes his findings on the sexual behavior of Christian teenagers:

> Evangelical Protestant youth may hold less sexually permissive attitudes than most other religious youth, but they are *not* the last to lose their virginity, on average. Not even close . . . evangelical teenagers don't display just average sexual activity patterns, but rather above-average ones. There are several explanations for this anomaly, but I give most weight to the clash of cultures that evangelical adolescents are experiencing: they are urged to drink deeply from the waters of American individualism and its self-focused pleasure ethic, yet they are asked to value time-honored religious traditions like family and chastity. They attempt to do both . . . and this serving of two masters is difficult.[7]

The problem goes even deeper. I would suggest that many churches today have responded to the sexual crisis of our age by grafting the individualist narrative onto Christian teaching and practice, much as the traditionalists did in the middle of the last century. The church has accommodated the ethic of individualism in many quarters. An increasingly common theme in religious books and sermons, for example, is pursuing pleasure in our sex lives.

We should, of course, teach that God created sex and that it is good. Yet I have to wonder if we in the church have immersed ourselves too deeply in the all-American river of self-satisfaction. One older teen we interviewed told us about a leader in his church who talked to the young men in the youth group about going to Victoria's Secret to buy sexy apparel for his wife: "He said he was trying to show us how much pleasure his sex life brings him. But I kept thinking, *Really? Too much information!* I didn't see what lingerie choices had to do with being a Christian." There is a big difference between frank, nurturing talk about sex and self-centered bragging.

I have also started to wonder if we have embraced the individualist narrative by agreeing that students should finish their education, pay off debt, get a job, and get settled before marrying—that is, expecting young people to get their lives nice and ordered as American consumers before committing to marriage. This late-marriage approach is unrealistic for many, especially if we advocate celibacy until marriage. I do not intend to suggest that everyone should beat a path to the altar before age twenty, but we need to think clearly about the reasons behind the demands we make of young adults.

Based on our research, I also worry that some of the Christian community's teaching on abstinence focuses too much on the personal, individualist benefits of delaying sex until marriage. I am certainly not questioning the motives of those who urge the next generation toward sexual purity but I do wonder if some of the methods reflect a mindset influenced by individualism. "Save yourself for marriage and have fantastic sex with one partner, the way it's meant to be. Sex as God intended will blow your mind. Be safe; avoid the risks of STDs and an unwanted pregnancy. Think about your future." Much of the abstinence messaging, however well-intended, capitulates to culturally cultivated individualism: *sex is about me.*

In the tension between traditionalism and individualism, could we be missing a richer story, a truer narrative about sex? Lauren Winner, in her influential book *Real Sex*, points to the gap in her own experience after coming to faith in Christ as a young woman:

> I did not write this book because I want to challenge or overhaul traditional Christian teachings about sex, but rather because I want to challenge the way the church typically helps people practice those teachings. I have, by now, read countless books and heard countless lectures on

singleness, chastity, and refraining from premarital sex. Many of these lectures and books seem out of touch with reality. They seem naïve. They seem designed for people who get married right out of college. They seem theologically vacuous. Above all they seem dishonest. They seem dishonest because they make chastity sound easy. They make it sound instantly rewarding. They make it sound sweet and obvious. . . . Somehow the tools we give people to live premarital chastity are not working as well as we might hope.[8]

It seems that the way we communicate about and live the truth of sexuality has produced a generation of torn souls.

## REPRESSIVE TURNS TO RELATIONAL

My goal in this final section is not to outline a complete sexual ethic or to answer every (or even most) questions. Instead, my objective is to spur our thinking about the biblical narrative of sexuality to a relationally minded generation. Frankly, God has stretched me through the process of writing this chapter, and my posture in these paragraphs (indeed, I hope in the entire book!) is not know-it-all researcher but rather fellow broken soul.

We need a new mind to cultivate a deeper, more holistic, more Christ-filled ethic of sex. Neither traditionalism nor individualism is working—nor are they biblical. Most of us sense this, but what can we do? We need to rediscover the *relational* narrative of sexuality.

Sex is about selflessness, not primarily about self. It is about serving, not only about personal pleasure. It is about God's creativity intersecting human action, not our personal identity and self-expression. Rather than saying that *sex is taboo* (traditionalist) or that *sex is about me* (individualist), the relational approach to sexuality says, *sex is good and it is about us.*

We need to approach the issue of sexuality with utter humility. Because of sin, our relationships with God, each other, and our community are broken. Jesus saved us from sin by his death on the cross, sent his Spirit, and gave us his written Word so that these relationships can be fully restored. Yet as we read the Bible, we find every kind of distortion of and troubles with sexuality, even among God's people. By humbly acknowledging our common brokenness, we can deal with problems when they arise rather than sweeping them under the rug.

One way we accept our common brokenness is by keeping up our guard when it comes to sexual temptation. But how can we help each other avoid temptation without becoming legalistic rule makers? We can do it by understanding the impact of sexual beliefs and actions on our whole community.

Mosaics, remember, embody a relational identity. While they are often narcissistic and thoroughly immersed in a culture of individualism, young Christians show enormous capacity for and aspiration toward relational connection and "staying true" to family and peers. So I hold out a great deal of hope that this generation is ready for a different, more biblical approach to sexuality. In other words, we have a great opportunity to help the next generation live a new narrative of sexual life—the *relational* narrative. We can begin by doing two things—making sex everybody's business and making sex God's business.

### Making Sex Everybody's Business

Sexual sin is not worse than other sin but it does have profound consequences for relationships. I remember talking one day with my brilliant friend Eric Twisselmann about all sins being equal in God's eyes. He said, "That's true; Jesus said that sexual fantasies are no less sinful than actually having an affair. But the social consequences *are* different. Don't believe me? Just ask your wife."

Sex matters to everyone. It is integral to the health and wholeness of families, churches, and communities. Don't think that's true? Just ask someone who has had an abortion how it affected the relationship with her significant other, her parents, and her church family. Ask a young man dealing with an addiction to porn how his relationships with his mom and other women have changed. While most Americans believe that their sexual appetites are a matter of personal preference, the fact is that our sexual practices and beliefs have a far-reaching impact on those around us. The relational story of sex powerfully counters the individualist view in this respect. "Sex is not about me," it says. "Sex is about us."

Because sex is about us, we need to talk about it. One unfortunate effect of traditionalism was the church's reluctance to talk openly about sex and sexuality. There *are* clear scriptural injunctions against vulgar speech, but only a traditionalist would argue that all talk about sex is vulgar. I believe we must cultivate an environment in the faith community that invites open conversation about the power, beauty, darkness, and full reality of sex. Mosaics *will* find out what they want to know and *will* connect with others who are asking the same questions—they have the world at their fingertips! When the Christian community is hesitant to dialogue about sex, we lose the opportunity to apprentice the next generation in transparent, trusting, Christ-centered relationships. We need to initiate respectful, frank (not vulgar or self-congratulatory) conversations that will help young people develop a deep, nuanced, and livable sexual ethic beyond "Sex is dirty; save it for the one you love."

I also believe our conversations need to be courageous and reflect our refusal to take ourselves too seriously. Sometimes our discussions will be earnest and quiet. Other times they may be lighthearted, self-deprecating, even comedic. The connective tissue must be a sincere desire for flourishing relationships.

I think we need to reconsider doing "sexual formation" on a mass scale. Our research leads me to be skeptical of the long-term transformational power of events and rallies. I'm not saying we should never have large-scale worship events or that proclaiming the gospel in public places is pointless. It is not, and doing so is clearly a biblical pattern. Yet if we measure our impact solely by the number of students making pledges or raising their hands, I think we have to wonder if we are really committed to making disciples.

Finally, we need a willingness to talk about and "own" our struggles with sex, even as we stay on high alert for pretense or judgmentalism in our hearts. Hypocrisy might be defined as *leniency toward ourselves and strict standards for everyone else.* The comments made by the older gentleman, Max, about "kids nowadays" belie a willingness to wield this double standard. I pray that, in our relationships with young adults, we will be governed by honesty and grace, and that we will refuse to withhold love, respect, or mercy from those who do not comply with the biblical, relational narrative of sex. Leaders may have to exercise church discipline on occasion but they must do so with mercy in mind—for God has shown us mercy! Remember that those who don't conform to traditionalists' standards are outcasts, and those who don't conform to individualists' ideology are prudes. We who live by a new Way reject rejection in favor of grace.

Topics we need to start talking (and listening) about include:

- *Marriage.* The Bible uses marriage as a powerful metaphor for the self-sacrificing love God has for humanity, demonstrated ultimately on the cross of Christ. In contrast, much of our marriage talk today, both inside and outside the church, is me-centered. How can we rediscover, with the next generation, the profoundly sacred and sacrificial nature of both marriage and sex? How can we reclaim marriage as a communal, not just personal, covenant?

- *Gender.* In the relational narrative of sexuality, women are given full and complete responsibility to be their God-given best. They are neither walking wombs (traditionalism) nor walking vaginas (individualism). How can we mentor young women to become confident Christ-followers who are honored and respected in the church? How can we shape young men to become strong, compassionate servants of God, their family, and their friends?

- *Sexual orientation.* Christian or not, younger adults tend to be more accepting of gay, lesbian, bisexual, and transgender individuals than older adults. Although I do not personally view this as a positive trend, any discussion on sexual ethics with the next generation must not ignore this critical arena of human sexual experience. (The chapter on homosexuality in *unChristian* covers our research and my views on this subject.) How can we engage in meaningful dialogue, reflecting our relational priority even when we disagree with others?

- *Birth control and reproduction.* In chapter 7 (Anti-science), we met Colleen, who was trying to decide whether to donate her eggs to make money for college. As we consider the relational nature of our sexual ethics, reproduction and birth control are two more self-versus-community issues. How can we help the next generation think through reproductive decisions from a communal, relational perspective?

This list is certainly not exhaustive but it represents key themes we must address together in our communities of faith.

## Making Sex God's Business

Both traditionalism and individualism use God-talk to manage behavior, rather than responding to and strengthening relationships with God. Traditionalists use the threat of divine punishment, while individualists use the promise of divine blessing. The relational narrative about sex says that behavior management is a poor substitute for a whole, integrated, restored life with God. It seeks to reclaim sex as sacred and truly good. In other words, it makes sex "God's business"—because *life* is God's business.

Most Christians will tell you that their faith is a relationship with Christ, not a laundry list of duty-bound obligations. That's "religion." Our approach to sexuality should take the same view. The purpose is relationship with each other and with God. Any rules we put in place, rather than keeping people "in" or "out," like the rules of the traditionalists, are to help relationships thrive—and we stay on guard against rules taking on a life of their own, multiplying and expanding for their own sake. Biblical rules—like you shall not commit adultery—are absolutely necessary, of course. But the purpose is thriving relationships, not sexual repression.

A research study we conducted for Chip Ingram's ministry, Living on the Edge, provides ample evidence that young Christians embrace less of a rules-oriented spirituality than older Christians. It's possible that people become more rules-focused as they get older, but the generational gap is so extreme that I believe the difference is a fundamental shift in the next generation's orientation toward rules. Perhaps, with some level of optimism, we might describe young Christians as fertile ground for grace.[9] This is good news when it comes to making sex God's business, because the truth is that we all screw up and are in desperate need of restoration.

## Grace Generation?

Survey question: Do you agree or disagree with the following statement: Spiritual maturity means trying hard to follow the rules in the Bible?

Percentage of self-identified Christians who agree strongly:

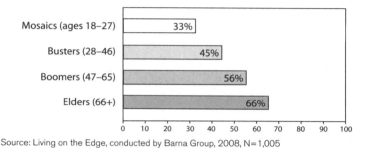

Source: Living on the Edge, conducted by Barna Group, 2008, N=1,005

Christian young adults who are living with split selves, divided at a soul level between their pelvic urges and their saintly aspirations, need to be made whole. Eugene Peterson puts it masterfully in *The Message*: "If someone falls into sin, forgivingly restore him, saving your critical comments for yourself. You might be needing forgiveness before the day's out" (Gal. 6:1). When we make sex God's business, he will give us the grace we need to restore lives, families, and communities.

He will also help us nurture lives, families, and communities in the relational narrative, heading off problems before they begin. Research shows the huge impact of fathers on the sexual formation of their children, particularly daughters. Are we providing tools and encouragement to parents that will help them grow whole, sexually integrated kids? Are we connecting teens and young adults from single-parent and blended homes with couples and families so they can learn (or relearn) patterns of healthy relationships?

Making sex God's business also means that our sexual ethics are based on the revealed truth of God through the Bible. Yet that's not as easy as it sounds. When one of my Christian friends in high school became sexually active, I rushed home to find the verses in Scripture that clearly condemned his actions. It was harder than I thought it would be, much more difficult than my Sunday school experiences had led me to believe. I found that the Bible's sexual ethic is much more complex, more nuanced, than I expected.

This generation needs us to be honest about the fact that the Bible is not crystal clear on *all* matters of sexuality. Together, we need to search it, test it, probe its essential meaning in its historical, cultural, and literary context.

This generation also needs us to live as if the Bible has a claim on our lives. Where we discover the clear teaching of God's Word, we need to be willing to pursue its role in every facet of our lives.

## PEOPLE OF SECOND CHANCES

On a trip to Chicago, I met a young woman (we'll call her Amanda) in her early twenties. She'd had several abortions during her teen years. She told me how much these choices had hurt her and her mother because "my mom always allowed pregnant teens into our home. If there is anyone on the planet who would have understood, it was my mom."

Now as a twentysomething, Amanda is trying to use her experiences for good. She has talked four pregnant teens out of abortions and is determined to help other girls avoid the same choices that, still today, fill her with regret.

At the same time, Amanda believes strongly in second chances. "I have another friend who still chose to have an abortion. Even though I tried to help her consider giving away the baby for adoption, she didn't choose that. That hurt, you know? But even though many of my Christian friends told me to cut off contact with my friend after she had the abortion, I couldn't do it. I still love her. I still accept her. I still believe in her. I still believe in what God wants to do in her life."

It is stories like this that bolster my appreciation for the next generation—imperfect but eager to extend grace. This hyper-relational generation is searching for the meaning of one of the ultimate expressions of human relationships: sex. They want to share their stories, and they are blunt, irreverent, and sometimes crude when they do. And in a no-privacy, socially networked world, this bare-all impulse tempts them to share anything and everything with anyone who clicks through.

But there is also the positive side, as my friend Mike Foster points out. He is the founder of People of the Second Chance, so named because there are, as he says, "a lot of young people in this generation who are dealing with unfulfilled expectations. Life isn't working out the way the American Dream scripted it." Mike puts the grace generation in a whole new light: "It's amazing what God can do once people reach a point where they really don't care what you think of them."

They might even start a new kind of sexual revolution.

# 9

# EXCLUSIVE

*Disconnection:* "I felt like I had been punched in the stomach. . . . It was a very sad and lonely night. I remember thinking . . . , *My non-Christian friends would* never *do that to me.*"

—Sarah

*Reconnection:* "When I have empathy, I begin to understand the love Christ has for the hurting and begin to see the situation from their point of view. It is a way of humbling yourself and putting others' needs and emotions before your own."

—Taylor

After high school graduation, Sarah moved to Winnipeg and started work at a trendy restaurant, where she was embraced by a circle of warm, wonderful friends—few of whom, as it happens, were Christians. She even started dating Steve, who had grown up Catholic but no longer practiced the faith. The following summer, Sarah was hired to work at the Christian camp she had attended as a high school student. She was thrilled—the summers she had spent there had been meaningful seasons in her life and her walk with God and she was excited to return.

Sarah and Steve felt strongly enough about each other that they decided to stay together long distance while she was away for the summer. They wrote and talked every day, and their relationship continued to deepen. But after the camp director's wife found out that Sarah was dating a non-Christian, Sarah became her "project." Sarah says, "Morning meetings, lunch meetings—she even sent me to talk with another woman who came from a 'mixed' relationship—all with the sole agenda of trying to convince me to break up with Steve." The all-out assault on Sarah's relationship took its toll and, after a few weeks, she and Steve decided to take a break. She remembers, "He didn't want to pull me away from my beliefs but he also knew that he wasn't going to change. We were both crushed but felt like it must be the right thing to do. The director's wife was elated. It was literally an answer to her prayers. I found out later that the entire senior team was having meetings about me.

"That was a tough week at camp. As much as I tried to tell myself that it was for the best, it just didn't feel right."

When Sarah and Steve saw each other the following weekend, they decided that in spite of their religious differences and the pressure Sarah was under, they wanted to try to make their relationship work. (They've been together ever since—seven years and counting.)

The day Sarah returned to camp was her last. She recalls, "That night after the kids were in bed, I was called down to the director's office. He told me that, because I chose to date Steve, I had become a 'spiritual block' at the camp. I needed to pack my things and leave first thing in the morning. I wasn't allowed to tell any of my friends—the director and his wife would explain everything at the morning meeting, which I would not be welcome to attend. After the meeting I could say my good-byes and leave.

"I felt like I had been punched in the stomach. They let me use the office to make arrangements to be picked up in the morning and that was that. It was a very sad and lonely night. I remember thinking on the way home, *My non-Christian friends would never do that to me.*"

# INTOLERABLE

Sarah's story illustrates one of the most pervasive perceptions among young adults: the church is *exclusive*. Many in the next generation believe that Christians have an insider-outsider mentality that is always ready to bar the door to those who don't meet their standards. This flies in the face of the Mosaics' collective values and reference points. *Tolerance* has been the cultural North Star for most of their upbringing. Inclusiveness, diversity, and political correctness are ideals that have shaped this generation. And these values are more than aspirations—multiculturalism already defines the experiences and friendships of many young adults. Whether or not we like this fact, we must grapple with these generational realities and make sense of them if we are to relate well for the sake of the gospel.

Take *ethnicity*. In 1960, as the Boomers came of age, more than four out of five of the eighteen- to twenty-nine-year-old demographic in the United States were white.[1] Now, just slightly more than half of young people are white. Look at *faith*. In 1960 more than nine out of ten young adults identified as Christian. That proportion is now 62 percent. Notice *family makeup*. In 1960 just one out of every twenty births (5 percent) were to unwed mothers. Now that percentage is 42 percent. Young people are growing up with peers who are more ethnically, religiously, and relationally diverse than the peers with whom their parents came of age.

Furthermore, gender equality, sexual openness, and awareness of the gay and lesbian community were new to the cultural consciousness of the 1960s. Now, egalitarianism, hypersexuality, and sexual orientation are part of the scenery. Most twentysomethings assume that the voices of lesbian, gay, bisexual, and transgender people should be heard in cultural conversations of any consequence.

And that's just the beginning. Mosaics are more globally interconnected than previous generations (greater levels of access, remember?). This has attuned many of them to the immense gap between the world's rich and poor. Even as many of them grow up to consume just as lavishly as their parents, they are keenly aware of economic and social disparities.

Sitting in the stands at my daughter Annika's recent basketball game, I noticed a huge banner on the middle school's gymnasium wall. Created by students to look like the Declaration of Independence, the banner proclaimed that these ten- to thirteen-year-olds would "stand up for anyone who is bullied because of their race, religion, or income." I'm all for rejecting bullying—as are most people of any age—but I was struck by the banner's patriotic design. Could it really be that, for America's younger generations, intimidation and intolerance are on a level with oppression by a foreign power? Even if not, their affinity for tolerance poses a significant challenge for the church, in four related ways.

## Agreement versus Disagreement

Founder of Off the Map, Jim Henderson, has described eighteen- to twenty-nine-year-olds as "the great agreement generation," because young people prefer finding areas of common ground rather than emphasizing differences that may lead to conflict. They look for ways to come together, rather than for issues on which to divide. Whatever your views on President Obama, for example, there is no denying his appeal to Mosaics. His themes of unity and collective action resonate with and continue to inspire the younger generation.

The history of the church, both in the distant and the recent past, points to a willingness on the part of Christians to split from other believers if the stakes are high enough. We could talk all day (and probably never agree) about the worthiness of various issues over which churches have split, even as we agree that there are good reasons to stand firm on matters of Christian theology and practice. But the point remains: fewer Mosaics than previous generations would be willing to make these same divisive choices. "No compromise!" has been the slogan of the Western church, but it does not make sense to the next generation, for whom negotiation and cooperation are facts of life. As the church moves together into an unknown future, we may find Mosaics' compulsion toward unity a gift.

## Peer Responsibility versus Individuality

Young adults also look to their peers to be their moral and spiritual compass. They tend to base their views of morality on what seems fair-minded, loyal, and acceptable to their friends. This peer-centeredness poses many challenges for other generations. One of the challenges businesses face, for example, is the fact that many young employees have no moral qualms about giving away goods and services to their friends. Again, this is not entirely new. Previous generations have done favors for each other. But institutional loyalty is faltering, while tribal or peer loyalty has intensified.

In the Western church we tend to emphasize the individual over the group. We focus on personal responsibility to a fixed standard, rather than on collective negotiation with a world absent of absolute truth. This is the exact opposite of how young adults relate to their world. Yes, it is important that we in the church continue to tell the truth about personal morality, but I believe the next generation can remind us of our collective responsibility to each other and to the world. Christians are Christians in community, and the next generation can teach us a thing or two about what that means.

## Fairness versus Rightness

Another hallmark of the next generation is their emphasis on fairness over rightness. Teens and twentysomethings tend to determine the rightness and wrongness of their choice by what seems *fair, reasonable,* and *accessible.* Just ask the executives (and former executives) in the music industry. One of the major forces—along with digital tools and digitized content—that undermined the conventional model of the music biz is the fact that young people came to believe (collectively) that the system of music distribution was unfair. According to their thinking, it is unfair to charge the price of an entire album when a customer wants only one song. Unfortunately for music execs, younger customers were not willing to go along with the established model. Once technology made album purchases unnecessary, young music lovers began to share individual songs—even though doing so was (and is) illegal.

Digital piracy isn't *right*, but music sharing seems *fair*. Many young people are redefining their ethical decisions by what seems fair, rather than by an outside standard of right and wrong. How can the church, which flies the flag of God's unchanging moral standards, deal with such a shift?

## Participation versus Exclusion

With all this emphasis on peer acceptance and agreement, it should come as no surprise that the majority of young people hate to be out of the loop. They dread being excluded. They want to participate. This expectation is driven to some extent by the interactivity (rather than passive transmission) of information, and by a flood of "reality" entertainment, which promises everyone fifteen minutes (okay, maybe less) of fame. Yet a core motivation for their participatory mindset is the fundamental belief that *everyone has the right to belong.* No one should be excluded for any reason.

In the church we tend to make belief a prerequisite to belonging— you're not "one of us" until you have signed off on our Statement of Faith. Yet young people start with the basic assumption that everyone belongs and they have a hard time understanding spiritual communities that feel like insider-only clubs.

# EXCLUSIVITY AND ALL ITS FRIENDS

Recently I emailed Sarah, whom we met at the outset of this chapter, to ask where she's at with church and Christianity now that she's a few years removed from her bad camp experience. She wrote, "Over time I stopped going to church. It didn't make sense to leave my wonderful group of friends every Sunday to try to build new relationships with people I didn't know or really connect with. I already had a community that loved, supported, and challenged me; what else did I need? I decided that I was never again going to try to make friends based on religious beliefs. If they happened to be Christian, fine, but going forward I was going to invest in those relationships that genuinely grow out of a true enjoyment of each other's company. So far, that has been working much better for me. I don't think that my faith in God is ever going to change. There have been profound experiences in my life when I have felt the presence of God. Whenever I start to have doubts, I look back on those moments and know they were real. God will always be a part of my life. I just don't think the church will be."

By relating Sarah's story, I do not mean to debate the biblical correctness of the camp director's decision. Instead, I want to suggest that exclusivity, applied legalistically and without a relational foundation, leaves a bitter taste. Being excluded is tough to swallow for any generation, but it is especially tough for today's all-access, low-authority young people who would rather do just about anything than choose to end a relationship.

As we noticed previously in this chapter, young Christians have had greater exposure to a wide range of theological and religious viewpoints than previous generations. They maintain more non-Christian friendships than any previous generation of Christian youth. They have more relationships than did their parents with those of various sexual orientations and identities.

Contrasting with their being "for" all these relationships is the church, which appears to be against them. Today the Christian community exists in society's vortex of discontinuously different thinking about the world and relationships. One of the sentiments we uncovered in our research was that many young Christians, particularly young exiles, feel "forced to choose between my faith and my friends." In other words, many young Christians and ex-Christians feel as though the church makes them choose between faithfulness to friends and faithfulness to faith.

### Exclusive | In Their Own Words

*Percentage of 18- to 29-year-olds who have a Christian background*

|  | completely true of me | completely or mostly true of me |
|---|---|---|
| Churches are not accepting of gays and lesbians. | 19% | 38% |
| Christians are afraid of the beliefs of other faiths. | 13% | 29% |
| I feel forced to choose between my faith and my friends. | 12% | 29% |
| Church ignores the problems of the real world. | 9% | 22% |
| Church is like a country club, only for insiders. | 8% | 22% |
| I have never really been accepted by church people. | 6% | 14% |

Barna Group | 2011 | N=1,296

The specific comments we uncovered in our research included the widespread belief that churches are not accepting of gays and lesbians.

Another common perception is that Christians are afraid of the beliefs of other faith groups.

There is a reason why Christianity is perceived to be exclusive. One of our faith's central claims is that God's coming in Jesus was incomparably unique, a one-time event never to be matched or repeated. Jesus himself told the disciples, "I am the way and the truth and the life. No one comes to the Father except through me" (John 14:6).

But what does the next generation believe about the claim of Christ to be the only way to the Father? What do they believe about the necessity of salvation? And do their beliefs translate into personal faith sharing with others? If we look at the overall picture, eighteen- to twenty-nine-year-olds are more likely than the previous generation of Americans to believe in religious pluralism, which holds that there are many different paths to God. More specifically, they are likely to believe that most or all religions teach essentially the same spiritual truths.

We found that young nomads and prodigals are particularly focused on exclusion as an unpalatable aspect of Christianity. We see an example of this in John Sullivan, a *GQ* writer who says that the "hell stuff" really caused him to rethink his faith in Christ (read John's story in chapter 10). Yet the findings among exiles and other faithful young adults suggest that they are just as likely to believe in the exclusivity of Christ as were their parents and grandparents. For instance, there are no differences between younger and older Christians when it comes to rejecting the following beliefs: that people can lead a meaningful life without accepting Jesus as their Savior; that Christians and Muslims worship the same God; that the Bible, the Koran, and the Book of Mormon are all different expressions of the same spiritual truths; and that it doesn't matter what religious faith you follow because they all teach the same lessons. Most young committed Christians have a great deal of theological consistency with their parents' viewpoints on these issues. Aside from exiles and other committed believers, however—that is, among the wider population of young Christians and former Christians—we find significantly more religious pluralism than among the older generations.[2]

What, then, is the difference between young Christians and older believers? It's their context. The younger Christian community is "doing theology" in an environment different from that of the past; not everyone within the community connects with the historic faith's truth claims. This fact is causing younger Christians, especially exiles, to rethink theology and practice in at least three areas: evangelism, denominations, and the "other."

## Evangelism

Young Christians are less likely than Christians a decade ago to share their faith with others.[3] They are reluctant to try to convince a friend to become a Christian. This is an unfortunate response to the chasm between their beliefs and those of the broader culture, which says that it's offensive or even hateful to argue for a specific religion or truth claim.

If there is one thing the church might learn, however, it's this: young Christians who *are* willing to share their faith consistently explained that they do not believe evangelism can be separated from action. As we have already mentioned, this generation doesn't want to be merely hearers of faith but also doers. This desire explains the next generation's focus on social justice. For better or worse, many young Christians believe that evangelism must be connected to actions on behalf of others.

Kate, one young Christian we interviewed, captured this sentiment when she said, "I don't want to attend a church that constantly rails against sin and sinners. I want to be a part of a church that also helps people who are *affected* by the results of sin. This seems like what Jesus did."

Candidly, my concern as a researcher and as an observer of this generation is that they will focus so much on "doing" that the message and the motivation—Christ's work on the cross—will be lost. I worry that their concerns for "causes" will be spent, used up, without the potency of the gospel at the core of their efforts. And I wonder what we could do as older Christ-followers to represent both the words and deeds of Christ, so that the next generation has a healthy model to follow.

## Denominations

For the most part, denominations are of less importance to younger generations than to older adults. Don't get me wrong. Denominations are and will continue to be significant shapers of American religion, and millions of young people are quite loyal to their particular "brand" of

Christianity. As I have said, I believe institutions matter because they are the mediators of our collective culture; therefore, the appropriate reinvention of these institutions matters to our future. Similarly, theology matters—and so too differences of theological opinion between various Christian traditions. We should help the next generation see why respectful, honest conversations about these differences are important.

Yet we shouldn't miss the larger pattern here. There is a growing sensibility among many young Christians that denominations emphasize believers' differences while they would rather celebrate what Christians share in common. They don't want to be defined exclusively by denominational categories. Many Protestants want to understand their Catholic sisters' and brothers' viewpoints. Young Christians of all stripes want to move beyond "theological feudalism" in favor of a shared vision of their role in Christ's kingdom. Yes, the anti-institutional impulse of the next generation is a driver of this perspective but it is more than that. Exiles, in particular, are raising potent questions about why Christ talked so much about unity, and about how we might reconcile his instructions with the downside of denominationalism.

One study we conducted among pastors of a specific denomination is a case in point. Young evangelical clergy from this denomination were far less willing than older leaders to sign an exclusive statement about their denomination's theological position. Rarely have I seen as huge a gap between young and old as was uncovered in that study.

While denominations will continue to be an important part of organizing and mobilizing churches and churchgoers, we are finding that young people (including younger pastors) do not want denominational differences to get in the way of Christianity's broader story. They do not want to neglect the church's mission just so they can live or die on a denominational hill.

## The "Other"

When you marry highly valued diversity to a theological belief in the necessity of Christ, you get a love for the "other"—the outsider, the marginalized. Passionate, mission-driven exiles seem to share the conviction that the North American church has somehow lost its heart for the very

kinds of people Jesus sought out during his earthly ministry—the op-
pressed, the poor, and the physically, emotionally, and socially crippled.
The more critical among the younger generation might say that the
typical church is good at reaching "recycled Christians"—believers who
are uncommitted to another church body—but not at reaching those
who are truly on the outside looking in.

A young church plant here in Ventura, California, where my friend
and fellow thirtysomething Chris Hall is the pastor, has focused its vision
on reaching those who are "far from God." Chris has been criticized by
other Christian leaders in our community for his expressions and actions of solidarity with homeless people, drunks, and junkies. (Sound
like criticism Jesus heard?) Yet Chris and his church family know that
there is a world of difference between claiming that Jesus is exclusively
the Christ and excluding people from fellowship with the church.

## EXCLUSION TURNS TO EMBRACE

My young friend Lucas works at one of my favorite coffee shops in Ventura. A few months ago, Lucas—who is somewhere between a nomad
and an exile—described to me the upside-down ethics of a recent encounter with a customer. "There is this guy who comes in pretty regularly," he said. "And he always buys the cheapest thing on the menu,
usually a small coffee, and then asks for an extra large cup. He goes over
to the sugar and cream station and puts a little milk in his small coffee.
Then he fills up the *entire extra cup* with 2% or whole milk. And then
he leaves.

"Recently I got promoted to shift lead and was really tired of seeing
him blatantly steal milk. I mean, it's basically shoplifting, right? So when
he asked for the extra cup the other day, I told him, 'You know, if this
is for your milk, I really need to charge you for it.' He was really ticked
off. So guess what happened next?" Lucas asked, ramping up the drama.

"What?"

"The guy got so angry that he complained to the manager. And Monic,
my supervisor, guess what she did? *She wrote me up.* I got disciplined.
Why? Because I 'failed to leave the customer with a positive experience.' "

I was genuinely flabbergasted. "Dude, are you serious?"

"Completely," Lucas confirmed. "Is that not the craziest thing you have ever heard?"

"Pretty close."

"Monic tells me not to worry about it, but it's on my employee record. I just don't understand how a company makes it okay for someone to steal and then is hard on me as an employee for trying to protect their property. That's just messed up."

Lucas's experience with the milk shoplifter epitomizes the dark side of inclusiveness—a culture so enamored with tolerance that an employee who could not tolerate stealing was punished. An understandable rejection of this twisted ethic lies at the root of the church's reluctance to grapple with the next generation's concerns about our exclusiveness. After all, we serve a God who is utterly dependable in his moral character and who has revealed in the Bible the standard by which right and wrong are to be measured. Rightly, I believe, we question our culture's fixation on political correctness and "peace at all costs." Yet I also think the next generation's impulse to include everyone is an invitation God is extending to the church to rethink our posture toward the world.

I want to suggest that when we accept the terms of the debate— exclusion versus tolerance—we lose. When we choose exclusion, the church circles the wagons and becomes a fortresslike, members-only organization overcome by a siege mentality. We bar the door to everyone who looks scary or asks questions that make us uncomfortable.

When we choose tolerance of every person and ideology, on the other hand, we shrink from sharing the very, very good news of God's love, demonstrated like never before or since in Christ, and from confronting sin and the suffering that is sin's result. Exclusion lacks love; the wrong kind of tolerance lacks courage.

At the heart of the Christian story, however, is the Triune God's rejection of both exclusion *and* tolerance. The Creator was not content to exclude those who had rejected him, but neither was he prepared to tolerate our hatefulness and sin. So what did he do? He became one of us, one of the "other," identifying with us to embrace us in solidarity, empathy, and selfless agape love—all the way to the cross.[4]

What would it look like for the Christian community to do the same? How would the church be different if we were to reject exclusion as unacceptable and tolerance as not good enough? What would we do differently when discipling young adults to help them cultivate Christlike empathy that identifies with the least, the last, and the lost?

## Embracing Scripture

We might start by seeking a fully biblical view of Christ's message and mission. A good place to begin this endeavor is with the stories Jesus told about the "other." Let's enter into the story of the wealthy host who invites the dregs of society to his lavish banquet after the elite turn down his invitation (see Luke 14:15–24). Let's meditate on the tale of the shepherd who leaves ninety-nine of his sheep to seek the one that is lost (see Luke 15:1–7). Let's find ourselves in the parable of the loving father who wants nothing more than to reconcile with his wayward son (see Luke 15:11–32). In each of these stories—and by his own actions—Jesus invites us to glimpse God's heart for the outsider.

The apostle Paul's writings to the fledgling early churches show a similar compassion for those on the outside looking in. "God demonstrates his own love for us in this: While we were still sinners, Christ died for us" (Rom. 5:8). Don't forget that we were *all* outsiders, he says to the church in Rome. To the church in the city of Corinth, he writes:

> When I wrote to you before, I told you not to associate with people who indulge in sexual sin. But I wasn't talking about unbelievers who indulge in sexual sin, or are greedy, or cheat people, or worship idols. You would have to leave this world to avoid people like that. I meant that you are not to associate with anyone who claims to be a believer yet indulges in sexual sin. . . . Don't even eat with such people. It isn't my responsibility to judge outsiders, but it certainly is your responsibility to judge those inside the church who are sinning. God will judge those on the outside.
>
> 1 Corinthians 5:9–13 NLT

Paul's instructions are crystal clear but are tough to apply, even for the most devout and lifelong Christian. Most of us are more than happy to judge those who are not "one of us"! What would it look like for us to take Paul's admonition seriously and teach our young people to do the same?

"Live wisely among those who are not believers, and make the most of every opportunity," Paul writes to the young church in Colossae. "Let your conversation be gracious and attractive so that you will have the right response for everyone" (Col. 4:5–6 NLT). What a wonderful snapshot of our responsibility as Christians! Such a livable piece of advice! Are we cultivating this gracious posture toward non-Christians and teaching young disciples to live wisely as well?

A while ago I heard of a group of teen-conference planners who considered teaching young people catchy one-liners "to use on an atheist," simple phrases that could be taught in a short seminar session that could then be lobbed at a person who doesn't believe in God. (I wondered, *Is "Go to hell" on the list?*) Although this is an extreme example, the fact this idea was seriously considered points to our heart's preference for slogan making over living wisely and speaking graciously.

Scripture must also be our guide as we grapple with the singularity of Christ and what this means for the church's mission. I know a youth pastor who leads a one-month study of the Gospel of John with his group *every year*. He says, "It's really hard for people to read the book of John and miss what Jesus was saying about himself. He was making a reality-altering claim about his nature. Even my best teaching falls flat trying to convey this. The best way is for young people to learn Christ through the Scriptures. That's the only way I have found for any of us to truly grasp the exclusivity of Christ's message."

## Embracing Practice

What methods are we using to help young adults understand and experience Christ's message? What practices can help them develop their missional empathy, producing actions of love for the hurting and hopeless because of their love for Christ? Are we making service to the outsider a central component of discipleship?

Our rich and varied traditions can help us in this regard. Every tradition, whether Wesleyan, Reformed, Orthodox, Anabaptist, or Anglo-Catholic, has formulated missional practices that can help the broader church shape a generation of mission-minded and passionately evangelistic Christ-followers. As we share practices and fellowship across denominational lines, we reject both exclusion and tolerance and can truly embrace each other as sisters and brothers in Christ.

## Embracing Empathy

The next generation needs workable, biblical, grace-filled ways to relate with people who are not believers. For the sake of Christ and the church's mission, we must give them better tools and a thoughtful, livable theology to match. I wish I had easy suggestions, but the truth is that relationships are hard, complex work. No two are alike. Yet learning how to love others with the courage of our God-given convictions is the fine art of following Christ. Teaching younger Christians how to do this is the fine art of discipleship.

One piece of good news is that the next generation has more to offer than we might imagine. I think many of them—like our family friend, Taylor, who is a nineteen-year-old now studying at Seattle Pacific University—are already working out a thoughtful, livable theology. I ran into Taylor recently at a shop in our hometown of Ventura. As she gabbed with a friend, I couldn't help but notice that she had "Empathy" embroidered across her handbag. Frankly I was curious why that word so resonated with her.

When I asked about it, Taylor said, "Empathy is the ability to see a situation, an emotion, an action through Christ's eyes and through the other person's heart. When I have empathy, I begin to understand the love Christ has for the hurting and see the situation from their point of view. It is a way of humbling yourself and putting others' needs and emotions before your own."

"But aren't you concerned that some Christians might think 'empathy' just means accepting everyone no matter what they do?" I asked.

"Yeah, a few people have kind of looked at me strangely. But empathy is taking on the nature of Christ. It's the ability to understand and take on yourself the burdens of others. I have a huge heart for those caught up in sex trafficking. It's an evil that rips away the innocence of children and treats women as if they are less than dirt. Though I cannot relate at all to their situation, it is through empathy that I am able to realize the inner hurt and despair created by this slavery. In our yearning to become Christlike, we have the opportunity to embrace his character."

Beyond the false choice between exclusion and tolerance, let's help the next generation see the Way—Jesus.

Discover how different generations view and use the Bible at www.barna
.org/generations-and-the-Bible.

**10**

# DOUBTLESS

*Disconnection:* "The hell stuff—I never made peace with it. Human beings were capable of forgiving those who'd done them terrible wrongs, and we all agreed that human beings were maggots compared with God, so what was his trouble again?"

—John

*Reconnection:* "Being here, with people I like, *doing something* despite my unbelief is better than not doing anything."

—Helen

Faith and doubt can creep into the strangest places—even into the pages of *GQ*.

This research project has been years in the making, starting with Barna Group's 2003 study, which identified a generational shift with real implications for the future of the church. Yet it took on new energy after I read an article in *GQ*.

A long feature from the February 2004 issue describes the culture and fans of Christian rock music and satirizes the fusion of spirituality and rock 'n' roll. The subtitle gets the party started: "Rock music used to be a safe haven for degenerates and rebels. Until it found Jesus . . ." An illustration of Jesus as a rock star completes the setup. He wears a sly smile and, of course, shoulder-length hair. He is ripped and muscular, clad in jeans and a white shirt—and his right arm is inked with a heart-and-cross tattoo.

This is how the editors of GQ envision the Christian-rock version of the Savior of the world.

What captured my attention most, though, is the backstory of the article's author, John Jeremiah Sullivan. Sullivan is in a good position to provide an insider-turned-outsider viewpoint because he lived it—Christianity was a key aspect of his personal faith journey. As the feature unfolds, he describes his teen years, a period during which he considered himself a committed, born-again Christian. He recounts active involvement in Bible studies, as well as discipleship and mentoring throughout his teenage "Jesus phase."

Here's the kicker: Sullivan's crisis of faith, as he terms it, came years ago *at a Christian rock concert,* where he had been recruited by his church to provide spiritual counseling to concertgoers. Anyone who made a new commitment to Christ would receive one-on-one counseling so they could better understand the ramifications of their decision. While trying to help a group of neophyte believers understand what it means to become a Christian, Sullivan's answers began to sound hollow—to himself. Perhaps it is mere journalistic flair, but Sullivan indicates that he walked out of the concert that night as *less Christian.* He was a changed person and, evidently, on the path to walking away from faith.

Because of his doubts, the church lost him.

## SHADES OF DOUBT

It may seem redundant to say that doubt causes people to struggle with faith, but it is important to remember that doubt is not always faith's opposite. Theologian and Pulitzer-nominated novelist Frederick Buechner once said, "Doubt is the ants in the pants of faith." Often doubt acts as a powerful motivator toward a more complete and genuine spiritual life, and our research confirms that not everyone who doubts walks away from faith. Still, our study also shows that doubt is a significant reason young adults disengage from church.

We have learned too that doubt comes in more than one flavor. This is a good time to reemphasize one of the most important themes of our findings: every spiritual journey is unique. We must pay attention not just to macro trends but also to individual stories. If we want to capture the big picture of the next generation's relationship to the church and to Christianity, a paint roller will only help us prep the canvas. We need a fine-tipped artist's brush to render the details.

*Every story matters.*

In our modern evidence-based, logic-oriented culture, we may have a certain picture in our head of what it means to be a doubter. Many Christians believe that people who experience doubts simply lack the proper evidence or depth of conviction. But doubt is a far more nuanced and slippery experience that involves personality, lack of fulfillment, notions about certainty, relational alienation, and even mental health.

Is the Christian community capable of holding doubt and faithfulness in tension, welcoming hard questions even as we press together toward answers? Or will the church continue to be seen as a place where doubters don't belong because certainty is the same as faith? Will we push doubters to the margins in order to be people with *no doubts*?

Let's look at some common avenues of doubt, and then explore how we might better respond when someone's spiritual journey takes him or her down one of these roads.

## Intellectual Doubt

Let's begin with the doubters we expect: those who struggle with evidentiary forms of doubt, who are not satisfied with rational proofs that God exists or that Jesus was resurrected. Most Christian teenagers and young adults are not racking their brains (or their souls) in an effort to bring logical consistency to their faith claims. However, these types of concerns do affect millions of younger (and older) Americans and should not be minimized. We learned in our interviews with eighteen- to twenty-nine-year-olds who have a Christian background that one-quarter (23 percent) have "significant intellectual doubts about their faith." This is not a majority, but remember, individual stories matter. About one out of every nine young Christians (11 percent) said that college experiences caused them to doubt their faith. Again, this is not a large percentage, but it represents tens of thousands of people.

What are the implications? There is still an important part to be played by traditional apologetics in dealing with intellectual questions that stand in the way of faith commitment—though the *form* apologetics takes must be adapted for the next generation. We might consider shifting away from a focus on "experts" toward a more relational approach. One faith community in Oregon hosts a weekly worship service that invites anyone to ask any question they have about faith. To fit with the uber-connected world of young people, the church accepts questions submitted via text and Twitter. My guess is that this can be nerve-racking for the pastoral staff, who willingly put themselves on the spot to wrestle with people's most pressing questions—but I imagine it's worth it, and not just to those who get the answers they seek. The entire community gets to witness, on a weekly basis, what it looks like to wrestle with doubt, to confess our questions without abandoning faith.

For those of us who have strong faith convictions, it can be difficult to imagine how people struggle with unbelief. One of the qualitative interviews we did with a young man named Matt helped me understand the potency of intellectual questions. He said, "Sometimes I wish I could just push the belief button. I really do wish I could say yes to Christianity. But it doesn't work. I can't get past some of these big questions about faith, about God, and about Christianity."

John Sullivan, the *GQ* writer whom we met earlier, explains in his article that he could not understand God's damnation of sinners, among other intellectual and theological questions. His words summarize the feelings of thousands:

> The hell stuff—I never made peace with it. Human beings were capable of forgiving those who'd done them terrible wrongs, and we all agreed that human beings were maggots compared with God, so what was his trouble again? I looked around and saw people who'd never have a chance

to come to Jesus; they were too badly crippled. Didn't they deserve—more than the rest of us, even—to find his succor, after this life?[1]

Some of the doubts we encountered in our research echo similar struggles, which comes as no surprise; these are questions people have wrestled with since the dawn of the faith. We found that those who experience intellectual doubt are most commonly prodigals—those who decide not to be Christian any longer. Prodigals are the most likely of all dropouts to say they have one or more "big questions" that they cannot get around, such as:

- Why does God allow suffering? Or evil?
- Isn't the fact that I was born into a Christian family or society an accident of geography? I could just as easily have been born Hindu or some other faith.
- What should I believe about the Bible? Why?
- Don't all religions say basically the same thing? Why is Christianity so exclusive?

Of course, most people—not just prodigals—ask themselves these questions at some point along their faith journey. Yet questioning does little to stop most people in their spiritual tracks. The research shows that, as students enter their junior and senior years of high school and then college, these types of doubts increase in significance and impact. But even at their peak, it is not typically intellectual doubts that drive a wedge between most young Christians and their beliefs. Nomads and exiles, for example, are likely to consider intellectual questions, but often find other kinds of doubt more undermining to their faith commitment.

## Institutional Doubt

A particular type of doubt experienced by the next generation is a form of institutional skepticism directed at present-day Christianity. Singer-songwriter David Bazan, whom we met in chapter 3, exemplifies this perspective. These young adults may be frustrated by the classic philosophical questions much like intellectual doubters, but they are also deeply at odds with expressions of modern-day Christianity, which many would categorize as distortions or abuses of Christ's teachings. In other words, some young adults doubt God—but for others, "doubt" might best be described as a deep, visceral sense that the church today is not what it could or ought to be.

I think this helps to explain one of the surprise findings I wrote about in *unChristian*. Many young Christians, just like millions of young non-Christians, have a negative perception of the church, particularly of evangelicalism in America. In that research project, I was shocked to find so many young believers who harbor negative views of the church. The surveys we did for this project helped to clarify and define those earlier findings.

### Doubtless | In Their Own Words

*Percentage of 18- to 29-year-olds who have a Christian background*

|  | completely true of me | completely or mostly true of me |
|---|---|---|
| I don't feel that I can ask my most pressing life questions in church. | 14% | 36% |
| I have significant intellectual doubts about faith. | 12% | 23% |
| My faith does not help with depression or other emotional problems. | 10% | 20% |
| I have or had a crisis in life that has made me doubt faith. | 9% | 18% |
| The death of a loved one has caused me to doubt. | 5% | 12% |
| College experiences cause me to question my faith. | 5% | 11% |
| I am not allowed to talk about my doubts in church. | 5% | 10% |

Barna Group | 2011 | N=1,296

As we described in the chapters on nomads, prodigals, and exiles, one out of five young people (21 percent) with a Christian background said, "I am a Christian, but the institutional church is a difficult place for me to live out my faith." Exposure to some of the darkest parts of religious life can also sow seeds of doubt. Among the young adults with a Catholic background, one-fifth reported "the priest-abuse scandals have made me question my faith." Another doubt breaks my heart and has dire implications for the leadership of tomorrow's church. Nearly one out of every eight young Christians (13 percent) said they "used to work at a church and became disillusioned." Our research did not probe whether they were church staff or church volunteers, but either way, there are tens of thousands of twentysomethings disconnected because of firsthand negative experiences serving in a congregation. How can we do a better job of monitoring the experiences young people are having in leadership?

The arena of institutional doubt is one of the places where we see the rise of the exiles, young Christians who are seeking ways of following Jesus outside typical footpaths. Recall that in chapter 4 we said more than one-third of young Christians (38 percent) "want to find a way of following Jesus that connects with the world I live in." One-fifth (22 percent) want to "do more than get together once a week for worship."

Sometimes exiles make an effort to stay connected to the institutional church to speak prophetically to the broader Christian community, challenging us to reform and renew. Shane Claiborne and his friends at The Simple Way, a new monastic community in Philadelphia, are a notable example of this posture. They are committed to living out a decidedly countercultural vision of Christianity, yet Shane shares their vision at mainstream church conferences and events, exhorting believers of many traditions to examine and reevaluate our ways of being Christ's followers.

Not all of us may agree with everything these young exiles say and do. I believe, though, that we ignore the institutional doubts of the next generation at our peril. God always seems to work at the margins and speak through prophetic voices. Frequently young leaders are bold and catalytic, and God will use young women and men to start new enterprises that serve the church. Billy Graham was a young man when his evangelistic ministry took off. Mother Teresa arrived in India when she was just nineteen. Many young leaders can envision the future in ways that are not perceptible to established leaders.

Some may be too quick to act on their institutional doubts and define themselves by their leaving, yet some of their criticisms hit close to the mark and can help us identify the shallowness of our worship and practices. While I am convinced that every Christian needs to be part of a community of fellow believers—and many young dropouts need more true community in their lives—we must be willing to listen and respond to the heartfelt institutional doubts of the next generation.

## Unexpressed Doubt

Sitting over breakfast several months ago at one of my favorite local spots, Kevin and I talked about the choices that had led him away from church. He grew up Catholic, and it was his parents' breakup that had begun to undermine his confidence in the faith. "At first it was hard for me to accept that my parents were getting kicked out of the church as a result of their divorce," Kevin said between sips of coffee. "But probably just as important was how the church handled my doubt . . . or didn't handle it." He hesitated before admitting, "I kept my doubts to myself, because I didn't think my leaders would want to know that I really didn't believe. Maybe they could have helped me more, but I never believed they would be able to."

I suspect that, if Kevin had talked about his doubts, he would have found more help than he expected. Sadly, we'll never know.

I believe *unexpressed* doubt is one of the most powerful destroyers of faith. Our research reveals that many young people feel the church is too small a container in which to carry their doubts. Fully one-third of young Christians (36 percent) agree that "I don't feel that I can ask my most pressing life questions in church." One out of ten (10 percent) put it more bluntly: "I am not allowed to talk about my doubts in church."

This statistic signals one of the challenges that the next generation of Christians brings to the church. They are used to "having a say" in everything related to their lives. As we noted earlier, communication, fueled by technology, is moving from passive to interactive. Yet the structure of young adult development in most churches and parishes is classroom-style instruction. It is passive, one-sided communication—or at least that's the perception most young people have of their religious education. They find little appetite within their faith communities for dialogue and interaction.

There is an isolating element to unexpressed doubt as well. When a person feels as though church is not a safe place to be honest, he or she feels compelled to pretend, to put on a show, which all too often results in a faith that is no more than skin deep. When young believers hang back, holding their doubts, concerns, and disillusionments in private, they cut themselves off from leaders and peers who might help them deal with their doubts in a constructive, faith-building way.

People remain silent about their doubts for all sorts of reasons. And let's be honest, it's not always the church's fault. Many youth leaders and pastors are ready, willing, and able to listen to young people, to encourage them in their quest for answers to their biggest questions, and to walk beside them in honesty and authenticity.

There are too many instances, however, when faith communities create a toxic environment where doubts are allowed to fester. Or they never create space for questions to be raised, where pressing life issues can be openly discussed. In these places, young adults don't feel accepted, safe, or secure. Perhaps their church does not invite transparency but is instead a place where the "expert" makes those who express doubt feel stupid or out of sync with "true" belief. Some perceive they will be judged for being honest, while others want to believe more deeply and articulating doubt feels traitorous.

We cannot solve doubt like a puzzle but we can create communities that hold doubt and faith in proper balance. God is not afraid of human doubts. "Doubting Thomas" is remembered for his unbelief, yet in his mercy, Christ allowed Thomas to renew his faith when the risen Lord displayed the evidence of his crucifixion and resurrection. King David is called a man after God's heart, even though many of his psalms questioned God's intentions toward and provision for him—many times in raw, angry language that leaves very little emotion unexpressed. Job too voiced his doubts and disillusionment in very strong terms.

We need communities where it is safe for people to talk about their deepest, darkest concerns, where expressing uncertainty is not seen as abnormal or apostate. Radical transparency, for better and worse, is the norm in young adult culture; just check out the magazines and gossip websites so popular with the younger generation. Better yet, notice how most young people are willing to live totally "in public" on Facebook and other social networking sites. As pastor and technology sage Shane Hipps describes, this is "a generation of exhibitionists." Most of them do not shy away from asking honest questions (at least within their circle of friends), though they sometimes do not have the patience or determination to pursue good answers.

Still, after studying the role of faith communities and families in spiritual formation, I believe that the problem is *not only* the next generation's short attention span, exhibitionism, or lack of intellectual rigor. Rather, I think faith communities have not done a good job creating environments and experiences where students can process their doubts. Our posture toward students and young adults should be more Socratic, more process-oriented, more willing to live with their questions and seek answers together. We need guides who know how to strike a better balance between talking and listening.

Dealing with doubt is a fully relational task. German pastor and theologian Dietrich Bonhoeffer was concerned for the spiritual development of young people, especially young men, and became a partner-mentor to many of them. One of his students, Ferenc Lehel, recalls Bonhoeffer's response to his doubts:

> In my intellectual difficulties he stood by me, as a pastor, brotherly and friendly. When he recommended Karl Heim's *Glaube und Denken* to me he pointed out how Heim was able to feel at one with the doubter; how he did not indulge in cheap apologetics which from their lofty base fire upon the battlements of natural science. We must think with the doubter, he said, even doubt with him.[2]

As we shape communities where young people can express and process their doubts in secure, accepting relationships, we must also avoid making doubt a way of life. In our firm's research and in my interactions with young pastors, I have encountered "faith" communities where doubt is so entrenched that it has taken over completely, choking off Christian hope with cynicism and passion for the church's mission with apathy. Asking great questions can become an excuse for doing nothing. In *The Myth of Certainty*, Bethel University professor Daniel Taylor writes about his refusal to allow doubt to paralyze him when it arises: "I have learned to live with the rise and fall of the thoughts and feelings of faith, to co-exist with honest doubt, to accept tension and paradox without clinging to it as an excuse for inaction."[3]

The idea that action—*doing* faith—can disarm doubt's most crippling effects is a theme we'll return to in this chapter.

## Transitional Doubt

Two out of every five young people (38 percent) say they have experienced a time when they "significantly doubted their faith." We offered an array of options in our survey for why doubt arises, and a substantial number of respondents indicated that their doubts were rooted in personal, rather than intellectual, reasons.

- 12 percent said, "The death of a loved one has caused me to doubt."
- 18 percent said that they "have or had a crisis in life that has made me doubt my faith."
- 20 percent indicated that "church does not help me with depression or other emotional problems," which negatively affects his or her faith journey.

We might classify these types of doubt as *transitional*, arising out of a deeply affecting personal experience. Most believers experience transitional doubt at some point in their lives, yet not all receive the kind of support and encouragement from fellow believers that can catalyze it into a sustaining faith. Let me offer an example that may surprise you.

I met Helen at a Christian conference. After the first day of presentations, I was talking with the conference organizer, Jim Henderson.

"Did you meet Helen, the atheist?" Jim asked.

"You mean short Helen?" I remembered a vertically challenged woman with whom I'd had a brief conversation over lunch.

"Yeah, that Helen. She's not a believer. You should talk with her more tomorrow."

The next day when the training event for Christians resumed, I did just that. Helen confided that she had been a very committed, born-again

Christian for many years. Yet she had entered a season of serious mental health problems. "I'd had an active prayer life, but I began hearing voices—it was not normal or healthy. Sometimes I thought it was the voice of God, but at times it was other personalities I was developing for myself. It finally reached a point that I was literally going crazy and on the verge of a breakdown."

Helen paused and then said, "I had to act on my doubt and become an atheist, to save my mental health."

About one in four adults in the United States suffers from a diagnosable mental disorder.[4] Clinical depression is especially widespread, even among Christian leaders. My own father, a lifelong pastor in Phoenix, Arizona, has dealt with depression most of his adult life. He has spoken on the challenge of being in ministry while struggling with the disorder and has even written a critically acclaimed book on the subject, *Understanding Depression and Finding Hope*.

Of those Americans with a diagnosable mental illness, 6 percent are, like Helen, seriously ill.[5] It goes without saying that poor mental health can cause debilitating family, work, and personal problems—but it can also plant the seeds of soul-bending doubt. As common as these issues are, however, the Christian community does not always know how to respond. Helen experienced this: "When I went to talk about all of this with my pastor—a very good man who meant well and had been very important to my faith—he said I was silly to become an atheist. He understood I was struggling but said I should not abandon my faith in God. His capacity to really understand and relate to the conflict inside me was very superficial."

With all she had been through, I couldn't wrap my brain around Helen's presence at that Christian conference. I just had to ask, "What are you doing *here*?"

Her answer underscores the importance of faith in action as a corrective to unbelief: "I am here to help. I respect Christians. I love Jim and this conference. I don't know where my life will take me but I am definitely an atheist. I just can't bring myself to believe that there is a God who speaks because I am always on the edge. And I have a husband and kids to take care of. Being here, with people I like, *doing something* despite my unbelief is better than not doing anything."

## DOUBTING TURNS TO DOING

Creating faith communities where doubts of all kinds can be honestly, openly, and relationally explored is one way to make the turn with the next generation. Another is giving young adults an opportunity to put feet to their faith. Many of the deepest truths of Christianity become clear when we put our faith into action; in the *doing*, believing makes sense. Sometimes the best thing we can do with our unbelief is to stop fixating on it and get busy for the sake of others. We need to help young adults *do something* with their faith in order to contextualize their doubts within the church's mission.

Recently my father, who led a large church for many years, reminded me that his congregation encouraged anyone to participate in mission trips and service activities, regardless of where the person was spiritually. Even non-Christians could participate. Of course, they had committed Christians leading and teaching on these trips and activities but they did not require a person to be a Christian to serve.

"This caused a lot of challenges," he said, "because some church insiders thought people should know what they believe before being associated with the church. No one knew how to handle it when a young woman came up to one of our team leaders on an outreach to Guatemala and said, 'You know, I didn't really believe in God before this trip. But now I see what you are doing—what *we* are doing for these people. Now I want to follow Christ.'"

There is a place for winsome apologetics, yet to capture the heart of the next generation, we also need to help them become *doers of faith*—a phrase that comes from Scripture itself. James encouraged his fellow Christ-followers to be not merely hearers of the word, but doers (see James 1:22). How can we help young people turn their intellectual, institutional, unexpressed, and transitional doubts into something more than questions?

We cannot argue anyone—young or old—out of doubt. Only the Holy Spirit can do that. But we can try to appreciate how doubts affect real individuals and walk with them as they face vexing questions about life, God, and themselves—real individuals like John Sullivan. His confession—smack in the middle of *GQ*, mind you—still grabs me: "Once you've known [Jesus] as God, it's hard to find comfort in the man. The sheer sensation of life that comes with a total, all-pervading notion of being . . . the pull of that won't slacken. And one has doubts about one's doubts."[6]

Like Sullivan, there are millions of young adults rethinking church and faith—and they have doubts about their doubts. How can we help them act in faith, allowing their doubts to be "ants in the pants" of their quest for God?

Part 3

# RECONNECTIONS

# 11

# WHAT'S OLD IS NEW

## (Or, Three Things I Learned Studying the Next Generation)

The church in the West is struggling to connect with the next generation. We are dealing with the immense technological, spiritual, and social changes that define our times—the changing nature of access, new questions about authority, and increasing relational and institutional alienation. We are learning how to pass on a faith worth claiming in a new context. How can we prepare the next generation to live meaningfully and follow Jesus wholeheartedly in these changing times? And how can the next generation rise to the challenge of revitalizing the Christian community for our mission to and in the broader culture?

Now that we have met the nomads, prodigals, and exiles and explored their perceptions of the church and Christianity, allow me to share three things I have learned from studying the next generation: (1) the church needs to reconsider how we make disciples; (2) we need to rediscover Christian calling and vocation; and (3) we need to reprioritize wisdom over information as we seek to know God. As I have argued throughout this book, *the Christian community needs a new mind—a new way of thinking, a new way of relating, a new vision of our role in the world—to pass on the faith to this and future generations.*

As it turns out, this "new" mind is not so new. After countless interviews and conversations, I am convinced that historic and traditional practices, and orthodox and wisdom-laden ways of believing, are what the next generation really needs. This may sound like great news, and it is—but it is not a shortcut. Walking the ancient pathways of faith together in this new environment will not be easy. Yet I also believe that as we dig deeper into the historic Christian faith to nurture younger generations, the entire Western church will be renewed. Young Jesus-followers need older Christians to share the rich, fulfilling wine of faith, and the established church needs new wineskins into whom we can pour the church's future. We need each other.

Let's take a closer look at the three areas in which I believe God is calling us to renewed thinking.

## RETHINKING RELATIONSHIPS

Our modern idea of generations is overrated and may even distort our vision of how the church is designed to function. While generational demographics will remain an important way of approaching what I do as a market researcher, I have come to believe that we in the church must recapture the biblical concept of a generation. Chris Kopka is the one who turned my thinking upside down in this area. "David," he said one day, "you seem to assume that the church is a collection of separate generations, with the older generations given the responsibility of raising young people."

"Yes, I think that's true. Don't you?" To me, this way of thinking was obvious.

"That may be *part* of the picture, but there is a much bigger reality. A generation is every living person who is fulfilling God's purposes." Chris paused, probably because I looked confused. "In other words, while it is true there are different age groups represented in the church, the Bible seems to say that everybody in the church at a particular time make up a 'generation,' a generation that is working together in their time to participate in God's work."

The picture Chris painted that day was an aha moment for me.

*Original assumption:* The church exists to prepare the next generation to fulfill God's purposes.

*New thinking:* The church is a partnership of generations fulfilling God's purposes in their time.

What does this mean? The Christian community is one of the few places on earth where those who represent the full scope of human life, literally from the cradle to the grave, come together with a singular motive and mission. The church is (or should be) a place of racial, gender, socioeconomic, and cultural reconciliation—because Jesus commanded that our love would be the telltale sign of our devotion to him (see John 13:35)—as well as a community where various age demographics genuinely love each other and work together with unity and respect.

Flourishing intergenerational relationships should distinguish the church from other cultural institutions. The concept of dividing people into various segments based on their birth years is a very modern contrivance, emerging in part from the needs of the marketplace over the last hundred years. As goods were mass-produced, marketers sought new and effective ways to connect a given product or service to a specific niche or segment. Age (or generation) became one of those helpful "hooks"—a way to pitch, advertise, or attract a certain kind of buyer to one's wares.

In a misguided abdication of our prophetic calling, many churches have allowed themselves to become internally segregated by age. Most began with the valuable goal that their teaching be age appropriate but went on to create a systematized method of discipleship akin to the instructional model of public schools, which requires each age-group be its own learning cohort. Thus many churches and parishes segregate by age-group and, in doing so, unintentionally contribute to the rising tide of alienation that defines our times. As a by-product of this approach, the next generation's enthusiasm and vitality have been separated from the wisdom and experience of their elders. Just to be clear, I am not saying that we should suddenly do away with children's Sunday school or programs for youth. I am saying that our programs need to be re-evaluated and revamped where necessary to make intergenerational relationships a priority.

Rather than being defined by segregated age groups, however practical they may seem, I believe we are called to connect our past (traditions and elders) with our future (the next generation). Christians are members of a living organism called the church. In Scripture we find the infinite variety and eternal cohesiveness of this organism described in mind-blowing detail:

> You have come to Mount Zion, to the city of the living God, the heavenly Jerusalem, and to countless thousands of angels in a joyful gathering. You have come to the assembly of God's firstborn children, whose names are written in heaven. You have come to God himself, who is the judge over all things. You have come to the spirits of the righteous ones in heaven who have now been made perfect. You have come to Jesus, the one who mediates the new covenant between God and people.
>
> Hebrews 12:22–24 NLT

Intergenerational relationships matter on earth because they are a snapshot of Zion, a small but true picture of the majesty and diversity of God's people throughout the ages, who are citizens of the new reality God inaugurated in Jesus Christ. How can we recapture that sense of historical continuity, of a living, breathing body of Christ—of a divine assembly of the saints alive today and throughout the ages?

If you are a young Christian, whether a nomad or an exile, pursue wisdom from older believers. I want to really emphasize the idea of *pursuing* wisdom. One of the overriding themes of Proverbs is that wisdom is elusive. It's like love. It seems obvious and easy at first but then turns out to require patience and long-term commitment. Likewise, finding a wise and trustworthy mentor doesn't happen by accident. Knock on doors, send emails, make calls.

If younger generations are to avoid the mistakes of the past, young leaders desperately need a sense of what has gone before—and you can only get that sense from soul-shaping friendships with older Christians. Often I am surprised at how teenagers and young adults believe they are the first to think of an idea, a cause, or a way of doing something. (I know because I have thought this very thing.) Eventually most find that their idea was not so revolutionary after all; it just *seemed* hip and new. Meaningful relationships with older adults who are following Christ will help to ensure that your fresh ideas build on the incredible work of previous generations and that your passion to follow Jesus in this cultural moment is supported and upheld by this whole, living generation of believers.

If you are a Boomer or an Elder, I encourage you to come to grips with the revolutionary nature of the Mosaics' cultural moment. Young Christians are living through a period of unprecedented social and technological change, compressed in an astounding manner, and the longer we take to acknowledge and respond to these changes, the more we allow the disconnection between generations to progress. Ask yourself how available you have been to younger Christians. The generation gap is growing, fueled in part by technology, so it takes extra effort to be on the same page. Frankly, deep relationship happens only by spending time, and big chunks of it, in shared experiences. I encourage you to be ready for a fresh move of God, buoyed by young adults. Are you open to "reverse" mentoring, wherein you allow younger leaders to challenge your faith and renew the church?

If you lead a faith community, prioritize intergenerational relationships. For the most part, these connections won't happen by accident. You will need to catalyze them in your community and model them in your own life. This means you may have to challenge prevailing assumptions of "cool" ministry or chasten elder Christians focused on traditionalist preferences.

Perhaps you will have noticed that the "turns" in each of *You Lost Me*'s chapters in Part 2 have a relational aspect.

*Overprotective* → *Discernment*

We cast out fear by discerning our times and embracing the risks of cultural engagement.

*Shallow* → *Apprenticeship*

We leave shallow faith behind by apprenticing young people in the fine art of following Christ.

*Anti-science* → *Stewardship*

We respond to today's scientific culture by stewarding young people's gifts and intellect.

*Repressive* → *Relational*

We live by a relational sexual ethic that rejects traditionalist and individualist narratives of sex.

*Exclusion* → *Embrace*

We demonstrate the exclusive nature of Christ by rekindling our empathy for the "other."

*Doubting* → *Doing*

We faithfully work through our doubts by doing acts of service with and for others.

The relational element is so strong because relationship is central to disciple making—and, as we've said, the dropout problem is, at its core, a disciple-making problem. As we rediscover the centrality of relationship, I believe we must be willing to reimagine our structures of discipleship. Not all the programs we have put in place should be abandoned, but as we identify systems that are not effective, will we be willing to give them up?

*God-centered relationships create faithful, mature disciples.* In the final chapter, you'll find ideas for forming these meaningful relationships from older Christian leaders and from young nomads, prodigals, and exiles. It is my prayer that these practical ideas will start conversations in your community that lead to reconciliation between generations and fearless disciples of every age.

## REDISCOVERING VOCATION

The second thing I have learned through the process of our research is that the Christian community needs to rediscover the theology of *vocation*. There is confusion about this term, the use of which is often limited to trade or "vocational" education. But in Christian tradition, vocation is a biblically robust, directive sense of God's calling, both individually and collectively. Vocation is a clear mental picture of our role as Christ-followers in the world, of what we were put on earth to do as individuals and as a community. It is a centuries-old concept that has, for the most part, been lost in our modern expressions of Christianity.

For me, frankly, the most heartbreaking aspect of our findings is the utter lack of clarity that many young people have regarding what God is asking them to do with their lives. It is a modern tragedy. Despite years of church-based experiences and countless hours of Bible-centered teaching, millions of next-generation Christians have no idea that their faith connects to their life's work. They have access to information, ideas, and people from around the world, but no clear vision for a life of meaning that makes sense of all that input.

I believe God is calling the church to cultivate a larger, grander, more historic sense of our purpose as a body and as individuals. Let me illustrate with baseball.

I was privileged to meet the lead architect of PNC Park, the new stadium that the hapless Pittsburgh Pirates call home. Talking about his design, David Greusel said, "The old Three Rivers Stadium was built the same basic way as the donut-style, industrial-looking stadiums in Philadelphia and Cincinnati. It was a very cookie-cutter design. Even though it required enormous amounts of engineering and architectural planning, there was this sense that doing it the same as everyone else would save money and make for a congruent look to all these stadiums. But none of these stadiums were built to look like they belonged, embedded in the cities and contexts where they were built. They looked like alien ringed saucers, just landed from outer space.

"In designing the new ballpark, I spent weeks and weeks on the ground, walking downtown Pittsburgh, thinking about how the new stadium could *belong*. I wanted it to fit the work ethic and beauty of this city."

David accomplished that, as anyone could tell you who has seen Pittsburgh's skyline from the iconic yellow bridge that spans the outfield gap. I asked David about that picturesque view.

"We wanted fans to be able to see the city, the bridge, the river. The irony is that old Three Rivers Stadium was originally designed to have an outfield gap, which would have had a similar panorama of the city. But the owners at the time told the architect to take it out. You know why?"

"More seats?" I guessed.

"Exactly. It was all about getting more paying customers into the stadium. I am convinced that if Three Rivers had been built with that gap, it would still be here today. Sure, it would have needed refurbishing. And yes, the owners would have had to make do with fewer seats to sell," he said. "But it would have lasted. Their vision for what a stadium should be was shortsighted, and it cost the people of Pittsburgh more in the long run to build, tear down, and rebuild. PNC Park is a stadium that will last, not simply because of its beauty, but because it takes into account the city of Pittsburgh, its unique geography and ethos, and the people who built it."

Why do I tell you this story? Because I think we have a shortsighted vision for our ministries to young people. I think we are constantly building, tearing down, and rebuilding our youth and young adult development regimens based on the fallacy that more is better. The more "disciples" we can cram in our programs, the better. The more seats we can fill, the more good we will do . . . right?

We need new ways of measuring success. If you are in church ministry, one metric of success might be to help young people make one or two relational connections, younger to older, that lead to significant mentoring bonds that will last for several years. These relationships would not be solely focused on spiritual growth, but should integrate the pursuit of faith with the whole of life. What would it look like to begin measuring things like teens' and young adults' knowledge of and love for Scripture, their clarity about their gifts and vocation, their willingness to listen to the voice of God and follow his direction, the fruits of the Spirit in their lives, and the depth and quality of their love and service to others?

I can almost hear you saying, *Kinnaman, are you kidding? How could we ever measure those things?* I think it *is* possible to make accurate assessments, not in a mechanistic way, but from a place of relationship and apprenticeship. A mentor knows intimate details about the progress of his or her protégé. An effective, discerning parent has a pretty decent sense of what's working and not working in a child's life. Jesus was in close enough contact with his disciples that he was able to shape the rough-hewn edges of their faith and ministry. *Jesus knew his followers.* If our churches are too large to cultivate this type of knowing, then our ministries are likely too large to disciple as Jesus did.

If you are a parish or church leader or direct a faith-based institution, think about how the story of PNC Park also shows the importance of discerning institutional decision makers. Our work at Barna Group has given me an up close and personal look at the power of great leadership to transform lagging businesses, churches, and other organizations. And even though one factor in the you-lost-me problem is that we have tried to mass-produce disciples, this does not mean that institutions are unimportant or should go away; nothing could be further from the truth. The reality is that the reinvention of our colleges, schools, ministries, and local churches will play a significant role in helping the church as a whole develop our "new mind." Whether you influence a civic organization, ministry, church, business, or nonprofit, your wise, intentional choices can produce different and better outcomes for the next generation. We need new architects of faith formation within our established (and soon-to-be initiated) institutions.

If you are an older believer, become a mentor who is committed to nurturing the faith and life of a young Christian. When you spend time with the teen or young adult whom you are mentoring, don't just talk about the Bible (though that's important). Get together because you enjoy each other's company and friendship. Be attentive to what matters to the young adult. Help him or her get into the right school. Offer money for tuition. Be ready to guide decisions about gap years and dating relationships. Humbly share your struggles and your wisdom. Avoid impatience and the intent to control. Help the young person find God's unique and empowering vision for his or her life.

If you are a parent, cultivate your own sense of vocation and calling. Your life should reverberate with the rhythms of a life in pursuit of God's presence and mission. Sadly, many young people do not have a sense of vocation because millions of Christian parents have a vision of following Jesus that avoids anything more demanding than faithful church attendance. Our children can't "catch" what we don't already have. I pray that God will give us a vision for our lives and for theirs.

If you are a young person, take responsibility for your life and your future. Whether you are a prodigal, nomad, or exile—or on some other kind of journey—God isn't done with your story. I urge you to open your imaginative spirit to a larger, historic vision of the church, the one depicted by the writer of Hebrews: an assembly of saints, past and present, of angels, of God, and of Jesus Christ. You are called to be a part of that assembly, empowered by the Spirit to work alongside your sisters and brothers to serve and restore God's world.

*Following Jesus means finding a vocation.* In the final chapter, you'll find further ideas from young nomads, prodigals, and exiles and from older Christian leaders for rediscovering a deep sense of vocation within the body of Christ. I hope that these practical ideas will lead your community, young and old, to see visions and dream dreams of the work we can do together.

## REPRIORITIZING WISDOM

Finally, I have learned that the Christian community needs to reprioritize wisdom in order to live faithfully in a discontinuously different culture. Submerged as we are in a society that values fairness over justice, consuming over creating, fame over accomplishment, glamour over character, image over holiness, and entertainment over discernment, we need a blueprint for what life is meant to be. How can we live in-but-not-of lives in the world that surrounds us? In a culture skeptical of every kind of earthly authority, where information is dirt cheap and where institutions and leaders so often disappoint, *we need God-given wisdom.*

Wisdom is the spiritual, mental, and emotional ability to relate rightly to God, to others, and to our culture. We become wise as we seek Christ in the Scriptures, in the ongoing work of the Holy Spirit, in the practices and traditions of the church, and in our service to others. As we come to know and revere God—which, according to Proverbs 9:10, is the beginning of wisdom—he will make us wise. But this is often a painful process, as Hannah's story shows.

Through this research project, I have interviewed many young adults who are not yet willing to submit their lives to Jesus or to commit fully to the church. As one young nomad, Hannah, wrote: "It wasn't until five years after leaving home that I finally found my way back to God. Those five years were life changing and devastating. I told the church that they lost me, that this was somehow their fault. But really, I lost myself. I lost the sense of who I was in Christ. I stopped seeing that it mattered. If I couldn't even find myself, how could church leaders? I might blame other people for the mistakes I made, the choices I made, the friends I made—but in the end, the only pronoun I was using was 'I.' This was between me and God."

Hannah may have seemed lost along her faith journey, but she is on the path toward wisdom, toward a right relationship with God, with others, and with the world. We can all learn from Hannah, even those of us who have been faithful. When the Holy Spirit speaks to us as we read Jesus's parable of the prodigal son, for example, we may see ourselves in the rebel younger brother or the hypocritical older sibling.

If you identify with the younger brother, ask God if it's time to "come to your senses" as the wayward son did (see Luke 15:17). If you're a nomad or a prodigal, I urge you to search your heart with the help of the Holy Spirit. Maybe it's time to return home. If you've experienced the ugly side of Christian community, I hope that you will ask God to help you forgive those who hurt you—and that hurts from the past will no longer keep you from reconnecting with those who are stumbling along behind Jesus. These Christians, like me, are trying their best (but sometimes doing their worst) to follow him.

Perhaps, after some soul-searching, you discover yourself in the older brother's story. I have interviewed older churchgoers who lament the disrespect of teens and twentysomethings in their congregation but have never bothered to learn the names of those very same young people. Like the "older brother," we may find comfort in the rules and regulations of religion while inwardly nursing offense toward those who are accepted by the Father even when they fail to follow the rules. Let's be honest with ourselves and release the resentments that have kept us from celebrating God's children in the next generation. If you identify with the older brother, your faithfulness is to be commended, but only so long as it is not a roadblock to reconciliation. Will you let go of anxiety, fear, control, and impatience and enter joyfully into the feast God has prepared to welcome home his lost ones?

In this iconic parable, Jesus offers a glimpse of the Father's heart. Through his life, ministry, death, and resurrection, Jesus pulls back the curtain of heaven to show us the very face of God. As we follow Christ, teach and study God's Word, live in the Spirit, and practice community with the saints, we will become the kind of disciples who make disciples.

*Wisdom empowers us to live faithfully in a changing culture.* In the final chapter you'll find further ideas from young nomads, prodigals, and exiles and from older Christian leaders about reprioritizing wisdom. I pray that these practical ideas will ignite in you and in your community a thirst for Jesus that will be quenched only as you seek him together.

Share your faith journey or discover how you can serve the next generation at www.youlostmebook.com.

# 12

# FIFTY IDEAS TO FIND A GENERATION

Whem we wrote *unChristian*, my coauthor, Gabe Lyons, had to convince me that contributions from Christian thinkers and practitioners would add to the project. I'm so glad he did, because the whole point of that book was to start people thinking and talking about the public's perceptions of Christianity. In retrospect, it's easy for me to see that the ideas offered by our contributors are among the significant ways God has inspired readers to move from thinking and talking (both important) to doing and changing (where necessary).

Now that we have reached the end of *You Lost Me*, it's my hope that—whether you are young or old, prodigal or nomad, exile or dedicated member of an established church—you will be inspired to take a similar journey. To spark some thinking and talking (and eventually doing and changing), I have asked a number of people to contribute their best ideas for how the Christian community might cultivate a "new mind" for understanding and discipling the next generation. Some of these contributors are well-known, while others are not. Some have seen a majority of their years pass, while others are just emerging as adults.

Some offer ideas for older believers and institutional leaders to consider, while others speak directly to young Christians and dropouts.

Not every idea will relate to your particular situation (every story matters!), but you are likely to find at least one that resonates with you, your parents, your children, your youth or college group, your organization, or your church community. When you do, I hope the conversations you start will lead to deeper, whole-life discipleship that shapes your relationships, your vocation, and your pursuit of God.

Two notes before we dive in. First, contributing an idea is not an endorsement of everything in this book. Likewise, I do not agree with every idea you find here—and that's intentional. One of the big lessons I have relearned through this project is that we don't have to agree on everything to remain in Christ-centered community. Second, these fifty ideas are only the beginning. At the *You Lost Me* website, www .YouLostMeBook.com, you'll find more ideas from contributors such as Mark Batterson, Margaret Feinberg, Adam Hamilton, Reggie Joiner, Dan Kimball, Mac Pier, Greg Stier, and many more. You can also share your own best idea for creating the "new mind" we need to be and make disciples as Jesus commanded.

Here are fifty to get us started.

## IDEAS FOR EVERYONE

### 1. First, Be Honest

In this book, you've received an invitation into an honest conversation. When you're honest with your story, when you share the truth about who you are and what you struggle with, you give others a tremendous gift: the gift of going second.

It's so much harder to go first. None of the rules have been set. The boundaries have not been drawn. The borders of the land have not been clearly marked, especially when it comes to Christian circles. But that's what we're called to do, to throw ourselves on the honesty grenade. To share and live the truth. When we do, we give everyone the gift of going second. It's so much easier to go second. You don't have to perform or shine up your mistakes to look like a "real Christian" or a "good Christian." The monster of pretending to be perfect has already been laid to rest.

If you want to reach this generation and every generation to come, go first with your story and give everyone around you the gift of going second.

**Jon Acuff**
speaker, launcher, and author of *Quitter: Closing the Gap Between Your Day Job & Your Dream Job* and *Stuff Christians Like*

## 2. Confess

Most Christian organizations create a culture that dissuades confession. We create codes of conduct for youth that we either don't live by or strive to live by without confessing our failures. All this does is create a dissonance that eventually deconstructs into a hypocritical church. Instead of policies that help sinners rebound, we create communities that isolate sinners, either from the community by expulsion or within themselves because they have to keep sin hidden (leading a double life). Honor codes essentially become "don't ask, don't tell" documents—it's no wonder so many churched young adults leave the church!

The Bible says we create a community of healing and joy by confessing our sins to God *and to our brothers and sisters* (see James 5:16). Let's wear our mistakes like a red badge of courage, for the blood soaked in our bandages is not ours, but from the One who healed us.

So go ahead. Confess and get kicked out. Confess and lose respect. Confess and lose your job. Confess and sleep on the couch. Confess and be saved from your sin. Confess and be part of a true Christian community. Confess and never be apart from the One who truly loves and truly forgives.

**Michael DiMarco**
CEO of Hungry Planet and author of *God Guy: Becoming the Man You're Meant to Be*

## 3. Increase Your Expectations

We have done everything humanly possible to make church "easy." We kept the services short and entertaining, discipleship and evangelism optional, and moral standards low. Our motives were not bad. We figured we could attract more people by offering Jesus with minimal commitment. But we ended up producing nominal Christians whose unchanged lives have deterred others from being interested.

There is a new generation rising up. Young adults are studying the Bible without missing the obvious. They see how shallow methodology is incongruent with the Jesus of Scripture who asked everything of his followers. They are bored with Sunday morning productions and long to experience the Holy Spirit. They need to be challenged with the awesome responsibility of praying for, baptizing, and making disciples of their acquaintances. They need to be reminded of the Spirit who supernaturally empowers them for this task.

The days of merely bringing our friends to an event so the pastor can save and disciple them need to end. New churches must be formed where *all* believers are expected to do the work of evangelism and discipleship. This generation sees the potency of a church where pastors equip and shepherd disciple-makers rather than service-attenders.

**Francis Chan**
author of *Crazy Love* and *Forgotten God* and host of the BASIC.series

## 4. Preach a Better Gospel

The consumer gospel that promises a life of happiness from now until eternity is wearing thin for street-smart, networked young adults. This gospel of personal fulfillment is either bolted onto the busy lives of twenty- and thirtysomethings as a lifestyle improvement app or dismissed as a cheap marketing pitch. Either way, this gospel is powerless to help the next generation resist the riptide of consumerism, individualism, and materialism that is the dark side of our modern culture. We need to rediscover the Bible's grand narrative and teach an all-encompassing, multi-dimensional gospel. By showing how the life and death of Christ brings reconciliation with God, neighbor, creation, and self, young adults will hear the call to live as a prophetic sign of God's coming kingdom.

**Krish Kandiah**
executive director of Churches in Mission, England, director of UK Evangelical Alliance, and author of *Destiny: What Is Life All About?*

## 5. Hand-Craft Disciples

If we really want to help someone grow, we will have to help them in a way that fits their wiring. Our great model for this is God himself, for he always knows just what each person needs.

He had Abraham take a walk, Elijah take a nap, Joshua take a lap, and Adam take the rap. He gave Moses a forty-year time out, he gave David a harp and a dance, and he gave Paul a pen and a scroll. He wrestled with Jacob, argued with Job, whispered to Elijah, warned Cain, and comforted Hagar. He gave Aaron an altar, Miriam a song, Gideon a fleece, Peter a name, and Elisha a mantle. Jesus was stern with the rich young ruler, tender with the woman caught in adultery, patient with the disciples, blistering with the scribes, gentle with the children, and gracious with the thief on the cross.

God never grows two people the same way. God is a hand-crafter, not a mass-producer. And now it is your turn.

God has existed from eternity, but he wants to do a new thing with you. The problem many people face when it comes to spiritual growth is that they listen to someone they think of as the expert—maybe the pastor of their church—talk about what he does, and think that is what they are supposed to do. When it doesn't work for them—because they are a different person!—they feel guilty and inadequate. They often give up. But spiritual growth is hand-crafted, not mass-produced. God does not do "one-size-fits-all."

**John Ortberg**
senior pastor of Menlo Park Presbyterian Church, Menlo Park, California, and author of *The Me I Want to Be* and *The Life You've Always Wanted*

## 6. Recover Imagination

There's a reason the Bible begins with creativity, anthropology, and vocation—because these are what it means to be human. Miss this and you'll miss a whole lot about what it means to be a follower of Jesus in the here and now and in the life to come. Why Christians fail to emphasize imagination and creativity when God's Book about being human clearly does is a great mystery to me.

The greatest gift we can give future followers is to recover the imaginative, creative life that is born through the saving grace of God and hold it out as an invitation to follow. What if an invitation to follow Jesus went something like this: Come meet Jesus. He has the power to forgive sins and the power to renew all of life. He is inviting you to come alongside him as his kind of imaginative, loving person in the creative life of caring for earth and people. He is renewing all that he loves. He is the maker whose Word to us begins and ends with creativity. He has made all things and he's making all things new.

This is the big story God has invited us into.

**Charlie Peacock**
musician, producer, and co-founder of Art House America

## 7. Recognize Giftedness

A breakthrough moment for me was the realization, found in Exodus chapter 31, that spiritual gifts are not limited to what we call "ministry." In shockingly plain language, God tells Moses that he has filled Bezalel and Oholiab "with the Spirit of God" for working in design, craftsmanship, and decoration to guide their work on the tabernacle. While their task was to create a place for the people to meet with God, their gifting was for design, not for ministry per se.

Understanding this passage made clear to me that my calling as an architect is not secondary to work that I do in and for the local church. In fact, it may be that God wants me to be the best architect I can be even more than he wants me to teach Sunday school. This idea seemed somewhat heretical to me a few years ago, but as I have lived into it, I have come to see its truth. God has gifted and called people to be butchers and bakers and website designers. Some of that work can benefit the church, but the vast majority of it is intended to benefit the world at large, beyond the doors of the church.

It's tremendously freeing to realize that what God has uniquely created you to do is exactly what he wants you to do—that you don't have to spend three-fourths of your life toiling at insignificant work so you can afford to go on a mission trip. All legitimate work is significant, all of it is valuable, because it's all part of God's common grace for the common good.

**David Greusel**
owner of Convergence Design and lead designer of PNC Park, Pittsburgh, Pennsylvania and Minute Maid Park, Houston, Texas

## 8. Invite Participation

I am convinced that both the church and art are fully realized when they are fully participatory. There is art that is created by professional artists, and it is there to be observed and appreciated. Then there is the kind of art that says, *Come one, come all*—picture preschoolers in smocks finger-painting and memory-care patients making beaded crafts. It is inclusive and valuable because it is simply creative. I'm afraid our quest for "excellence in worship," which has been a focus in the church for several years now, has set the stage for congregants to sit in our services like Simon Cowell, judge on *American Idol*, deciding over lunch what part of the service had the "X-factor," instead of asking themselves how they might engage and contribute.

While I can't get on board with a general cynicism about the church, I can appreciate the desire, especially in young people, for an opportunity to participate, the rejection of commodity and performance-based services, and the longing for real mission and service together. Art at its purest is not a commodity or a performance, and the church is alive when we are problem-solving, studying and serving together, and engaging our local communities and the issues facing them with the kingdom creativity of the gospel.

**Sara Groves**
singer-songwriter and music producer

## 9. Take Risks

In a post-9/11 world, the word *radical* makes us nervous. It reminds us of religious extremists, so to avoid confusion we dial down Christian passion. But to mute the radical nature of God's love in order to avoid religious extremism is like turning down the radio in order to stop the car. Extremism operates at ideology's thin and brittle edges, whereas the radical shape of God's love is found at Christianity's pulsating core: the life, death, and resurrection of Jesus Christ. The root of Christian faith is the cross, the consequences of God's love for us.

Doing radical things for our faith means imitating Christ even if it makes us look silly, or if it loosens our grip on some part of the American dream. Yet these risks are not lost on young people who know in their toes that Christianity is a dangerous thing. They know, perhaps better than we do, the price to be paid for trading in travel soccer for Sunday morning worship, for choosing a low-paying job instead of dealing drugs, for seeking a vocation and not just a profession. What about giving away 20 percent of our income? Casting our lot with a struggling faith community instead of a thriving one? Using vacation money to build an orphanage or risking ridicule by practicing chastity? In some communities, staying in school through graduation is a radical measure; in others, risking a promotion to be home with your kids is.

Radical faith is not about doing edgy things, but about embodying the self-giving love of Jesus Christ—a love that that risks suffering and matters more than life itself. Is Christianity worth the risk? Young people are watching and waiting to find out.

**Kenda Creasy Dean**
professor of youth, church, and culture at Princeton Theological Seminary and author of *Almost Christian: What the Faith of Our Teenagers Is Telling the American Church*

## 10. Re-center on Jesus

We undersell Jesus. We merely describe Jesus as a partner, Jesus as a means, Jesus as an escape. We seldom present Jesus as the source and center of joy that he is. In our failure to do so, we leave young seekers hungry and unsatisfied. We lead them to think that they must satiate their God-given desire for joy in something else. They look for it in fun, family, business or cultural goods, holiness or purity, sex or adventure. All of these are good, but none of them are ultimate. And so these young seekers wander. Looking, but never finding. Tell the next generation the truth: Jesus is the only source and must be the center of joy for every person.

**Britt Merrick**
founder of the Reality family of churches and author of *Big God: What Happens When We Trust Him*

# IDEAS FOR THE NEXT GENERATION

## 11. Don't Overreact

When challenging old conclusions, assumptions, and paradigms of thought, it is sometimes difficult to determine what to keep and what not to keep. We must be more thoughtful than to merely react to what we don't appreciate about the past, or we'll succumb to our own set of cultural blinders even as we despise the cultural blindness of the previous generation.

Simply put, reactionary thinking plagues much of evangelicalism—whether to conservatism or to liberalism, whether to perceived moral laxity or to perceived legalism, whether by resisting all cultural change or by accommodating it at all cost.

"We won't do it like them!" is no solution. We need a rich understanding of church history to inform our criticisms, a humble respect for the Holy Spirit's work in the lives and times of our spiritual parents to overshadow confidence in ourselves, and a courageous commitment to biblical authority to frame any efforts at reform.

**John Stonestreet**
speaker and writer for Summit Ministries and the Colson Center for Christian Worldview and the voice of *The Point*, a daily radio feature on worldview and culture

## 12. Be a Rebel—Get Married

A key reason why emerging adults are MIA from their congregations is the collision of sexual and religious impulses in their lives. The two seem incompatible. In fact, emerging adults are marrying on average five years later than their parents did. (Those are five libido-packed years, let me remind you.) The impulse toward sexual oneness is a strong one, but young Christians are beginning to resist the centuries-old narrative that marriage is good, earthy, and feasible—that it's what Christians in love are supposed to do next. Too many emerging-adult Christians are settling for cohabitation, convinced that in a divorcing culture they're being shrewd to proceed with caution. Moving in together, however, has a way of squashing the religious impulse—the one that motivates us to meet together in public worship, which has long been a hallmark of our common faith. Rising together for Sunday morning worship just seems odd in that scenario. So it goes dormant in favor of other forms of spirituality. Cohabitation, however, isn't a rebellious act—not when it's the norm. No, the countercultural move for emerging-adult Christians is marriage.

**Mark Regnerus**
associate professor of sociology and faculty research associate at the UT Austin Population Research Center and author of *Premarital Sex in America* and *Forbidden Fruit*

## 13. Take a Gap Year

Taking a gap year before going to college creates a remarkable opportunity for students to think more deeply and intentionally about the person God is calling him or her to be. Many students who struggle in college do so because they are not able to articulate reasons or explain goals for going to college. College has become the assumed next step after high school, with very little thought about *why*.

A growing trend among Christian camps, churches, and parachurch ministries is to provide a gap year experience for students that forces them out of the routine of "schooling" and into a deeper relationship with God. These residential programs typically last nine months; focus on worldview, identity, and service; and include a cross-cultural experience. While not for everyone, many students who participate in gap year programs are far more prepared for the transition to college and adulthood.

As followers of Christ, we are challenged to "not conform to the pattern of this world" (Rom. 12:2). This is a reminder that the church is shaped by a different story with a different definition of success. Too many students and parents allow the "world's story" to direct their higher education decisions and fail to think critically and biblically about the best steps for life after high school. Participating in a gap year program is a helpful way to counter this trend.

**Derek Melleby**
director of College Transition Initiative and author of *Make College Count: A Faithful Guide to Life and Learning*

## 14. Take Education Seriously

Education should lead us to know, love, and serve God. We know God through faith and reason, and this is what education must strive to achieve.

As Pope John Paul II wrote, "Faith and reason are like two wings on which the human spirit rises to contemplation of the truth; and God has placed in the human heart a desire to know the truth—in a word, to know Himself—so that, by knowing and loving God, men and women may also come to the fullness of truth about themselves" (Encyclical Letter, September 15, 1998).

I write this as a brand-new graduate of Thomas Aquinas College, ready to take on the world. I've been blessed with four years of Catholic liberal arts education—four years of theology, philosophy, mathematics, science, and literature—that has led me to God through both faith and reason. I feel anchored in the truth and ready to share it with others. I know many are unwilling to hear it. I only wish they too could see what I see and think what I think—not because I wish to conquer them, but because I want the truth to set them free. I feel the contagion of my own happiness and wish only for the chance to spread it to others. I can't help believing that if they had the chance to see the marriage of faith and reason, they too would embrace the Way and the Truth and the Life.

**Monica Shaneyfelt**
class of 2011, Thomas Aquinas College

## 15. Interpret Culture

The Bible begins with the marriage of Adam and Eve and ends with the marriage of Christ and the church. Right in the middle, we find an unabashed celebration of erotic love called the Song of Songs. I believe that every love song ever written (and oh, how many have been written!) is an attempt, however broken, to enter the Song of Songs. All we need do is turn on the radio and—*if we listen*—hear the cry of the heart for love, which is to say, the cry of the heart for Christ. Inasmuch as a culture's songs provide a window into its soul, I think the rise of rock music in the 1950s and '60s is very telling. If we can recognize the Song of Songs as the "soundtrack" of Christianity, I think "rock and roll" could be described as the "soundtrack" of the sexual revolution. I'm not saying this to condemn rock music. I'm saying it so we know how to *redeem* it.

The Song of Songs expresses properly directed eros. Rock music often expresses misdirected eros. "Untwist" the distortions of rock music and what do we find? We glimpse the love of the Song of Songs, and we discover that we've been looking for Christ all along.

**Christopher West**
research fellow and faculty member of the Theology of the Body Institute and founder of theCORproject

## 16. Find the Family of God

Family is a catch-22 for my generation. Many of us, me included, carry deep wounds from the circumstances of our journey to adulthood. Yet most of us—according to some studies, 9 out of 10—desire to be married and raise families of our own. How can these conflicting emotions be reconciled?

Nothing short of the Christian faith is adequate to the task. We Millennials must absorb the "whys" of God's design for families. And we must not be discouraged from pursuing an understanding of these truths just because those who came before us modeled them poorly, or because culture has no use for them, or because we don't like the white-hot rhetoric of fellow believers who advocate for them in the political arena.

Millennials have been called the "justice generation." It's time we seize some of that justice for ourselves, by refusing to settle for the counterfeits to marriage and family we have inherited. We must harness the passionate conviction that makes us yearn to live a story larger than ourselves, then focus on processing and promoting God's script for marriage and family. If we embrace this cause the same way we embrace many others, we will see hearts heal, restore hope, and turn this world upside down.

**Esther Fleece**
special assistant to the president for millennial relations, Focus on the Family

## 17. Find Calling in the Marketplace

As men and women in the marketplace, we must first figure out what purpose God has for our businesses, and then lean on biblical principles and theology to actually shape and grow these businesses. Thankfully, we have some role models. Mars Inc.'s economics of mutuality creates sustainable communities in East Africa. Chick-fil-A's servant leadership equips its owner-operators to celebrate the stories of its employees and customers. DEMDACO emphasizes aesthetics in order to lift the spirits of everyone it touches. Servicemaster uses the principle of subsidiarity to empower its entrepreneurs. While these efforts may seem "soft," they reflect an attempt to find a "marketplace shalom" that leads to human flourishing—an attempt to find convergence between the real marketplace and the real kingdom.

Unlike many entrepreneurs before us, we need not wait to find significance in God's call for us until we have had our success. We can accept God's call in Genesis: to be co-creators in this majestic playground he calls his kingdom.

**Evan Baehr**
Harvard Business School

# IDEAS FOR PARENTS

## 18. Strengthen Family Ties

When I started my journey away from the Christian faith, I was worried about how my parents would take the news. They are both ordained ministers, and I grew up in the church—we even spent five years as missionaries in Africa. My sister encouraged me to be honest with them, and after a few months, I got up the courage and dropped the bomb.

I don't think they were disappointed in me—more sad and wondering where they went wrong. But true to their usual goodness, they let me know that they love me and that nothing can change that. I felt and still feel the same about them. Yet there is an inevitable disconnect that developed as a result of my walking away. A family like mine is rooted in the foundation of the Bible and faith in Jesus—careers, relationships, weddings, funerals, most holidays, and weekend activities. I have respect for my family and their faith, for how it has formed their lives and, in turn, informed mine. But by my own choice I no longer share in those beliefs so I find myself the odd man out, even though I know they don't think of me that way.

In the end, we are family and the love we hold dear is something none of us will let go of, ever.

**Tim Hawkins**
nonprofit administrator, Ojai, California

## 19. Think Christianly about Media

One of my greatest struggles as a believer has been the battle to integrate my faith into all of life. If the gospel is truly transformative for *all* of life, which areas of my life have I kept sheltered from its touch? This same struggle is front and center in the lives of the emerging generations today . . . with some unique nuances. One glaring area of omission in our ministries to youth and young adults is our failure to teach them how to integrate their faith into their media use. The most recent research tells us that the average 8- to 18-year-old is spending more than seven hours a day engaged with media.

If all we can muster up is a few media "don'ts" that keep our kids from media violence, sex, and profanity, we're continuing to fail. We must go out of our way to disciple kids into thinking Christianly and biblically about their media use by teaching them to recognize worldview elements, evaluate those elements in light of God's Word, and then make media choices that bring honor and glory to God. Let's stop thinking about media *for* them. Instead, take the time to think Christianly *with* them, so that they might be prepared for a lifetime of integrating their faith into their media use and practices.

**Walt Mueller**

founder and president of the Center for Parent/Youth Understanding and author of *Engaging the Soul of Youth Culture*

## 20. Avoid "Proxy Wars"

When the topic of faith gets too contentious, debate often gets channeled to other arenas. Rather than talk about God, we end up fighting "proxy wars" over inessentials. Yes, it's tempting to vent irritation over a young doubter's party lifestyle or political views or choice of relationships, but these are bad hills to die on. Avoid getting sucked into debates about peripheral issues. Too often we become embroiled in these proxy wars and unintentionally alienate our loved ones who are struggling with doubt. Even if we manage to convince them that, say, our morality and politics are superior, will that really lead them back to the faith?

Instead, focus on nurturing the relationship and building bridges of trust. And save your most impassioned words to talk about the gospel—the life, death, and resurrection of Jesus. Their lifestyles and opinions may well be contrary to Christian truth, but our job isn't to straighten out all their opinions; it's to light the path back to Christ. In theological terms, don't expect sanctification to precede salvation. Only when they've had a dynamic encounter with Christ will he resume his transformational work in their lives.

**Drew Dyck**

managing editor of *Leadership Journal* and author of *Generation Ex-Christian: Why Young Adults Are Leaving the Faith . . . and How to Bring Them Back*

## 21. Refuse a Religious Veneer

You lost me too when I was about fifteen or sixteen. I wanted no part of an institution filled with hypocrites who "talked the talk" without "walking the walk." But in my early twenties I began searching for truth instead of searching for a church. My search led me right back to Christ. I realized I had thrown the baby out with the bathwater. Most people who leave the church are not really rejecting God or Christ. They are rejecting an institution or specific people who claim to represent him. We can make the good news sound like bad news by distorting and obscuring the amazing, all-loving God who wants to embrace us in spite of our sins, our shortcomings, or our legitimate questions.

Young people are looking for answers and for authenticity. When they see a church or Christians seemingly more concerned with appearances than with truth, more concerned about rules than love, and more concerned with money and success than poverty and justice, is it any surprise that they flee? And parents, what do your own children see when they look at you? Do they see lives deeply dedicated to following Christ in every dimension of life or do they see only a religious veneer with a walk that doesn't match your talk? Young people have a sensitive nose for phonies and for hypocrisy. And when they smell them, they run the other way.

**Richard Stearns**
president of World Vision US and author of *The Hole in Our Gospel*

## 22. Travel as a Family

Our family's growth has been accelerated by our international travel. Our children have grown up consistently exposed to the truths of Scripture but, like many, find the allure of the world quite distracting. They can become disinterested in Truth. We trust the Holy Spirit's work in their hearts in this regard, but we also seek to compliment his work by giving them experiences that challenge their notions of what it looks like to really follow Jesus. Something happens inside when you find yourself getting to know someone who makes less than a dollar a day but who, at the same time, rejoices in giving to their local church. Our kids have been impacted deeply by seeing that although much of the world does not live like them, as brothers and sisters in Christ we all share the same joy of salvation.

Travel is not a "quick fix," but allows for connection with the global church and an understanding of the small role we play in making up the body of Christ. Our children have stared at poverty's brutality and the world's injustices. And because of this, they rejoice in the beauty of Christ all the more.

**Todd and Susan Peterson**
former NFL player, Atlanta, Georgia

## 23. Be Present

If you can do one thing that will preserve your faith in the faith of your child or children, it is being present. The essence of love is presence—presence with someone, knowledge that you are together regardless of what happens and what they do, and a conviction that you are on a shared journey into the goodness God has planned.

There are three practical ways you can be present with your child. First, eat together five evenings or more per week. Second, know what your kid does every day throughout the day. Third, include your child in your life so they know what you like, what you don't like, what you do and where you go. These ideas may sound mundane, but presence is practiced in the everyday of life.

As you eat together and participate in each other's lives, *guide them to Jesus.* I don't mean church and I don't mean salvation and I don't mean Christianity, though each is part of it. But these make absolutely no sense until they are connected to Jesus. Talk to your kids about Jesus, read the Gospels with them, tell them about how the apostles preached Jesus as Messiah and Lord. But above all, make sure you are a follower of Jesus and show them how Jesus shapes your life. If Jesus is in your life, then guiding your kids to Jesus is taking them to the center of the presence of your life with God and their life with you.

**Scot McKnight**
Karl A. Olsson professor in religious studies at North Park University and author of *The Jesus Creed* and *One.Life: Jesus Calls, We Follow*

# IDEAS FOR PASTORS, CHURCH LEADERS, AND CHRISTIAN ORGANIZATIONS

## 24. Be Intentionally Intergenerational

For too long, we have assumed that we do good youth or young-adult ministry when we separate kids from the rest of the church. Of course, there are times when 6 and 16 and 66 year-olds need to be on their own with folks in their same life stage, but we have swung the pendulum too far. We have *segregated* (believe me, this is not a verb I use lightly) students and young adults from the rest of the church—and it's hurting their faith.

Our *Sticky Faith* research shows that the more high school and college students are engaged in the overall life of the church, the stronger their faith. We're seeing churches experimenting with countless intergenerational connections, ranging from short-term service to hobby mentoring (e.g., cooking, gardening, art) to intentional small groups. Plus lots of churches are taking the "adult" events they already do (e.g., women's breakfasts, men's dinners) and strategically inviting kids to join in.

I believe the future of youth and young-adult ministry is intergenerational. It's good for students and young adults, and it's great for the church.

**Kara Powell**
executive director of the Fuller Youth Institute and co-author of *Sticky Faith*

## 25. Disciple Like Jesus

When he walked this earth, Jesus ministered to crowds but invested the majority of his time, energy, gifts—his life—in the next generation of young leaders. He invited them into close relationship and challenged them to take responsibility in God's mission. His life was accessible, and from him they learned not only about God's Word, but how an intimate relationship with the Father flows with kingdom power. His life was transparent, and so they learned how he treated the opposite sex, how he handled money, success, pressure, and pain. Jesus was secure enough to invite this young, inexperienced team to share his calling. He gave them opportunity to grow, fail, and mature. Then he gave them the movement to lead and stepped away. And the world was transformed.

The "new mind" we need for today's young adults is an ancient path called discipleship.

**Jo Saxton**
director of 3DM and author of *Real God Real Life* and *Influential*

## 26. Make Connections

We don't need leaders to create atmosphere, we need them to cultivate relationships. It's in the context of relationships that we gain a sense of belonging. And it's out of a sense of belonging in the church that we embrace our identity in the world.

The reason college age people are not connecting to churches is because they lack relationships with those in them and therefore don't feel like they belong. Churches that are intentional about connecting college age people with older adults, evaluating themselves based on quality of relationships rather than only quantifying measurements, and holding older adults accountable for discipling younger people will provide sustainable connections between generations.

**Chuck Bomar**
founder of CollegeLeader.org and author of *Worlds Apart: Understanding the Mindset and Values of 18–25 Year Olds*

## 27. Release Your Successors

What if we older, more established church leaders who hold the authority, property, money, and other church resources were to hunt down eclectic, somewhat ragtag, young women and men, and give our power and stuff to them with the instruction, "We choose you precisely because you are *not* like us. Here is your charge: Go after those who are seeking God. *Do not* copy our ways. *Do not* do what we have done. Innovate. Try. Fail. Succeed. Forge a new path. Build new kinds of churches and communities. Show us a new world founded on love, not doctrine. We will help and give advice only when asked. Now get on with your task. We are with you!"

The probable result? Some losses and many wins. The biggest winners will be the young adults who would otherwise be left out of and leaving our traditional churches—not because of any distaste for Jesus but because we're just plain out of touch.

**Ken and Deborah Loyd**
authors of *They're Gentiles for Christ's Sake* and pastor of HOMEpdx, Portland, Oregon

## 28. Meet a Need

I've never thought of myself as a "church-planter." After all, our neighborhood has a ton of "churches." What we really need is not more churches but *one church*, working together as a body—missionally, redemptively—on our streets. We are "community planters," starting up Christian communities that join the local congregations and indigenous neighborhood pastors around us. We're not parachurch. We're pro-church.

One of the coolest things that we've got going here at The Simple Way emerged from men in the neighborhood and local pastors who had seen enough kids grow up in a fatherless society and become statistics. They started a discipleship program for young men called *Timoteo*\* (Spanish for "Timothy"). It is now a flag-football league with nearly 200 youth on a dozen or so teams— and every team is sponsored by a local congregation. Young men feel loved, develop character, discover Jesus, and learn conflict resolution (where better to learn gospel nonviolence than on the football field?). But here's what else has happened: Timoteo has become a mission to the church, getting folks out of buildings and onto the football field. Pastors who might not usually get together unite in a common mission to mentor young men and love them into Jesus.

**Shane Claiborne**
author of *The Irresistible Revolution: Living as an Ordinary Radical* and founder of The Simple Way, Philadelphia, Pennsylvania

\*If you'd like to sponsor a team, or buy some jerseys for us, check out timoteofootball.com.

## 29. Reclaim Hope

Faith and hope are inextricably linked. Faith is trust in the absurd reality that, through Christ's death, the God of the cross is now found in dead places bringing new life. Faith is trust that, next to your own thousand little deaths, the God of life will be present. Faith is the willingness to stand in the reality of death and seek for God.

If faith is trust in "the foolishness of the cross," then *hope* is anticipating the coming of God's new reality (new creation, new humanity, new life). Faith is a life in the heaviness of the now, bent toward the future that is coming—hope is the anticipation of this future. The father in Mark 9 who says, "I believe, help my unbelief!" has faith, even next to his doubt, because he is willing to risk hope. *There is no faith without hope.*

Our problem in youth ministry is not that we don't take faith seriously, but that we don't take hope seriously. To help young people have faith in the crucified God, we need to nurture hope in God's new reality breaking in even now. We need to imagine with them the mystery of God's future and recognize the places of longing for that fulfillment within ourselves and our world. Practicing hope gives us and them eyes to see and courage to trust the God who brings life out of death.

**Andrew Root**
assistant professor of youth and family ministry at Luther Seminary and author of *The Theological Turn in Youth Ministry*

## 30. Seek Diversity

Faith development needs to look different from what a traditional white church has historically provided. Youth need to hear from people that look and think differently than they do. This means actively seeking ethnic, gender, socioeconomic, and ability diversity. Our demographics are changing, and we need to face the fact that our churches and parachurch organizations need to change. Story is central in this development, so churches and parachurch organizations need to provide a safe space for youth to share their stories. Only then, I believe, will our young people be able to develop their faith in a vibrant way. We need to acknowledge and talk about our differences in order to understand who God is.

**Joel Perez**
dean of transitions and inclusion at George Fox University

## 31. Use Time Wisely

Time has become a precious commodity for this generation, and they have many choices about where and how to spend it. Whether they are rich or poor, popular or unknown, smart or of average intelligence, they only have

24 hours to spend each day. What are we as a church offering that is a better value for their time than other opportunities? The answer is not better programming, creativity, or special effects. These teens are interested in the kind of power and community that only come from Jesus.

Once I realized this, I began to ask myself as I interacted with teens, "Where is the power?" Too often I summarized Scripture rather than sharing it with them directly. I promised to pray for them at some later, undisclosed time rather than praying for them right then and there. I allowed the distraction of my mobile device to keep me from fully being present.

Young people are asking, *What's the church got that I can't get anywhere else?* How will you answer?

**Mark Matlock**
executive director of Youth Specialties and author of *Real World Parenting: Christian Parenting for Families Living in the Real World*

## 32. Be Nonpartisan but Not Apolitical

Young Christians' flight from church mirrors a disassociation from formal political institutions. Caught between negative associations with the "Religious Right" and an inability to square certain policies of the Left with their values, many young Christians paradoxically go about the political task of enacting justice while remaining avowedly apolitical. Too often this results in the neglect of effective professional techniques in favor of harmful amateurish activism.

Pastors and teachers should challenge Millennials to slow down, lest the opportunities presented by their unique blend of characteristics be wasted. They should encourage youths to inform their passions, to study and abide in the tutelage of those who have gone before. They should remind youths that lasting impacts rarely follow hot zeal, but are often the result of a cold, steeled commitment over a lifetime.

Simultaneously, leaders should recognize the many commendable traits of Millennials. Their confidence, preference for teams, prioritization of relationships over ideas, and desire to manifest their values through action make them uniquely suited to refresh and use political institutions for good.

Finally, the church has too often avoided political teaching. Paul affirmed the ordained role of government; therefore Christians must develop a theology of political engagement. Leaders must develop an understanding of the congruence between Christian faith and the spheres of civil life and devote time to exploring these concepts with those they lead.

**Eric Teetsel**
program manager of the Project on Values and Capitalism at the American Enterprise Institute

## 33. Tell On Yourself

Sadly, the church often excels in artificiality. For most people, church is a public speaker who, following public singing, teaches and motivates neat rows of decently dressed, passive people. Nobody's totally real. Families fight on the way to church, put on their Christian behavior as they step out of their cars, then resume the fight on the way home. Sometimes the pastor's family does it, but he wouldn't ever tell you.

The Bible, though, is as real as it gets. Into humanity's mess, God sent his fully human Son. Jesus feels everything we feel: happiness and joy, family and friendship, betrayal and temptation, sorrow and pain. Read, too, the apostle Paul's letters. In the context of his face-saving culture, Paul's self-disclosure—about his angst, his anger, his depression and doubts—is nothing short of remarkable. "I will glory in my weaknesses," he announced. Yet what preacher does that?

Tell on yourself! Like Paul or the writers of the Psalms, let people know what's causing you pain, what makes you angry, what's difficult for you to overcome in your life—and how God and your closest friends are helping you deal with it.

**Gary Kinnaman**
pastor, Gilbert, Arizona

# IDEAS FOR SUPPORTERS OF THE NEXT GENERATION

## 34. Be Like Jesus

I want you to be someone I want to grow up to be like. I want you to step up and live by the Bible's standards. I want you to be inexplicably generous, unbelievably faithful, and radically committed. I want you to be a noticeably better person than my humanist teacher, than my atheist doctor, than my Hindu next-door neighbor. I want you to sell all you have and give it to the poor. I want you to not worry about your health like you're afraid of dying. I want you to live like you actually believe in the God you preach about.

I don't want you to be like me; I want you to be like Jesus. That's when I'll start listening.

**Emma Sleeth**
student, Lexington, Kentucky

## 35. Embrace the Radical Gospel

I have trouble reconciling the disconnect between what the church is saying and what its members are doing. I fail to understand the application when the church tells me to live in accordance with the Bible, but the "scripture" I see its members live by is titled "If I Work Hard I Am Entitled to Whatever Makes Me Happy." I understand the concept of providing for my family, but I'm disappointed when conversations about new granite countertops seem to carry more weight than those about following Christ. I see so much work for financial gain, by both church members and churches themselves, and I don't think that is what I should be pursuing for the sake of Christ.

If I can speak for my generation, we are presented with this dichotomy: your hard work has afforded us incredible opportunities, while at the same time your priorities and actions speak volumes. I've become thoroughly convinced that having more of anything other than love for God and neighbor will leave me dissatisfied with my relationships and possessions. I wonder how radical the church would be if our actions spoke louder than our words, and those actions reflected the Greatest Commandment.

**Stewart Ramsey**
cofounder of Krochet Kids International

## 36. Don't Condescend

I am misunderstood by my Christian community because I am young and because I am a woman. People often assume that my international development work is just a "phase," done for my own fulfillment, as if I do it for the thrill or for the snapshots I bring home. I would like my community to see my work for what it really is: the best thing I can do to act out the heart of Christ. It's not a phase, but an important part of who Christ made me to be.

Our work does not look like a traditional Christian ministry. The name of Jesus isn't in our title, and evangelism isn't the primary focus of our daily activities. But we are working for God's kingdom and believe this is the way God would have us reach people for his purposes. God has placed a dream and a calling within us, and we ask that the church, rather than seeing us as young and idealistic, would see us as warriors of God who are acting as the arm of Christ, reaching the world with love, hope, and empowerment.

**Kallie Dovel**
founder of 31 Bits Designs

## 37. Have Faith in the Next Generation

The majority of students at evangelical Christian colleges walk onto campus already deeply committed to the Christian tradition and to chastity in particular. Even if they have had sex already, they are typically trying to figure out what chastity means in light of this experience and how to honor it in their romantic relationships in the future. However messy their lives and choices may appear, we can trust their passionate faith commitments. Yes, many are confused and struggling with sexual decision-making in a society that constantly yanks them away from their religious commitments. But most are doing their absolute best to figure out how to be Christian in the midst of these struggles—and they deserve our faith in them. This is especially important as we all sit down at the same table, on an intergenerational level, to grapple with the church's approach to sex.

**Donna Freitas**
associate professor of religion at Hofstra University and author of *Sex and the Soul: Juggling Sexuality, Spirituality, Romance, and Religion on America's College Campuses*

## 38. Support a Student

The August after my freshman year at the University of Houston, I received word that my brother, Allen, had committed suicide. As you might imagine, this was devastating—doubly so because my mother was a paranoid schizophrenic who refused any sort of treatment.

But I was not alone. Four years earlier, a neighbor had invited me to church, where I had found joy and respite with many new friends. In my dark hour, I turned to my Christian family for comfort. My "church moms" encouraged me to go to a Christian university in the fall rather than returning to Houston, but I had no way to go—no money, no ride, no clothes. So they got organized. They started a fundraising phone campaign. Several got together to sew new clothes, while another took me to Neiman Marcus to buy a new coat. Just a few short days later, I found myself in Abilene, reaping the blessing that God and his people had provided in the wake of my brother's death.

After 18 years on the faculty at Abilene Christian University, I took a position with the Council for Christian Colleges and Universities because I believe that the potential and promise of young people's lives must be cultivated in order to grow. My church moms believed the same, and were willing to sacrifice to make it happen.

**Mimi Barnard**
vice president of the Council for Christian Colleges and Universities

## 39. Give Them What They Want

Some in previous generations felt the need to separate from culture, to insulate themselves in Christian cocoons constructed of Christian movies and

Christian music and Christian schools. Millennials reject such an approach. As the social structures of our world keep piling us on top of each other, they know separation is both ineffective and impossible. They desire to live *within* culture where they can repair the fallen places, but they need to be discipled and encouraged. They need trans-generational partners who possess the wisdom to undergird their efforts.

Confusion often reigns across generations, forcing a separation between the young and the old, the rising and the fading. But such separation works against a Christian mission that needs us—all of us—leveraging our collective enthusiasm to restore the brokenness of our world.

We all agree that the gospel of Jesus Christ is "the thing of first importance" (1 Cor. 15), and we echo the desire of the church eternal that has worked over two millennia to announce God's kingdom. Both generations recognize that God created a "good" world in the beginning (Gen. 1:31), and his ultimate desire is to "make all things new" (Rev. 21:5). The question for us now is whether or not we will work together to see this story progress in individuals, neighborhoods, cities, industries, and entire nations.

Even as we enter a post-Christian moment in the West, I'm hopeful about our faith's future. I've witnessed the desire of a new generation of Jesus-followers who see the world as it ought to be and want to push it toward that reality. What they want is what the world needs *and* what God has called his people to do. So why wouldn't we just give them what they want?

**Gabe Lyons**
founder of Q, co-author of *unChristian,* and author of *The Next Christians: The Good News About the End of Christian America*

## 40. Be the Right Kind of Mentor

Young people often have a save-the-world mind-set. While we might be extremely idealistic, we also have a great ability to get things done. We are not satisfied with letting the injustices of the world work themselves out over time, but want to do something to help. Now. Neither are we satisfied with easy answers or sugar-coated truths. We need to explore for ourselves the world and how we fit into it, to challenge the rules and systems already in place, and to have our findings listened to and respected.

This is not to say that we have all the answers. Far from it. Our idealism can be naïve at times, and our goals can be fickle and short-lived. We need mentors, guides, and role models to whom we can bring our successes and failures and be comforted, applauded, and, most importantly, led into reflection, all without feeling judged or inferior. In a world more diverse and connected than ever before, we see salvation in the faces of others, and we seek as mentors those who treat others well and who—like us—are working to make an immediate and permanent difference by fostering a mutual respect with all. We recognize the ability to get things done, and seek those who listen to the word of the Lord.

**Samantha Thomeczek**
pastoral associate for children, youth, and young adults at the Cathedral of the Assumption, Louisville, Kentucky

## 41. Catalyze Innovation

The creative implementation of innovative ideas is at an all-time high. Rapid advancements in technology and human networks have exponentially opened up new pathways to actualizing one's passions. Unlike in past centuries, people no longer need to wait for "permission" from established institutions to pursue a dream. If a person genuinely cares about a product or cause and commits wholeheartedly to giving his or her life to it, he or she will find or be found by a tribe of like-minded people.

What does this mean for the church today?

- We must humbly recognize our inability to "manage" people. Most are not asking to be managed but rather loved.
- We must move from cultures like Britannica (i.e., closed and controlled) to that of Wikipedia (i.e., open and collaborative) in which new ideas are welcome, easily shared, and postured for refinement and collaboration.
- We must architect more communities that allow for innovation without threat and inspiration without judgment.

The alternative to all of this will be a growing trend of disinterest, pessimism, and abandonment.

**Charles Lee**
CEO of Ideation Consultancy

## 42. Un-market the Gospel

Today's young adults have been saturated by marketing since infancy. From Internet pop-ups to movie product placement, market messaging has harnessed every artifice imaginable to compel behavior: buy, join, wear, vote, acquire. Little wonder that religious messages easily end up in the same "junk mail" folder in the marketing-weary mind. If we are to reach the heart of the disillusioned, we must give up trying to equal marketing messages in hipness, volume, or entertainment.

Real substance is the one great foil to the faux world of marketing. That's why authenticity is viewed as today's highest virtue, even when it's ugly or vicious. In a world yearning for authenticity, any Christian message that draws its impact from technique, technology, or "new paradigm" methods will do no more than draw short-lived attention. We must make truth touchable. The Good News must be as tangible as the wood of a cross. Without a visible expression, words like *transformation*, *grace*, and *radical discipleship* will be quickly dismissed as just another hyperbolic sales pitch. But these words made visible—even imperfectly—will crash through competing messages like a bulldozer through a Hollywood set.

Emphasizing the visible doesn't mean downplaying the significance of words or ideas. Robust biblical vision and language are as vital as ever. But every idea we share must be paired with a tangible expression. We speak of God's adoption of us as we adopt the orphan. We describe grace as we visit the prisoner. We tell of God's provision as we provide for the hungry and destitute. This is the *un*-marketing of the gospel: incarnating eternal truth in wood, dirt, and skin.

**Jedd Medefind**

president of Christian Alliance for Orphans, author of *The Revolutionary Communicator*, and former head of the White House Office of Faith-Based and Community Initiatives

## 43. Lift Up the God of Justice

We are compelled by Jesus Christ to demonstrate with our lives that there is a kingdom breaking in that beckons the next generation to give all they have and all they are to the things that matter most. This generation knows that some of the greatest heartaches of our globe are wrought by human disasters of violent injustice, and they want to make it right. This, therefore, is the generation that will grow to know, love, and follow Jesus because they discover in Jesus the one true God of justice who restores a world breaking under the weight of darkness. When we seize opportunities to lead this generation by demonstrating how the body of Christ is a vessel of God's rescuing and restoring justice, we will see their hearts won by the King who has ultimate victory over the gravest evil.

**Bethany Hoang**

director of the International Justice Mission (IJM) Institute

## 44. Take a Note from the Amish

I am a preacher's kid—"PK" in the general parlance. Growing up, I had a front-row seat for both the passion of the church and a healthy dose of the politics. Religious life for me didn't stop with the benediction; it followed me home to conversations around the dinner table about baptisms and budgets, communion and controversy. It was overwhelming. In retrospect, I can see that the deluge of "stuff" from the church crowded out Christ.

I left the church altogether. I spent my first years of college six states away from my parents and a million miles away from my faith. It took that long to squeeze the church "stuff" out of me. It took that long for me to realize that the message of Christ isn't in a building or annual meeting, but at the foot of the cross.

The Amish send their young people away from home in a rite of passage called *Rumspringa*, a word that literally means "running around." When Amish youth hit the age of 16, their parents open the doors of their closed community and grant them permission to run around. *We won't make you choose this church and this life*, they say. *You make your own choice. We raised you right, but it's time for you to find your faith for yourself.*

I'm not saying that every Christian kid needs a full-on Rumspringa, but some distance from their parents' way of doing faith, in order to decide how they will make faith their own, can be a good thing. As the Amish have found, the vast majority of those who were "raised right" choose for themselves to follow Christ.

**Joshua DuBois**
executive director of The White House Office of Faith-Based and Neighborhood Partnerships and Pentecostal associate pastor

## 45. Reason Clearly

All human behavior and institutional structures reflect moral commitment to *something*—even if that commitment is so taken for granted that we no longer notice. The fact that slavery is illegal in the United States, for instance, is based on beliefs about the inherent dignity of the human person that were, at one time, bitterly contested. The 1960s sexual revolution rested on a belief in the separability of body, heart, and mind—but is this belief true to how humans really *are*? If not, then how are we instead? What are we *for*? How do we *know*?

When I taught comparative religion and ethics to extremely bright high school students, I found that they did not know how to confront even horrific human practices with reasoned argument. They resorted instead to slogans like, "It's not my job to decide what's right for other people." This, when discussing genital mutilation or even slavery!

One of the best things we can give the next generation is a philosophical vocabulary with which to understand the eternal questions of the human experience, and a clear understanding of the possible answers—and their consequences. I am not talking about Christian apologetics, or any kind of rationalistic attempt to "prove" that one worldview is better than another. I'm talking about a calm, thoughtful ability to probe the moral commitments of what we see and hear and ask, "Does this ring true with what I know of human nature and human need? If not, then why not? And what can I do about it?"

**Ashley Rogers Berner**
academic fellow and co-director of the program on education at the University of Virginia Institute for Advanced Studies in Culture

## 46. Avoid False Ultimatums

I've watched with a heavy heart as many of my peers have left the faith because they thought it required checking their brains at the door. We are losing some of the brightest young minds in Christendom to a false dichotomy: presenting faith and science as choice.

I am not asking that evangelical leaders change their interpretations of Scripture or their positions on origins. I am simply asking that they give young people a little more room to think, to study, to ask questions, and to maybe even change their minds without facing an impossible ultimatum. We don't need a church in which everyone agrees on the age of the earth. We need a church in which all who love Jesus are welcome.

**Rachel Held Evans**
author of *Evolving in Monkey Town*

## 47. Make Distinctions That Matter

"Daddy, God made a rainbow!" As a high school science teacher, I can't resist responding, "*How* did God make the rainbow?" My poor little six-year-old is baffled, and I relent with a smile. I don't lecture my little one on the mathematics of Snell's Law and the principles of dispersion and refraction, but my students are another story. They need to understand the fancy equations and scientific principles behind rainbow formation.

The distinction between "God did it" and "*This is how* God did it" is a helpful device I use in my classroom to defuse the tension between science and religion that many students presuppose. A student who concludes that "God did it!" and goes no further stifles curiosity and furthers the false notion that science and religion are enemies. Big Bang? Geologic time? Evolution? The multiverse? I preface any potentially inflammatory discussion by saying that we're going to discuss the contemporary scientific views on these matters. Then I tell students that, for those who believe in God, these theories can be viewed as "*how* God did it," while those who have no belief can understand these ideas simply as "how it happened." Sometimes a simple distinction can help overcome the false choice between Christianity and science.

**Jeff Culver**
high school science teacher, Colorado Springs, Colorado

## 48. Give Honest Answers to Honest Questions

Having spent most of my life listening to young people who long to find a place in the world, each one wanting to be taken seriously, I know that something I heard when I was their age is perennially true: *an honest question, an honest answer.* Adolescents on their way to adulthood still hope, as I did, that an honest question will be given an honest answer. What is true for everyone is that we yearn to make sense of life. We want what is offered to be true to the way the world really is.

Year by year, I invite folk in their early twenties to come along with me and learn to read the Word and the world at the same time. We read Augustine's *Confessions*, we read Wendell Berry's stories and essays. We talk a lot about sexuality, knowing that if we can't make sense of our bodies—what we know most intimately—then making sense of anything else is suspect. But we also talk about politics and the arts, about economics and globalization, about the theological imagination and philosophical questions, always working hard in the hope that truth is woven into the very fabric of the universe.

I do what I do because honest questions deserve honest answers, for everyone everywhere.

**Steven Garber**
director of The Washington Institute and author of *The Fabric of Faithfulness*

## 49. Don't Fear Doubt

I have the privilege of spending time with many atheists and agnostics. When I ask them to share their stories they often say something like, "I grew up in the church but it never made sense to me. My questions were suppressed and considered sinful. Eventually I just couldn't believe anymore."

This breaks my heart because not only is Christianity true, but we have good reason to believe it. And yet somehow in the church we have become afraid of doubt and questions. We prefer simple answers that validate our beliefs. This may have been less problematic in the past when culture was much more amenable to the Christian worldview, but it is a significant reason we lose many young people today. The Internet has leveled everything. Young people have equal access to Christian apologetics, Islam, Wicca, and every other conceivable worldview. Doubts are natural for this generation, and we ought to invite tough questions from young people. The key is not to give pat answers, but to teach them *how* to think (we can only do this if we have done our homework and worked through our own doubts). In my experience, this is best done in relationship by asking further questions rather than providing simple responses.

Knowing that Christianity is true should allow us to give students the latitude to doubt. Yet we can also have confidence that the Holy Spirit is working in their hearts. If we lovingly mentor them, they will find the truth.

**Sean McDowell**
educator, speaker, and author of *Apologetics for a New Generation*

## 50. Share Power

To build a bridge to Millennials, Boomers like me will have to begin thinking more like coaches and less like players (or bosses). The next generation *assumes* shared power. They know they will get it sooner or later. They would just prefer to have it handed over graciously rather than wresting it from the death grip of Boomers.

Electricity results when you connect positive and negative poles. Here's my point: *Innovation lies at the intersection of difference.* From my perspective, Boomers have an activist streak and Millennials an optimistic one. When these differences intersect, a unique force field is created that can facilitate the building of a bridge. When intergenerational activists and optimists collaborate, innovative practices and unpredictable acts of love emerge.

**Jim Henderson**
executive producer Jim Henderson Presents and author of *Jim and Casper Go to Church*

You'll find more contributions and opportunities to share your ideas at www.youlostmebook.com, or follow me on Twitter @davidkinnaman.

# ACKNOWLEDGMENTS

I owe the following people big-time:

**The Barna Group team**—Brad Abare, Grant England, Esther Fedorkevich, Katie Hahn, Lynn Hanacek, Pam Jacob, Jill Kinnaman, Elaina Perez, and Brandon Schulz. It's a privilege to serve God together.

**Bill and Lorraine Frey**—This project would not have been possible without your generous support and prayers!

**George and Nancy Barna**—You make it look so easy! (It isn't so simple, huh?) Thank you for being such great partners despite my slow learning curve.

**Aly Hawkins**—I look back on the day you offered to help with this project as one of the single biggest acts of grace God has given this book and my ministry. You took a heap of ideas and made them work! Thank you.

**Baker Books**—Especially Jack Kuhatschek. But not overlooking the significant contributions of Dwight Baker, Twila Bennett, Deonne Beron, Michael Cook, Trinity Graeser, Amanda Halash, Janet Kraima, David Lewis, Mary Suggs, Mary Wenger, and Mike Williams.

**Contributors**—Thanks for participating and sharing your ideas. I enjoy our friendship and partnership.

**Special thanks**—For reviewing copies of the manuscript and surveys, or offering other assistance along the way: Jamaica Abare, Mary Andrews, Todd Barlow, George Barna, Kate Bayless, Tom Beagan, Savannah Berry, Bob Buford, Scott Calgaro, Ed Carlson, Doug Colby, Eric and Jen Corbett, Jeff and Shari Culver, Bill Denzel, Kevin DeYoung, Lucas Dorward, the Drivel Crew, Rob Flanegin, Richard Flory, Mike Foster, Donna Freitas, Val and Terry Gorka, Carolyn Gorka, Bill Greig, Clint Jenkin, Stan John, Reggie Joiner, Katie Kuhatschek, Matt and Kate Kinnaman, Anna and Chris Kopka, Dale Kuehne, Michael Lindsay, Jason Locy, Gabe Lyons, Derek Melleby, Britt Merrick, Mike Metzger, Tasha Mitchell, Kara Powell, Rebecca Pratt, Eddie and LaDonna Ramos, Mark Regnerus, Larry Reichardt, Mark Rodgers, John Seel, Eric Twisselmann, Gabe Watkins, and Glenn Williams. Thanks to each of you. None of you are responsible for my bad ideas or inept expression of them.

**Mark Matlock**—Thanks for all the help, particularly with *Access, Alienation, Authority.*

**Michael DiMarco**—I appreciate the great title, *You Lost Me.* (I have a catchy and clever one-liner for ya!)

**Steve McBeth, Roger Thompson, Pete Richardson, and Kevin Small**—You are incredible advisors in every detail, on this book and on the Barna Group business. Thank you.

**My friends at Peet's Coffee & Tea**—Grateful for the fuel.

**Gary and Marilyn Kinnaman**—Thanks, Dad, for going through this book again and again. And thanks for your prayers, Mom. I love you both.

**Emily, Annika, and Zack Kinnaman**—Thanks for giving up so much of me to get this book done. I love you more than you can ever realize. Maybe someday you will find it helpful in your own faith journey. Or even your kids' journeys.

**Jill Kinnaman**—Only you know how much this book cost. Thank you for sacrificing. I am amazed that God gave me a person as strong and humble as you. Let's keep loving Jesus and serving his church together!

# THE RESEARCH

## TERMS USED FOR | FAITH JOURNEYS

**Nomads**—a type of faith journey in which a person wanders or drifts away from active involvement with a church or faith community. Nomads typically think of themselves as Christian, but they try new faith experiences or practices or allow their faith to become disconnected from spiritual priorities. See chapter 3, "Nomads and Prodigals," for more details.

**Prodigals**—a faith journey in which a person gives up on the faith of their childhood, i.e., someone who describes himself/ herself as an ex-Christian. Use of the term *prodigal* is not meant to suggest these individuals will return to faith at some point later in life; simply that they do not consider themselves to be Christian after at one time having been a part of Christianity. See chapter 3, "Nomads and Prodigals."

**Exiles**—a faith journey in which a person feels stuck between the comfortable, predictable world of church and the "real world" they feel called to influence. Often there is a disconnect between their calling or professional interests and their understanding of their Christian faith. While the journeys of prodigals and nomads occur during any kind of cultural setting, exiles are most common during periods of profound cultural, spiritual, and technological change. See chapter 4, "Exiles."

## TERMS USED FOR | GENERATIONS

A generation is an analytical tool for understanding culture and the people within it. It simply reflects the idea that people who are born during a certain period of time are influenced by a unique set of circumstances and global events, moral and social values, technologies, and cultural and behavioral norms. Barna Group uses the following generations:

**Mosaics**—those born 1984 through 2002; many of today's teenagers and twentysomethings, often referred to as Millennials or Gen Y. Barna Group uses Mosaics because it reflects their eclectic relationships, thinking styles, and learning formats, among other things.

**Busters**—those born from 1965 to 1983, similar in birth years to the generation often called Gen X.

**Boomers**—those born from 1946 to 1964, the "Baby Boom" generation that followed World War II.

**Elders**—those born prior to 1946, sometimes called the "greatest generation" or "Builders."

## METHODOLOGY

Throughout this book you will read about research that is not directly footnoted. Those statistics and data-based statements have been derived from a series of national public opinion surveys conducted by Barna Group in relation to the *You Lost Me* project between 2007 and 2011.

Those studies build on findings from two decades of national studies conducted prior to that time.

In addition to extensive quantitative interviewing with adults and faith leaders nationwide, the main research for this book was conducted among 18- to 29-year-olds. This was a multiphase project that began with qualitative (or depth) interviews, conducted both via telephone and in-person. The large-scale quantitative study among 18- to 29-year-olds was conducted online. The *You Lost Me* study also included pretesting of the survey instrument as well as parallel testing on key measures using telephone surveys, including cell phone sampling. This provided an additional validation of the online panel and helped to round out our understanding of young adults' faith journeys.

All of the following studies are referenced in this book and were conducted by Barna Group among a national random sample of the population identified. Upon completion of each survey, minimal statistical weights were applied to the data to allow the results to more closely correspond to known national demographic averages for several variables. In the case of all Barna telephone studies conducted since 2008, special effort was made to include people who no longer have a landline in their home but now rely solely on mobile phones.

All telephone studies relied on callbacks to households or churches not reached after the first attempt; a maximum of six callbacks were made to each nonresponsive household or church, with contact attempts made at different times of the day and days of the week. The average length of the surveys in these studies ranged from fifteen to twenty-two minutes.

The online studies (with the exception of the YouthLeaderPoll) used an online research panel called KnowledgePanel, created by Knowledge Networks. It is a probability-based online non-volunteer access panel. Panel members are recruited using a statistically valid sampling method with a published sample frame of residential addresses that covers approximately 97 percent of U.S. households. Sampled non-Internet households, when recruited, are provided a netbook computer and free Internet service so they may also participate as online panel members. KnowledgePanel consists of about 50,000 adult members (ages 18 and older) and includes persons living in cell phone only households.

| Survey | Data Collection | Dates Conducted | Sample Size | Sampling Error[†] |
|---|---|---|---|---|
| **18–29-year-olds** | | | | |
| Faith Journeys | online | Jan. 2011 | 1,296* | ±2.7 |
| Faith Journeys— parallel study | telephone | Jan. 2011 | 520 | ±4.3 |
| Faith Journeys | online— pretest | Aug. 2010 | 150* | ±8.0 |
| Faith Journeys | telephone— depth | Aug.–Dec. 2009 | 76** | qualitative |
| **U.S. Adults** | | | | |
| OmniPoll[SM] 1-11 | telephone | Jan. 2011 | 600 | ±4.1 |
| OmniPoll[SM] 1-11A | online | Feb. 2011 | 1,021 | ±3.2 |
| OmniPoll[SM] 2-09 | telephone | July 2009 | 1,003 | ±3.2 |
| OmniPoll[SM] 3-08 | telephone | Aug. 2008 | 1,004 | ±3.2 |
| OmniPoll[SM] 2-08 | telephone | July–Aug. 2008 | 1,003 | ±3.2 |
| Markets & States database | telephone | 1997–2010 | 47,733 | ±0.4 |
| **U.S. Pastors** | | | | |
| PastorPoll[SM] W-07 | telephone | Dec. 2007 | 605 | ±4.1 |
| PastorPoll[SM] S-08 | telephone | July–Aug. 2008 | 613 | ±4.1 |
| PastorPoll[SM] F-08 | telephone | Nov.–Dec. 2008 | 600 | ±4.1 |
| PastorPoll[SM] 1-09 | telephone | July–Aug. 2009 | 603 | ±4.1 |
| **Tweens and teens, ages 8–17** | | | | |
| YouthPoll[SM] 2009 | online | Dec. 2009 | 602 | ±4.1 |
| Barna teen & tween database | telephone / online | 1997–2006 | 4,161 | ±1.5 |
| **Youth Leaders** | | | | |
| YouthLeaderPoll[SM] | online | Oct. 2009 | 507 | ±4.5 |
| Youth Leaders | telephone— depth | Aug. 2009 | 25 | qualitative |

\* Surveys included interviews with 18- to 29-year-olds who self-identify as current or former Christians or as churchgoers during their teen years.
\*\* Young adults qualitative survey included 20 interviews with adults ages 18–35.
† percentage points; sampling error cited reflects 95 percent confidence level.

When researchers describe the accuracy of survey results, the estimated amount of sampling error is often provided. This refers to the degree of inaccuracy that might be attributable to interviewing a group of people that is not completely representative of the population from which they were drawn. The maximum amount of sampling accuracy is listed in the table above. That estimate is dependent upon two factors: (1) the sample size and (2) the degree to which the result you are examining is close to 50 percent or the extremes, 0 percent and 100 percent. Keep in mind that there is a range of other errors that may influence survey results (e.g., biased question wording, question sequencing, inaccurate recording of the responses provided, inaccurate data tabulation, etc.)—errors whose influence cannot be statistically estimated.

# THE RESEARCHER

David Kinnaman is the president and majority owner of Barna Group, a leading research firm focused on the intersection of faith and culture located in Ventura, California. David joined George Barna's research team in 1995 as an intern. Since then, David has designed and analyzed hundreds of market research projects for a variety of clients, including the American Bible Society, the Billy Graham Evangelistic Association, CARE, Columbia House, Compassion, Easter Seals, Focus on the Family, Habitat for Humanity, the Humane Society, NBC-Universal, The ONE Campaign, the Salvation Army, SONY, Walden Media, World Vision, Zondervan (HarperCollins) and many others.

In addition to client studies, he has overseen eighty-six nationwide, representative research studies among American adults, teenagers, tweens, and clergy on matters of faith, spirituality, public opinion, political attitudes, and cultural dynamics. This body of public opinion research is frequently quoted in major media outlets (such as *USA Today*, *The Wall Street Journal*, Fox News, *Chicago Tribune*, *The New York Times*, and *The Los Angeles Times*). In total, during Kinnaman's sixteen years at the firm, he has supervised or directed interviews with more than 350,000 individuals and leaders.

Kinnaman is the co-author of the best-selling book, *unChristian: What a New Generation Really Thinks about Christianity*, which explores the attitudes of 16- to 29-year-olds in relation to faith. He frequently speaks publicly on topics of trends, teenagers, vocation and calling, leadership, and generations.

You can reach him at dk@barna.org.

# NOTES

## You Lost Me, Explained

1. Andrew Sullivan, "The Lost Catholic Church in America," *The Daily Dish* (October 24, 2010; accessed October 30, 2010), http://andrewsullivan.theatlantic.com/the_daily_dish/2010/10/the-lost-catholic-church-in-america-ctd.html.

2. Check out Earl Creps's book, *Reverse Mentoring: How Young Leaders Can Transform the Church, and Why We Should Let Them.*

3. This is a statement I have heard John Ortberg make.

4. Eric Metaxas, *Bonhoeffer: Pastor, Martyr, Prophet, Spy* (Nashville: Thomas Nelson, 2010), 141.

## Chapter 1 Faith, Interrupted

1. This research was drawn from work we conducted for Gospel Light and Regal Books. The complete study can be found at http://www.barna.org/family-kids-articles/321-new-research-explores-the-long-term-effect-of-spiritual-activity-among-children-and-teens.

2. Kevin Selders, "No More Secrets for the Cold War Kids," *Relevant* (January–February 2011), 56–59.

3. Other books that point to this countertrend include *The New Faithful* by Colleen Carroll, *Young, Restless, Reformed* by Collin Hansen, and *The Next Christians* by Gabe Lyons.

4. Barna Group, "Do Americans Change Faiths?" (August 16, 2010; accessed October 2010), http://www.barna.org/faith-spirituality/412-do-americans-change-faiths. This research does not minimize the importance of working with children and adolescents;

in fact I believe it makes it all the more important.

5. The Pew Forum on Religion and Public Life, "Changes in Religious Affiliation in the U.S." (April 27, 2000; accessed October 2010), http://pewforum.org/Faith-in-Flux.aspx.

6. James K. A. Smith, "Letter to a Young Parent," *Comment* (Spring 2011), 20–21.

## Chapter 2 Access, Alienation, Authority

1. The Pew Research Center, "Millennials: A Portrait of Generation Next," (released February 2010; accessed November 2010), 12; http://pewsocialtrends.org/assets/pdf/millennials-confident-connected-open-to-change.pdf.

2. Nick Bilton, "Part of the American Diet: 34 Gigabytes of Data," *New York Times* (Dec. 9, 2009; accessed April 2011), http://www.nytimes.com/2009/12/10/technology/10data.html.

3. *The Economist*, February 27, 2010, University of California San Diego.

4. Kay S. Hymowitz, "Where Have the Good Men Gone?" *Wall Street Journal* (February 19, 2011; accessed March 2011), http://online.wsj.com/article/SB10001424052748704409004576146321725889448.html.

5. Robert Wuthnow, *After the Baby Boomers: How Twenty- and Thirty-Somethings Are Shaping the Future of American Religion* (Princeton, NJ: Princeton University Press, 2007), 11. I think Professor Wuthnow's book provides one of the best overviews of how today's young adults are growing up in a different social setting than the Boomers. For those who would like to really understand the nuances of social change, I recommend it.

6. *USA Today* http://www.usatoday.com/money/economy/employment/2010-05-19-jobs19_CV_N.htm.

7. *Business Week* cover story, October 19, 2009.

8. "Employee Tenure Summary," Bureau of Labor Statistics (Sept. 14, 2010; accessed April 2011), http://www.bls.gov/news.release/tenure.nr0.htm.

9. Christian Smith, ed., *The Secular Revolution: Power, Interests, and Conflict in the Secularization of American Public Life* (Berkeley and Los Angeles: University of California, 2003).

### Chapter 3 Nomads and Prodigals

1. "50 Reasons to Watch TV, Reason #1: The Subversive Joy of Stephen Colbert," *Rolling Stone* (September 17, 2009).

2. *Rolling Stone* online exclusive (accessed January 12, 2010), http://catholiccolbert.wordpress.com.

3. Vanessa Grigoriadis, "Sex, God & Katy," *Rolling Stone* (August 19, 2010), 41–47.

4. Jocelyn Vena, "Katy Perry Responds to Rumors of Parents' Criticism: 'They Love and Support Me,'" MTV.com (August 20, 2008; accessed September 2010), http://www.mtv.com/news/articles/1593166/20080820/id_1962774.jhtml.

5. Grigoriadis, "Sex, God & Katy."

6. Monica Herrera, "Katy Perry: The Billboard Cover Story," Billboard.com (June 23, 2010; accessed September 2010), http://www.billboard.com/features/katy-perry-the-billboard-cover-story-1004105908.story#/features/katy-perry-the-billboard-cover-story-1004105908.story?page=1.

7. Drew Dyck, "I Never Wanted a Hard Heart," *Christianity Today* (Feb. 3, 2010; accessed March 2011), http://www.christianitytoday.com/ct/music/interviews/2010/davidbazan-jan10-1.html.

8. Ibid.

9. Ibid.

10. Ibid.

11. This corresponds to other Barna Group research showing that, after the age of eighteen, adults have only a 6 percent chance of accepting Jesus Christ for the first time. See chapter 2 in *Transforming Children into Spiritual Champions* by George Barna.

### Chapter 4 Exiles

1. A helpful discussion of exiles in history and current culture can be found in Patrick Whitworth's book *Prepare for Exile: A New Spirituality and Mission for the Church* (London: SPCK, 2008).

2. As quoted in Michael Frost, *Exiles: Living Missionally in a Post-Christian World* (Grand Rapids: Baker, 2006), 8–9.

3. Ibid.

4. From the foreword of Robert A. Fryling, *The Leadership Ellipse: Shaping How We Lead by Who We Are* (Downers Grove, IL: InterVarsity, 2010), 12.

5. "About Jay," *Revolution New York City* (accessed November 2010), http://www.revolutionnyc.com/about/.

6. Tremper Longman III, *Daniel: The NIV Application Commentary* (Grand Rapids: Zondervan, 1999), 51.

7. Whitworth, *Prepare for Exile*, 58.

### Chapter 5 Overprotective

1. Austin Scaggs, "God, the Devil and Kings of Leon: Around the World with the Heartbreaking, Trouble Making, Earthshaking Band of Southern Brothers," *Rolling Stone* 1077 (April 30, 2009; accessed February 2010), http://www.rollingstone.com/music/news/god-the-devil-and-kings-of-leon-20090430.

2. Ibid.

3. Matt Conner, "Kings of Leon's Faith Journey," *Relevant* (accessed April 2011), http://www.relevantmagazine.com/culture/music/features/23184-kings-of-leons-faith-journey.

### Chapter 6 Shallow

1. Christian Smith with Melinda Lundquist Denton, *Soul Searching: The Religious and Spiritual Lives of American Teenagers* (New York: Oxford University Press, 2005), 165.

2. We conducted this study on behalf of my colleague Mark Matlock, who currently works with Youth Specialties and Planet Wisdom.

3. We have focused on the relational, missional, educational, and vocational outcomes partly due to limited space in the chapter and

also because we believe that pursuing a life of meaningful faith has to be played out in real life, not just "inside." Yes, we should also look at spiritual outcomes, such as participation in prayer, Bible reading, and personal connection to Christ. Barna Group continues to explore these matters with all generations, including teens and young adults. For more information, check out our website, www.barna.org. For instance, you may want to read the article "How Teenagers' Faith Practices are Changing," 2010.

4. Eve Tushnet, "Book Review: Teen Angels," *Weekly Standard* 16, no. 12 (December 6, 2010; accessed January 2011), http://www.weeklystandard.com/articles/teen-angels_519564.html?nopager=1.

5. Dallas Willard, *Knowing Christ Today: Why We Can Trust Spiritual Knowledge* (San Francisco: HarperOne, 2009).

### Chapter 7 Anti-science

1. Quoted in Marvin Olasky, "Riding the Rapids: Grand Canyon Rocks Challenge Christian Colleges' Divergent Stands on Evolution," *World* (September 11, 2010; accessed October 2010), http://www.worldmag.com/articles/17064.

2. Adam Bly, *Science Is Culture: Conversations at the New Intersection of Science and Society* (New York: Harper Perennial, 2010), xiii.

3. I am indebted to my friend Eric Twisselmann and ideas from J. P. Moreland for assistance with this section.

4. See several parallel commentaries on this verse at "Daniel 1:4," Biblios.com. http://bible.cc/daniel/1-4.htm; accessed November 2010.

5. Quoted in John H. Tiner, *Isaac Newton: Inventor, Scientist and Teacher* (Fenton, MI: Mott Media, 1981).

### Chapter 8 Repressive

1. Tyler Charles, "True Love Isn't Waiting," *Neue* 6 (April/May 2011), 32–36.

2. Mark D. Regnerus, *Forbidden Fruit: Sex and Religion in the Lives of American Teenagers* (New York: Oxford University Press, 2007), 205.

3. Donna Freitas, *Sex and the Soul: Juggling Sexuality, Spirituality, Romance, and Religion*

on *America's College Campuses* (New York: Oxford University Press, 2008), xiv.

4. Ibid.

5. Ibid., xv.

6. Regnerus, *Forbidden Fruit*, 206.

7. Ibid., 205–6.

8. Lauren Winner, *Real Sex: The Naked Truth about Chastity* (Grand Rapids: Brazos, 2005), 15.

9. You can read more about how American Christians have embraced legalism in my previous book *unChristian*, especially the chapter on hypocrisy. It's not too boring.

### Chapter 9 Exclusive

1. This figure does not include Hispanics.

2. "What Americans Believe about Universalism and Pluralism," *Barna Update* (April 18, 2011), http://www.barna.org/faith-spirituality/484-what-americans-believe-about-universalism-and-pluralism.

3. "How Teenagers' Faith Practices Are Changing," *Barna Update* (July 12, 2010), http://www.barna.org/teens-next-gen-articles/403-how-teenagers-faith-practices-are-changing.

4. I am indebted to Miroslav Wolf, *Exclusion and Embrace: A Theological Exploration of Identity, Otherness, and Reconciliation* (Nashville: Abingdon, 1996), for the ideas outlined here.

### Chapter 10 Doubtless

1. John Jeremiah Sullivan, "Upon This Rock," *GQ* (February 2004), http://www.gq.com/entertainment/music/200401/rock-music-jesus?printable=true&currentPage=5.

2. Eric Metaxas, *Bonhoeffer: Pastor, Martyr, Prophet, Spy* (Nashville: Nelson, 2010), 125.

3. Daniel Taylor, *The Myth of Certainty: The Reflective Christian and the Risk of Commitment* (Downers Grove, IL: InterVarsity Press, 2000), 145.

4. "The Numbers Count: Mental Disorders in America," The National Institute of Mental Health, http://www.athealth.com/Practitioner/mentalhealthstats.html.

5. Ibid.

6. Sullivan, "Upon This Rock."

# INDEX OF CONTRIBUTORS

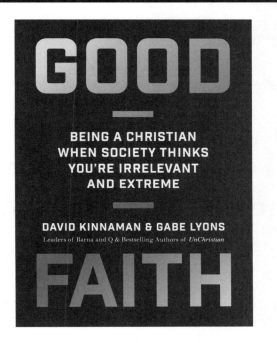

## Society says your faith is irrelevant and extreme.
## HOW WILL YOU RESPOND?

In a culture filled with contentious issues, many Christians find themselves overwhelmed as they try to live their convictions faithfully, while treating others who disagree with respect and compassion.

David Kinnaman and Gabe Lyons realize this is a problem that plagues the future of the American church. By inviting fellow Christians to discover ways that cultural challenges can be used for the common good, they show you how to be loving, life-giving friends despite profound differences.

## VISIT BARNA.ORG/GOODFAITH

# Knowledge to Navigate a Changing World

If you're like most Christians and church leaders, you're wrestling with how to navigate a complex and changing culture. You need a trusted advisor, someone who can help you figure out what's happening and the next steps to take.

Barna can provide you with relevant, data-driven insights on today's society. For more than 30 years, Barna has conducted over one million interviews through the course of thousands of studies, and has become a go-to source for insights about faith, culture, leadership and generations.

## Visit Barna.org

- Sign up for Barna's free research releases and newsletters
- Discover the latest Barna research and resources
- Find out more about custom research for your organization

🐦 @BarnaGroup    ⬛ facebook.com/BarnaGroup